NEW MEXI

MW01026236

Peace Officers Killed
In the Line of Duty, 1847-2010

For Ashley

Don Bullis

The Fourth Edition, May 2010

NEW MEXICO'S FINEST

Peace Officers Killed
In the Line of Duty, 1847-2010

by Don Bullis
The Fourth Edition, May 2010

© 2010, Don Bullis
Published by Río Grande Books
925 Salamanca NW
Los Ranchos, NM 87107-5647
505-344-9382
www.nmsantos.com

Book design by Paul Rhetts and Barbe Awalt

ISBN 13: 978-1-890689-69-8

Library of Congress Cataloging-in-Publication

Bullis, Don.
  New Mexico's finest : peace officers killed in the line of duty, 1847-2010 / by Don Bullis. -- 4th ed.
      p. cm.
  Includes bibliographical references and index.
  ISBN 978-1-890689-69-8 (pbk. : alk. paper)
  1. Police--New Mexico--Biography. 2. Peace officers--New Mexico--Biography. 3. Police murders--New Mexico. I. Title.
  HV8145.N6B85 2010
  363.2'30922789--dc22
                              2010003335

Cover: Photograph of "Guardian Angel" by Arthur D. Peralta ©1998.

Table of Contents

Introduction

It is an unfortunate aspect of law enforcement work that officers are called upon to participate in events which may result in serious injury or death. Since New Mexico became a part of the United States in the 1840s, at least 190 men and women have died, in one way or another, as a result of participating in law enforcement activities. Some have died in mishaps—airplane, car, helicopter, motorcycle and truck accidents—while others died violently from gunshot or stab wounds. Each of them gave everything they had for the people they served: the citizens of New Mexico.

Efforts to honor these officers began with the establishment of a memorial monument at the Law Enforcement Academy in the 1980s. By the late 1980s, 88 names were engraved there, and at the same time, efforts were undertaken to research the circumstances surrounding the on-duty deaths. The first edition of *New Mexico's Finest* was published in 1990, the second 1996, the third in 2000. The fourth edition contains the most up-to-date information available. However, I am aware that other New Mexico officers have died in the line of duty over the years, and efforts continue to identify them and honor them on the pages of future editions and by etching their names on the monument.

While it is my fervent wish that these pages will serve to honor the sacrifices these officers made, it is also my hope that the causes of these deaths will be examined by law enforcement personnel so that future injuries and deaths can be avoided. Every one of the officers on these pages left home with the intention of returning at the end of his or her tour of duty. None of them made it. My hope is that every officer who reads this book will return home safely at the end of every tour; that not one of their names will ever appear on these pages.

Don Bullis
Rio Rancho, New Mexico
May 2010

Acknowledgments

Over the years, so many folks have helped with the New Mexico's Finest project that it is impossible to list them all. Some of them have been current or former police officers, others have been civilians, many them the survivors of slain officers; some have been historians, law enforcement and otherwise, while others have simply been interested citizens. In short, many New Mexicans have been generous with their time, input and encouragement.

Some, though, merit special mention.

Arthur D. C. Ortiz, Director of the New Mexico Law Enforcement Academy, took the initiative to re-establish the New Mexico's Finest project after a hiatus of nearly a decade. His interest in recognizing and honoring those officers who died in the line of duty is commendable. Director Ortiz was joined by Jim Burleson, Executive Director of the New Mexico Sheriff's & Police Association, in providing the resources necessary to make the effort succeed.

Bill Kuehl, former New Mexico State Police Captain and current professor of Criminal Justice at Eastern New Mexico University (Roswell), has been an important part of the New Mexico's Finest project since the beginning in 1990. Most recently he reviewed the updated text for accuracy and he proof-read the entire book. Paul Rhetts, publisher, who worked diligently to bring together all of the separate elements of this book, is also sincerely thanked for his efforts.

Janette Smith, retired member of the New Mexico Law Enforcement Academy staff, must be recognized for beginning the whole project in the first place some thirty-odd years ago.

NEW MEXICO'S FINEST

Peace Officers Killed
In the Line of Duty, 1847-2010

Abeyta, Luis

Alarid, Ike

Allison, Wayne G.

Aragon, Lloyd R.

Archuleta, James

Armijo, Richard

Arvizo, John B.

Aven, Joe Jr.

Avilucea, Michael

Baca, Ronald T.

Batton, George W.

Bedford, Thomas C.

Bell, James W.

Bencoma, Ventura

Bennett, Royce

Bolin, Harvey

Brady, William

Breen, Victor C.

Bugg, Leslie Delbert

Burgen, William A.

Bustamente, Dan

Butler, Robert B.

Candelaria, Emilio

Carbajal, Ruben

Carlyle, James

Carmichael, Mack R.

Carrillo, John Arthur

Carson, Joe

Casey, Germaine

Castillo, Luis

C de Baca, Mackie

Chacon, Philip H.

Chavez, Andres

Chavez, Leo

Chavez, Victoria

Chase, James M.

Clark, James Edward

Clark, Kelly Fay

Clifton, J. M.

Cline, Gerald Eugene

Cogdill, J. V.

Coker, David

Corn, Jasper

Cunningham, Charles

Daniel, Leonard E.

Davis, Oscar

Davis, Ray

Dow, James Leslie

Dunnahoo, Rufus J.

Farr, Edward

Filfred, Winsonfred

Fleshman, Warren G.

Fountain, Albert J.

Gallegos, Luciano G.

Garcia, Angelic S.

Garcia, Nash Phillip

Garcia, Ralph

Garcia y Griego, Manuel

Garrett, Patrick F.

Gene, Hoskie

Geoffrion, Gregory

Gomez, Richard

Gonzales, José María

Gray, O. C.

Green, Benjamin L.

Guerro, Vicente

Gurule, Leopoldo C.

Hall, Tom

Hall, Thomas H.

Harris, Joseph A.

Haynes, James F.

Haynes, Travis

Heard, J. H.

Hedman, Robert

Henry, E. D.

Herrera, Ben

Higginbotham, Ralph

Hindman, George

Hodges, Melvin Lee

Howard, Lowell D.

Huber, Glen

Hurley, John

Jaramillo, Antonio

Jerrell, W. L.

Jewett, Louis F. Jr.

Johnson, Bud

Johnson, William D.

Jones, James B.

Jones, Tom

Kearney, Kent

Kent, James I.

Kilburn, William H.

King, Michael R.

Knapp, Lewis A.
Koteen, Ishkoten
Landdeck, Owen
Lane, David A.
Larson, David P.
Ledezma, Rodolfo
Lee, Robert Earl
Lee, Stephen Louis
Leonard, Barney F.
Lopez, Tranquilino
Love, Henry M.
Magee, Gerald Peter
Martinez, Elfego
Martinez, Issac B.
Martinez, Jerry
Martinez, Juan
McCamant, Louis
McClure, J. A.
McGrane, James Jr.
McGuire, Robert
McWethy, Kenneth Shawn
Meador, William
Mestas, Emilio
Mickey, Lewis H.
Mirabal, Christopher
Mitchell, Larry B.
Montoya, Barney D.
Montoya, Gilbert
Moreno, Edward
Narvaez, Julian
Oldham, Max Ray
Olinger, Robert A.
Olivas, Manuel

Olivas, Philip
Ortiz, Filimon J.
Ortiz, Juan Leo
Peña, Lee Vicente
Phillipowsky, Lyon
Purcell, Robert F.
Quintana, José F.
Rainbolt, William
Ramsey, John T.
Redfern, Donald W.
Redhouse, Samuel
Richard, Bruce A.
Richmond, Thomas
Rivera, Daniel C.
Roberts, Austin A.
Rodriguez, Perfecto
Romero, Robert Seth
Rosenbloom, Robert
Ross, Peter
Rowe, Truett Eugene
Ruiz, Warren
Rusk, J. B.
Russell, Jeffrey C.
Rutherford, William
Salazar, Clemente
Sanderson, Andres P.
Sandlin, Stephen
Scarborough, George
Schulz, John "Kevin"
Schutz, C. B.
Seaman, Edward
Serna, E. C.

Shores, Ronald E.
Sibrava, William
Silva, Joseph Ralph
Silva, Louis
Sjolander, Frank A.
Smith, Charles B.
Smith, David
Smith, Dominique J.
Smith, Richard
Smithers, A. L.
Solis, Ramon Robert
Speight, William T.
Stedman, William M.
Stephens, Dwight B.
Sutton, Raymond Sr.
Taber, Walter G.
Talbot, Damon Kyle
Tingwall, Andrew F.
Tipton, William E.
Todecheene, Esther
Toler, Sherman Lee
Valdez, Antonio L.
Vigil, Frank X.
Vivil, James Monroe
Vocale, Carl E.
Walker, Charles
Wasmer, Charles E.
White, William F.
Wingall, Jay Elmo
Williams, Bennie D.
Woods, Horst H.
Woofter, R

LUIS ABEYTA*

Deputy Sheriff
Isleta Pueblo

In early January 1921, Luis Abeyta, a deputy sheriff from Isleta Pueblo, attempted to arrest James Williams, 19, who had shot and severely wounded 16 year old Lawrence B. Mackey Jr. in Albuquerque the day before. Williams shot Deputy Abeyta, too, and fled after firing at Mrs. A. G. Seis, wife of the Isleta postmaster. A posse of people from the Pueblo, along with several Albuquerque-area police officers, soon began tracking Williams and found him in a swampy area just northeast of the village. In the gunfight that followed on January 7, 1921, Albuquerque officer Pablo Lujan shot and killed Williams. Some sources report that the outlaw was hit by two bullets while others report four.

Young Mackey died of his wounds the following day and Deputy Abeyta died of his wounds on January 12.

The original shooting was the result of a squabble, the cause unknown, between Williams and Mackey, both of whom worked at the Alvarado Hotel in Albuquerque. Williams was a janitor and bootblack in the barbershop and Mackey was a "call boy."** Williams shot Mackey, twice, without warning.

Luis Abeyta, 38, at the time of his death, had served for six years as deputy sheriff for Isleta Pueblo and also as a special agent for the Santa Fe Railroad. He had previously served ten years as a federal Indian police officer. He was survived by a wife and five children ranging in age from two to 17.

His wife was granted a pension after it was confirmed that Abeyta was acting in his official capacity as a peace officer when he was killed, and that a recently enacted law made Mrs. Abeyta eligible. She was allowed $17.50 per month for herself (as long as she didn't remarry) and just over $3.00 per month for each of her children (until they reached 18 years of age), for a total of $33.33 per month. The U. S. Employees' Compensation Commission also provided payment for doctor and burial expenses.

A newspaper reported at the time, "He [Deputy Abeyta] had been in the service for a number of years and was considered one of the most trustworthy and invaluable of the force."

* One news story identified the deputy as "Louis" while another referred to him as "Pablo" Abeyta.

** A "call boy" was responsible for ensuring the members of train crews were notified and on hand for their assigned runs.

Albuquerque *Morning Journal*, January 8 & May 17, 1921
Las Vegas *Optic*, January 7, 8 & 12, 1921
Santa Fe *New Mexican*, January 8, 1921

IKE ALARID

Deputy Sheriff
Santa Fe County, New Mexico

On Thursday, November 3, 1932, Luis Moreno and Evaristo Garcia escaped from the New Mexico State Penitentiary at Santa Fe. The following day, Santa Fe County Sheriff Jesus Baca received information that the two men were hiding near the village of Rowe, southeast of the capital, and that a man named Frank Gonzales would pick them up there to complete their escape plan. The sheriff, along with deputies James Baca and Ike Alarid, followed Gonzales to Rowe to investigate. They soon observed an automobile occupied by two men who fit the descriptions of the escapees. Officers stopped the suspect vehicle, and Deputy Alarid drew his pistol as he got out of the sheriff's car. He accidentally pulled the trigger as he stepped down. The bullet entered his head, killing him instantly. Sheriff Baca arrested the escapees and returned them to prison.

Deputy Alarid, 47, had served under Sheriff Baca for about two years. He had previously served Santa Fe County as Sheriff and Assessor. A wife and one child survived him.

Albuquerque *Journal*, November 5, 1932
Clovis *Evening News-Journal*, November 5, 1932
Michael Taylor (Deputy Alarid's grandson), conversation, April 25, 2002

WAYNE G. ALLISON

Officer/Pilot
New Mexico State Police

Officer Wayne Allison, 32, died when the State Police twin-engine Cessna Skymaster he piloted crashed near Galisteo, New Mexico, on Saturday, February 13, 1988. He was alone in the plane and en route to Carlsbad in clear weather at the time. Investigators never determined a specific cause for the accident.

Officer Allison joined the State Police in November of 1985. He spent two years in the Gallup District before assignment to the Aircraft Section in Santa Fe in September of 1987. Allison earned his pilot's license in 1979. He had logged more than 630 hours of flight time when he was killed. He was also a certified flight instructor.

A native of Chicago, Illinois, he was survived by his wife Michelle. A memorial service was held for Officer Allison in Gallup on February 16, 1988.

Albuquerque *Journal*, Feb. 14 & 15, 1988
Chief John Denko (Ret.), New Mexico State Police
Rocky Mountain News, Feb. 14, 1988
Santa Fe *New Mexican*, Feb. 14 & 16, 1988
The Roadrunner (New Mexico State Police Association, Vol. 3, No. 2, Summer 1992)

LLOYD RAFAEL ARAGON

Senior Patrolman
New Mexico State Police

The Grants Police Department received a call at about 7:00 o'clock on the morning of August 1, 2001 reporting that two individuals had stolen non-prescription drugs from the Wal-Mart store at the east end of town. A store employee noted the description of the pickup truck the suspects used, along with the vehicle's license number. With that information in hand, Grants Police Sgt. Michael Trujillo soon stopped the vehicle. One suspect fled from the scene on foot while the other one sped away in the truck, driving east on Interstate 40. Officers, in the meantime, learned that the truck had been stolen in Albuquerque. State Police and Laguna and Acoma Tribal Police officers joined the chase.

State Police Officer Lloyd Aragon was on his way to Albuquerque to attend a Federal Court hearing, and was therefore well ahead of the action. In coordination with pursuing officers, he set up "stop sticks" which were designed to blow the tires on the fleeing pickup. The suspect driver, however, avoided the sticks in the roadway, and veered into the median.

He deliberately ran down Officer Aragon, killing him instantly.

Zacharia Dewitt Craig, 19, of Albuquerque, was captured near the I-40 intersection with State Road 6, just east of the point where Officer Aragon was killed. Craig's brother, Aaron, who had fled from officers at the initial vehicle stop, was also captured east of Grants. Zacharia Craig was charged with murder.

After a two-year delay, Craig was declared incompetent to stand trial and committed to the New Mexico psychiatric unit at Las Vegas. Finally, in September 2006, he was sentenced to 20 years in prison, and five years of supervised probation upon release.

Lloyd Aragon, 36, was born in Las Vegas, New Mexico. He grew up in Grants and graduated from Grants High School. He joined the Grants Police Department in 1986 and served eight years there before he joined the State Police in 1994. His wife, Monica and two children, Lloyd Jr., 11, and Audrianna, 4, survived him.

Grants Police Chief Fred Radosevich said, "He was probably one of the best police officers we've ever had. If I had to build a mold for an ideal police officer, I'd use him."

Lieutenant Robert Cook of the New Mexico State Police said, "Words can't describe the loss. It's hard to find good cops. This guy was exceptional. Losing him was just a tremendous blow."

Albuquerque *Journal*, August 2, 3, 4 & December 9, 2001; May 9, 2003; and September 2, 2006
Grants *Beacon*, August 3, 8, 15, 29 & November 14, 28, 2001; February 22, 2002

JAMES ARCHULETA

Patrolman
New Mexico State Police

Patrolman James Archuleta, 27, was responding to a local hospital to investigate a shooting, when he was killed during an accident in which his State Police vehicle, southbound on U. S. Route 84, ten or so miles north of Espanola in Rio Arriba County, collided with a cow in the road. The car flipped several times after striking the animal and the officer was ejected and struck by at least one northbound vehicle. The accident occurred on Sunday, June 4, 2006.

Officer Archuleta, a two year veteran of the State Police, was honored at a memorial service in Chimayo before he was interred at the National Cemetery in Santa Fe. His brother, Leon, an Arizona police officer, said James had a positive impact on everyone he met. "He was funny, sarcastic, protective and, most of all, loving.

Albuquerque *Journal*, June 10, 2006
The Associated Press, June 6, 2006

RICHARD ARMIJO

Patrolman
Albuquerque, New Mexico, Police Department

Officer Richard Armijo, 31, died on September 30, 1958, when the police motorcycle he was riding collided with a car driven by a 24 year old University of New Mexico student at the corner of Second and Coal in southwest Albuquerque. The officer was en route to an accident with his emergency equipment engaged when he entered the intersection against a red light. The driver of the car acknowledged that he'd heard the siren, but thought the emergency vehicle was behind him.

A six-year veteran of the Albuquerque Police Department at the time of his death, Officer Armijo had previously worked as a Bernalillo County Sheriff's deputy from 1949 to 1952. His wife, Esther Lee, and three daughters, Catherine, Linda, and a three-day-old baby, survived him. His last request was to have the youngest child named after his wife. Officer Armijo was buried in the family plot at Armijo Cemetery in Albuquerque.

The accident occurred during the New Mexico State Fair which that year featured noted television personality Arthur Godfrey. Mr. Godfrey quietly paid all of Officer Armijo's doctor and hospital expenses.

After the accident that killed Officer Armijo, his police motorcycle—Motor 41—was repaired and issued to Officer Max Oldham. While riding it on February 21, 1959—five months after officer Armijo was killed—Officer Oldham was struck head-on and killed by a drunk driver who was driving on the wrong side of Lomas Boulevard (see page 226).

Albuquerque *Journal,* October 1 & 2, 1958, February 22 & 24, 1959
Albuquerque Police Department

JOHN B. ARVIZO
Captain/Chief of Detectives
Gallup, New Mexico, Police Department

Gallup Police Chief Manuel Gonzales received a tip that the Navajo Motor Company would be burglarized either late on the evening of Friday, September 10, or early on the morning of Saturday, September 11, 1965. Captain John Arvizo and Detective Al Williams hid themselves in the motor company office and waited.

The tip was a good one. At about 4:00 o'clock on Saturday morning, Larry Ambler, 24, and Vincent Barraza, 19, approached the company's janitor as he arrived to do his cleaning chores. They handcuffed the custodian and used his keys to enter the building. The two then gathered some tools, including an acetylene cutting torch, from the garage and carried them into the office where they intended to cut their way into the company safe. Officers Arvizo and Williams revealed themselves and announced that the robbers were under arrest. Shots were fired immediately. Ambler shot Captain Arvizo in the chest with a .38 caliber revolver and the officer was able to return fire with one blast from his 12-gauge shotgun. The full load of buckshot hit Ambler in the chest at close range. Ambler managed to get from the office into the garage area where he fell dead. Captain Arvizo died on the way to the hospital. Barraza escaped from the scene, but his freedom was short-lived. Detective Williams recognized him and a citywide manhunt was quickly organized. A Gallup patrolman spotted Barraza on the street near his home and arrested him without incident.

(Another version of the story held that Ambler actually shot himself and that Barraza shot Captain Arvizo.)

Originally charged with felony murder, aggravated burglary, assault with intent to commit a violent felony, aggravated battery and aggravated assault, Barraza later pled guilty to second degree murder and received a sentence of from 10 to 50 years in prison. Ambler, a native of Oklahoma, had been employed as a jailer for the city of Gallup for about 13 months before he was killed. Chief Gonzales believed that Ambler was involved in other burglaries in the Gallup area.

Detective Arvizo, 59, had been with the Gallup Police Department for 15 years at the time of his death. He was survived by his wife and two grown children. When renovation of the Gallup Department of Public Safety building was completed in August of 1989, it was rededicated to the memory of Detective John B. Arvizo.

Albuquerque *Journal*, September 12, 1965
Gallup Police Department, Case and Personnel Files
Cpl. Sam Gomez, Gallup Police Department, correspondence, November 22, 1989

JOE AVEN, JR.

Patrolman
New Mexico State Police

State Police Officer Joe Aven and State Police Sergeant John "Jake" Ramsey (see page 241) were severely injured on August 6, 1953 in a head-on collision with a vehicle occupied by five members of a Chicago family on highway U. S. 180 about 14 miles east of Hobbs, New Mexico. Ramsey died at the scene and Aven died the following day. Three people riding in the other car were also killed. E. W. "Bill" Long, acting chief of the Hobbs Police Department, a passenger in the State Police car, was injured but survived.

The officers had been en route to Sweetwater, Texas, to complete an investigation and to attend the funeral of Sheriff Robert L. McReynolds of Gaines County who was killed in an automobile accident earlier that week.

Officer Joe Aven, 30, a native of southeastern New Mexico, was a four-year veteran of the State Police. He had previously served as a Hobbs city police officer. His wife, Edna, a three-month-old daughter, Teresa Jo, his parents, Mr. & Mrs. Joe T. Aven, Sr., and three sisters survived him. Joe Aven was highly regarded in the community and eulogized by the Hobbs *News-Sun*.

Frances Aven Brewer (Sister), correspondence, December 10, 1989
Hobbs *Daily News-Sun*, August 6, 1953
Roadrunner (New Mexico State Police Association, Vol. 3, No. 2, Summer, 1992)

MICHAEL C. AVILUCEA

Lieutenant
New Mexico State Police

Lt. Mike Avilucea served as commander of the New Mexico State Police Explosive Ordinance Disposal (EOD) team, as well as assistant commander of the Alamogordo district. In late May, 2008, he was given an assignment having to do with the disposal of explosives in northern New Mexico. On May 30, while driving south on U. S. Route 84, after completion of his assignment, near Tierra Amarilla in Rio Arriba County, he lost control of his State Police pickup, which then rolled over at least once, and jumped over a guardrail. Not wearing a seatbelt, Lt. Avilucea was thrown from the vehicle and severely injured. He was pronounced dead at La Clinica del Pubelo in Tierra Amarilla a short time later.

Lt. Avilucea, 51, was a 26 year veteran of the State Police. He was a native of Las Cruces and graduated from high school there in 1974. He subsequently attended Western New Mexico University and graduated Magna Cum Laude in criminal justice and sociology. He joined the State Police in 1981. He was an active member of the New Mexico State Police Association, the National Rifle Association, New Mexico Cattlemen's Association, the American Quarter Horse Association and the International Association of Bomb Technicians and Investigators. He was survived by his son, Lucas.

One of Avilucea's former supervisors described him "...a man of courage, first to get to the really bad calls for service [and] always a volunteer when something high-risk was happening."

State Police Chief Faron Segota said, "I have known him since I started with the State Police in 1982; he was a State Policeman's policeman. He was dedicated to serving the citizens of New Mexico and loved the department dearly. We will miss him very much."

Albuquerque *Journal*, June 3, 2008
Albuquerque *Journal*, Northern Bureau, May 31, 2008
William C. Kuehl, Captain, New Mexico State Police (Ret.)
New Mexico State Police Uniform Crash Report

JULIO E. BARAY

Air Interdiction Agent
United States Department of Homeland Security
Customs and Border Protection-Air and Marine

Julio Baray was killed in an aircraft accident on September 24, 2007, at the Moriarty Airport, in Torrance County, New Mexico, east of Albuquerque. He was undergoing training in a Cessna 210 with an instructor pilot who was also an Air Interdiction Agent. The instructor was seriously injured in the mishap.

Agent Baray was born in Matamoros, Tamaulipas, Mexico, but raised in El Paso, Texas. He graduated from El Paso High School in 1986 and earned a Bachelor of Science degree in criminal justice from the University of Texas in 1994. He earned a Master of Science degree in criminal justice from New Mexico State University in 1998. He joined United States Customs and Border Protection (CBP) in the same year. He served as K-9 handler before he joined the CBP Office of Air and Marine to become an Air Interdiction Officer in February 2007. He was a resident of Alamogordo, New Mexico at the time of his death. He was survived by his wife, Melissa and two sons, Angel Miguel and Victor Daniel. He is interred at the Immaculate Conception Catholic Cemetery at Alamogordo, and recognized at the Alamogordo Law Enforcement Officer's Memorial Garden.

Alamogordo Daily News, September 25, 2007
Lorraine Mackewich, Alamogordo, New Mexico

RONALD T. BACA

Patrolman
Gallup, New Mexico, Police Department

Officer Ronald Baca was officially off duty on the morning of Friday, January 3, 1986, but just before noon he picked up a departmental motorcycle and took it to be serviced. Along the way, a 70-year old man driving a pickup turned into Baca's path and the officer was unable to avoid a collision. Baca was not wearing a helmet. Police Chief Frank Gonzales said later that department policy required officers to wear helmets when on duty, but there was no such requirement when they were off duty, and no state law required the use of protective head-gear.

Ronnie Baca was pronounced dead at 2:23 that afternoon at Rehoboth McKinley Christian Hospital.

Officers cited the driver of the second vehicle for failure to yield to oncoming traffic. He pled no contest and was fined $15.

A three year veteran of the Gallup Police Department at the time of his death, Officer Baca, 22, was survived by his wife, Angela, and son, John, 2. Another son, Ronald, was born in August after his father died.

Albuquerque *Journal*, January 4, 1986
Gallup Police Department, Case and Personnel Files
Cpl. Sam Gomez, Gallup Police Department

GEORGE WASHINGTON BATTON

Sheriff
Eddy County, New Mexico

In early June, 1922, word reached Eddy County Sheriff George Batton that a Texas outlaw called the "Longhorn Will-O-Wisp" (Pedro Galindo) and two women were hiding at a house—some said a shack—in the town of Hope, about 20 miles west of Artesia in the far northwest corner of the county. Galindo had escaped from the Huntsville, Texas, prison while serving a life sentence for murder.

Batton, along with his deputies and a posse of local cowboys and citizens surrounded the place and ordered those inside to surrender. The women emerged and said no one remained inside.

The sheriff approached the front door and one of his deputies, Stone Wilburn, approached the back door. The "Will-O-Wisp," from concealment behind a dresser, opened fire immediately as the officers entered the house. A soft-nosed bullet bounced off Wilburn's rib and the sheriff took a bullet in the bowel near hip level. Both officers opened fire in a rapid succession of shots. The lights inside were blown out and the firing stopped. As Wilburn staggered outside, the women tried to escape, only to be caught by a couple of cowboys. The younger woman was then forced to go back into the house. She crawled in on her hands and knees and soon returned with Galindo's gun, a large caliber semi-automatic. She said both men inside were dead.

She was right. The posse found Sheriff Batton on the floor, dead. The outlaw was in a corner, shot through the neck and heart. Deputy Wilburn recovered from his wound.

George Batton, 58, previously served four years as deputy sheriff of Brown County in central Texas where he killed an outlaw who had shot and killed Sheriff Charles Bell in March 1898. Batton then served four years (1898-1901) as Brown County sheriff.

After he arrived in New Mexico, Batton served as Artesia town marshal and Eddy County deputy sheriff before he was elected sheriff in 1920. His wife, Lillie Bell, and four children—Sam, Grace, Cecil, and Dot—survived Sheriff Batton.

Sam succeeded his father as sheriff. Reports at the time showed that Sam was present at the gunfight that claimed his father's life, but his involvement is not known.

Albuquerque *Morning Journal*, June 5, 1922
Carlsbad *Current*, June 9, 1922
John Lewis, Eddy County Sheriff's Department
Sammy Tice, *Texas County Sheriffs*, privately published
Captain James B. Williams, Carlsbad Police Department

THOMAS C. BEDFORD, JR.

Deputy Sheriff
Lincoln County, New Mexico

A rash of burglaries occurred around the village of Nogal in Lincoln County, between Carrizozo and Ruidoso, in the fall of 1979. Though new to the area, Lincoln County Deputy Tommy Bedford was called upon to take reports and investigate many of them. On the evening of Sunday, October 7, Deputy Sheriff B. J. Barnes located a stolen, badly damaged and abandoned car in Nogal Canyon. Officers believed it was related to the burglaries.

On Monday afternoon, October 8, Deputy Bedford spotted two suspicious looking men—one of them armed with a rifle—walking along the road in the same area. He radioed the Lincoln County Sheriff's dispatcher and requested back up officers. He approached the two and ordered the man with the rifle to put the weapon on the hood of the patrol car and to produce identification. Bedford took a drivers license from one of the suspects and as he prepared to request a records check from the dispatcher, the older man removed a pistol from the younger man's hip pocket and shot the deputy. The first shot hit the officer in the chest and knocked him down. Then the killer stood over Bedford and shot him again and again. In all, the officer was shot five times: once in the hand, once in the stomach, once in the chest and twice in the head. When Deputies B. J. Barnes and John Cupp arrived, they found Bedford's car engine running, red-lights flashing and the radio microphone hanging out the left car window. Efforts to revive Bedford were unsuccessful.

A massive manhunt began immediately and before it was over as many as 250 officers from law enforcement agencies all over the state participated. With cars, pickups, horses, bloodhounds and a helicopter, they combed the rugged mountains in and around Nogal Canyon. On Tuesday, October 9, a 16-year-old escapee from the New Mexico Boy's School at Springer, Louie Salandre, surrendered himself first to rancher Bud Crenshaw who turned him over to State Police Sergeant Jack Johnson in the village of Nogal.

Salandre told officers that he met Robert Elton Cox, 40, in Albuquerque and together they stole a car and drove it to Lincoln County, where they wrecked it. Salandre claimed he had no part in killing Deputy Bedford. An Alamogordo magistrate issued a warrant for Cox's arrest, but the suspect, an expert woodsman who was somewhat familiar with the rugged Nogal Canyon area, was not immediately located. (Cox said later that he was out of Nogal Canyon by midnight on Monday, the 8th; the same day Bedford was killed.) On Thursday, roadblocks were dismantled but the search was not halted.

Just before noon on Friday, October 12, Otero County Sheriff's Deputy Hollis Bynum, on his way home to Alamogordo from the penitentiary in Santa Fe where he had delivered two prisoners, stopped in Corona, in far northern Lincoln County, for a snack. He recognized a man leaving the little store with a bag of groceries as fitting the description of Robert Elton Cox. Bynum radioed for assistance and was soon joined by Lincoln County jailer/dispatcher Donn Dosé and Carrizozo policeman Guy Brown. The three officers arrested Cox on a Corona street and though the killer was armed, he did not resist.

Cox had previously served prison time in Mississippi for grand larceny and New Mexico for fraudulent use of a credit card. He was sentenced to life in prison for the capital murder of Deputy Sheriff Tommy Bedford.

One of the officers who participated in the search for Cox was Lincoln County Deputy Sheriff Jim McSwane who later worked as a corrections officer at the prison near Santa Fe where he became acquainted with Robert Cox. Cox admitted to killing Bedford. He said he did it to avoid returning to prison. He also said that his main reason for being in the Ruidoso/Nogal Canyon area was to kill the warden of the corrections facility at Camp Sierra Blanca against whom he held a grudge dating back to the time Cox was incarcerated there. Jim McSwane was later elected sheriff of Lincoln County.

Deputy Bedford's wife, Beverly, and two small children survived him. The Lincoln County Sheriff's Department Substation in Ruidoso is named in honor of Deputy Thomas C. Bedford, Jr.

Albuquerque *Journal*, October 10, 11, 12, 13, 18, 19 & 25, 1979
B. J. Barnes, Sergeant, Ruidoso, New Mexico Police Department (Ret.)
Don Caviness, New Mexico Department of Corrections
James O. Jennings, Deputy Chief, New Mexico State Police (Ret.)
James McSwane, Former Sheriff, Lincoln County, New Mexico

JAMES W. BELL

Deputy Sheriff
Lincoln County, New Mexico

James Bell, 30,* also known as "Long" or "Lone" Bell, died after being shot by William H. Bonney, AKA, Billy the Kid, on April 28, 1881. Deputy Bell and Doña County Deputy Sheriff Robert Olinger were assigned the task of guarding Bonney, who had been sentenced to hang for the murder of Lincoln County Sheriff William Brady (April 1, 1878, see page 27). Legend may have eclipsed fact, but many believe that Bonney was provided a gun—probably hidden in a privy—which he used to kill Deputy Bell. He then secured a shotgun which he used to kill Olinger (see page 227). Research in the early 21st century indicated that Bonney may have attacked and disarmed Deputy Bell as the two of them returned to the courthouse from the privy. Bonney may have then used Bell's own gun to kill him.

Bell, a native of Maryland, migrated to Texas about 1875. He joined Company D, Frontier Battalion, Texas Rangers the same year. He arrived in New Mexico in time to marginally participate in the Lincoln County War (1878-1881). One source indicates that Bell may have also served as a Deputy U. S. Marshal but documentation is lacking. Described as quiet and soft-spoken, he was well regarded in the community. Bonney is even said to have regretted killing Bell.

Lincoln County Sheriff Patrick F. Garrett (see page 106) shot Bonney to death less than three months later, on July 14, 1881, at Fort Sumner, New Mexico.

Deputy Bell's obscure burial place was located at White Oaks, New Mexico, by members of the New Mexico Sheriffs' and Police Association. On July 19, 2003, the association erected a monument on the spot to honor his fidelity to duty.

* One source shows Bell's birth date around 1842. Another indicates that he was about 30 at the time of his death, which would mean he was born in the early 1850s.

George Curry, *1861-1947, An Autobiography*, University of New Mexico Press
William A. Keleher, *Violence in Lincoln County*, University of New Mexico Press
Jay Robert Nash, *Encyclopedia of Western Lawmen & Outlaws* Da Capo Press
The New Mexico Lawman, Vol. 10, No. 3
Marc Simmons, *When Six-Guns Ruled, Outlaw Tales of the Southwest*, Ancient City

Press

Dan L. Thrapp, *Encyclopedia of Frontier Biography*, University of Nebraska Press

Paul Trachtman, "The Gunfighters," *The Old West*, Time-Life Books

Robert M. Utley, *High Noon In Lincoln, Violence on the Western Frontier* University of New Mexico Press

John P. Wilson, *Merchants, Guns & Money, The Story of Lincoln County and Its Wars*, Museum of New Mexico Press

VENTURA BENCOMA

Jailer
Grant County, New Mexico

In the spring of 1921, Rumaldo Lazano and Elenterio* Corral, both teen-agers, were serving time in the Grant County jail on relatively minor charges. Lazano was nearing the end of a 30-day sentence for attempted larceny and Corral had been sentenced to reform school for robbing an elderly man. On April 2, they undertook to free themselves from confinement. First, using a piece of iron from a bunk, they scraped a hole in their cell wall. This allowed them into an adjacent room. They were then able to climb over a door and get into the jail's hallway.

The problems they faced at that point were twofold: the doors leading to freedom were locked and the jailer, Ventura Bencoma who had possession of the keys, was sleeping in a room that opened onto the hallway. One of the young felons found a hand ax in a room used to store firewood. With it, he struck jailer Bencoma in the forehead with such force that the wound extended from the top of the man's head to the center of his face.

With keys in hand, Lozano and Corral attempted to free prisoner Jesus Rocha, but they were unable to get the cell door to open. They also had Bencoma's gun which they used to threaten other prisoners before they fled. A female prisoner named Bradshaw set up the alarm and Sheriff John Casey was in pursuit of the escapees within an hour.

Bencoma died about five hours later.

Capture of Lozano and Corral came four days later at Santa Rita, northeast of Silver City. In June of 1921, both were tried for murder, convicted and sentenced to death. In spite of numerous pleas for clemency, Governor Merritt Mechem refused to intervene and Lozano and Corral were hanged at Silver City on January 20, 1922.

Ventura Bencoma, 60 years old at the time of his death, had been a Grant County jailer for 12 years. He was a large and muscular man who maintained a reputation for fearlessness when handling prisoners. He had been ill for a few days leading up to his death and officials speculated that he was sleeping more soundly than usual because of it.

News reports of the time indicated that Bencoma was well regarded as a jailer, and well respected in the community. His funeral was "…attended by hundreds of friends, being one of the largest ever seen here [Silver City]." He was survived by a wife and several children.

* The Name is also spelled *Elitrio* and *Eleuterio*, depending on the source.

Albuquerque *Morning Journal*, April 3, 1921, January 21, 1922
West Gilbreath, *Death on the Gallows: The Story of Legal Hangings in New Mexico, 1847-1923*, High-Lonesome Books
Santa Fe *New Mexican*, April 5, 1921
Silver City *Enterprise*, April 8, 1921, January 21, 1922

ROYCE BENNETT

Patrolman
Deming, New Mexico, Police Department

It was between 3:00 and 3:30 a.m. on Wednesday morning, July 25, 1979, when Officer Royce Bennett pursued a blue Chevrolet pickup truck operated by Billy Gibson, 25, into the parking lot of Klein's Kountry Klub [*sic*] Motel on U. S. Route 70-80 East near Deming. Bennett was aware that Gibson had been drinking and he had earlier warned him not to drive any more that night. Bennett was also aware that the pickup belonged to Gibson's wife, Lana, and the bank wanted it repossessed because it was uninsured.

Officers Bob Bowen and Benito Salas arrived to back up Bennett and both saw the officer with his gun drawn and pointed at the driver's side of the pickup. Both heard and saw an exchange of gunfire between Bennett and Gibson. Officer Bennett was hit in the chest with a single bullet fired from a .45-70 lever action rifle, and while his body armor offered a measure of protection, it was not enough. The impact of the heavy slug formed a "cone" in the vest which penetrated the officer's lung and caused severe, and fatal, internal injury. Billy Gibson was wounded slightly in the exchange of gunfire and arrested at the scene.

Gibson went on trial in January of 1980 charged with first-degree murder. The trial was held in Silver City on a change of venue requested by the defendant's lawyers. Officers Bowen and Salas testified that Gibson fired first and then Bennett fired, only to be killed with a second shot fired from the pickup. Gibson claimed that Bennett opened fire on him and that after five or six shots were fired into his truck, he fired just once in self-defense. A main defense contention was that Bennett's wound was so disabling that he could not have fired his own gun *after* being shot by Gibson. Therefore, the officer had to have fired first since the officer's gun was empty.

Other testimony in the trial indicated that officer Bennett had dated Lana Gibson at a time when the Gibsons were separated. Additionally, one of the prosecution's primary witnesses proved to be somewhat unreliable in his testimony. At the end of a five-day trial, the jury acquitted Gibson on the first-degree murder charge but could not reach a verdict on charges of second degree murder.

In June of 1980, Gibson was tried for a second time, charged with second-degree murder, and for a second time he was acquitted.

Officer Bennett, 25, a native of Hobbs, New Mexico, graduated from Deming High School in 1972. He served in the U. S. Army as a military policeman from 1972-75 after which he worked for his father until he joined the Deming Police Department on January 1, 1978. Royce Bennett was survived by a son, Casey, 5, of Grants, and his parents, LeRoy and Fern Bennett, and sisters Norene, Dena and Irene, all of Deming. The officer was buried in the Mountain View Cemetery in Deming with full military and law enforcement honors.

Albuquerque *Journal*, July 26, 1979
Deming *Headlight*, July 25, 26, & 27, 1979; January 21, 22, 23, 24, 25, & 28; June 23, 24, 25, 26, 27 & 30, 1980
Bill Kuehl, Deming Police Department
Capt. Jack Coussons, Luna County Sheriff's Department
Sixth Judicial District Court, County of Grant (CR-79-063)

HARVEY SAMUEL "HARVE" BOLIN

Deputy Sheriff
Lamb County, Texas

On July 15, 1932, a band of three or four robbers held up the bank at Olton, Lamb County, Texas. They made off with about $3800. An investigation by Lamb County Sheriff Bob Crim produced suspects Lee Pebworth, Glen Hunsucker and Jack Sullivan. The sheriff secured arrest warrants for the three and organized a posse made up of himself, Deputies Harve Bolin and Bob Miller, District Attorney Meade F. Griffin, and Roosevelt County, New Mexico, Deputy R. L. Hollis.*

Crim's investigation led him to Lee Pebworth's ramshackle homestead located near the village of Bluitt in far-southern Roosevelt County, between the communities of Milnesand, New Mexico and Bledsoe, Texas. Early in the morning hours of Saturday, August 20, 1932, the posse took up positions near the farmhouse. As four men walked from the farmhouse to the barn, Sheriff Crim identified himself and ordered them to "…stick up your hands!" Instead of obeying, the outlaws produced guns—Pebworth secured a rifle he'd previously hidden in a feed trough—and commenced firing at the officers.

Deputies Bolin and Hollis went down with the first volley. Shot in the head, Bolin died immediately. Shot in the mouth and hip, Hollis was severely wounded, but survived. The officers took cover and returned fire. Pebworth was wounded but, along with three other bandits, managed to escape from the scene.

Police departments and sheriff's offices all over eastern New Mexico and west Texas were alerted to be on the lookout for the killers. At about noon the same day, Sheriff Bob Beverly of Lea County, New Mexico, and a posse arrested Pebworth and Stanley Headrick at the Dalmont ranch, about 12 miles southwest of Tatum. Pebworth's wound prevented his escape. No trace of the remaining outlaws was immediately found. Headrick was arrested but claimed that he had no part in the shooting. Pebworth's son-in-law, Joe Jones, was also arrested, and he too claimed innocence. Charges against Headrick and Jones were subsequently dropped. Jack Sullivan and Glenn Hunsucker disappeared completely, but that wouldn't last.

Texas and New Mexico officers shot and seriously wounded Sullivan before they arrested him near Mountainair, in Torrance County, New Mexico, three weeks later on September 13, 1932. Texas authorities extradited him for the robbery of the Olton bank. He was held in the Lubbock, Texas, County jail, from which he escaped on November 19, 1932. Recaptured at Vernon, Texas just before Christmas, he was subsequently tried and convicted of the Olton robbery and an armed robbery he committed during his escape, and sentenced to 37 years in prison. He was not tried for the killing of Harve Bolin.

Glenn Hunsucker was shot and killed by a Lincoln County, New Mexico, posse in July of 1933. Before his death, he'd participated in the killings of four peace officers: Harve Bolin; Sheriff John Moseley of Swisher County, Texas; Deputy Sheriff Joe Brown of Wise County, Texas; and Chief Deputy Sheriff Tom Jones of Lincoln County, New Mexico (see page 159).

On October 5, 1932 Lee Pebworth, about 60 years old, appeared before a Portales judge and pleaded guilty to second degree murder to avoid the possibility of receiving the death penalty. He was sentenced to 99 years in prison. In 1938, New Mexico Governor Clyde Tingley commuted Pebworth's sentence to 30 years. He actually served about nine years before he was released from prison in 1941.

Born in Lee County, Virginia, Deputy Bolin was about 54 years old at the time of his death. He'd served as a police officer at Lockney, Texas, before he moved to Plainview where he served as policeman, police chief, and night chief of police. He also served as Hale County, Texas, deputy. He'd been a peace officer for about twenty-two years. His wife, Nellie, and ten children—nine girls and one boy—survived him. He was interred at Lockney, Texas.

* Different sources tell different stories about the number of possemen that participated in the gunfight at Pebworth's farm. One source indicates the group was seven strong. Most likely, the members were Sheriff Crim, Harve Bolin, Meade Griffin, and R. L. Hollis. Deputy Bob Miller may have been there—he said he was—but some sources do not mention him. Dozens of officers participated in the search for the killers.

Albuquerque *Journal*, August 21, September 14, December 21, 1932
Don Bullis, *Duels, Gunfights & Shoot-Outs: Wild Tales from the Land of Enchantment*, Rio Grande Books
Carlsbad *Current-Argus*, August 20, September 14, 1932
Clovis *Evening News*, August 22, 1932
Clovis *News Journal*, November 18, 1938
Lubbock *Sunday Avalanche Journal*, August 21, 1932
Plainview, Texas, *Evening Herald*, August 21 & 22, 1932
Roswell *Morning Dispatch*, October 5, 1932
New Mexico Department of Corrections records

WILLIAM BRADY

Sheriff
Lincoln County, New Mexico

Sometime between 9:00 and 10:00 on the morning of April 1, 1878, Sheriff William Brady along with deputies George Hindman, John Long, J. B. Mathews and George Peppin stepped out of the Lincoln County Courthouse, in Lincoln, New Mexico, and walked along the town's only street towards the John Henry Tunstall store. The quiet of the spring morning was shattered by a volley of gunfire and Sheriff Brady fell dead, his body pierced by at least a dozen rifle balls. Deputy Hindman was hit once and went down. A second bullet subsequently dispatched him (see page 141). The other deputies escaped unharmed.

Nine assassins may have made up the party that killed Brady and Hindman: William H. Bonney (Billy the Kid), John Middleton, Henry Brown, Jim French, Charlie Bowdre, Frank McNabb, Robert Widenmann, John Scroggins, and Fred Waite.* They all managed to escape the scene, although reports at the time indicated that Bonney and French were wounded slightly when J. B. Mathews opened fire as the killers picked over the bodies of Brady and Hindman (Bonney stole Brady's new rifle, according to one source).

William H. Bonney avoided capture until a posse led by Lincoln County Sheriff-elect Pat Garrett (see page 106) captured him two and a half years later, at Stinking Springs, near Tiaban, in December of 1880. Tried at Mesilla for the murder of Sheriff Brady, Bonney was convicted on April 13, 1881, and sentenced to death by hanging; the sentence to be executed on May 13 in the town of Lincoln. On April 28, Bonney escaped custody in Lincoln after killing deputies J. W. Bell (see page 19) and Robert Olinger (see page 227). Garrett finally shot and killed Bonney on July 14, 1881 at Fort Sumner. Of all the murders Bonney is alleged to have committed, the killing of Sheriff Brady is the only one for which he was ever convicted. Indictments were filed against several of the other ambush participants, but none of them were ever tried for the crime.

William Brady, 49, was born in Ireland and migrated to the United States in 1851. He joined the United States Army the same year and was posted to Texas and New Mexico. He left the Army in 1866 with the rank of Major. His wife, Bonifacia and eight children survived Brady. A ninth, Primitivo, was born in November after his father died.

* There is some dispute about the number of killers present, and who, exactly, they were. Different historians offer different lists of participants.

William A. Keleher, *Violence in Lincoln County, 1869-1881*, University of New Mexico Press

Lily Klasner, *My Girlhood Among Outlaws*, University of Arizona Press

Donald R. Lavish, *Sheriff William Brady, Tragic Hero of the Lincoln County War*, Sunstone Press

Robert M. Utley, *High Noon in Lincoln, Violence on the Western Frontier*, University of New Mexico Press

VICTOR C. BREEN

District Attorney
Tenth Judicial District of New Mexico
(Quay, Harding & De Baca Counties)

Vic Breen walked out of his house in Tucumcari at a little after 8:00 o'clock on the morning of December 1, 1971. He faced the second day of a murder trial and he was on his way to the courthouse. Two shots, fired from a car parked near-by, rang out and the 54 year old District Attorney fell dead in his driveway, shot in the back with a .30 caliber military-type rifle.

A massive investigation involving officers from the Quay County Sheriff's Department, the Tucumcari Police Department, the New Mexico State Police, the Attorney General's Office and the Southern Pacific Railroad police began immediately. Information from sources in Tucumcari led to a suspect and at about 8:00 the next evening, State Police officers arrested Jose Rosendo Garcia, 43, at a motel in Belen, south of Albuquerque. Garcia's vehicle matched the description of a car witnesses observed near the Breen home at the time of the shooting. Garcia also had in his possession a rifle that matched the weapon used in the assassination.

At the time of the killing, Garcia was free on convalescent leave from the State Hospital at Las Vegas where he'd been a court-ordered patient several times beginning in 1968. Breen had been instrumental in those commitments. Whenever Garcia misbehaved at home, his family would threaten to "...get Mr. Breen after him."

In February 1972, public defenders Benny Flores and Leon Karelitz represented Garcia before District Court Judge J. V. Gallegos who ruled that Garcia was incompetent to stand trial. The Judge issued an order sending the assassin to the state prison in Santa Fe for "safe keeping." A proviso of the commitment was that Garcia not be removed from the prison without a written order of the court. Less than three years later, in December of 1975, without notification to anyone, Garcia was moved back to the State Hospital. He subsequently gained outpatient status and returned to Tucumcari. Vic Breen's family was not notified when Garcia was released, and they were considerably distressed by the way in which the prosecution handled the entire matter.

Garcia died in 1988 without ever having been tried for the murder of Vic Breen.

Born in Forrest, New Mexico, and a graduate of the Kansas University Law School, Breen was described as a "vigorous prosecutor." He'd served as District Attorney for 20 years prior to his death. His wife, Lois, two daughters, Vicki Ann and Nancy survived him, along with his parents, Mr. and Mrs. Ed Breen of near Tucumcari.

Vicki Ann Breen (Daughter)
Office of the District Attorney, Tenth Judicial District, October 1989
Las Vegas (New Mexico) *Optic*, December 2, 1971
Tucumcari *Daily News*, December 1, 2, and 3, 1971
A. P. Wickard, Deputy Chief, New Mexico State Police (Ret.)

LESLIE DELBERT BUGG

Patrolman
New Mexico State Police

Patrolman Delbert Bugg, astride his State Police motorcycle, was patrolling U. S. Route 66 near Tucumcari on Tuesday, August 20, 1946, when he collided head-on with a car driven by a Texas man who was driving on the wrong side of the road. The officer suffered a broken pelvis, back and internal injuries. He was taken to the hospital in Tucumcari where he died the following day. Leslie Delbert Bugg had been with the State Police fewer than five months—he joined the department on April 9, 1946—when he was killed.

Officer Bugg, 26, was a native of Garden City, Texas, and graduated from Tucumcari High School in 1940. He joined the army in 1942 and served in both the Aleutians and Europe during World War II. His wife, Evalena and four stepchildren survived him.

Quay County *Sun*, May 18, 1988
New Mexico State Police records
Roadrunner (New Mexico State Police Association, Vol. 3, No. 2, Summer, 1992)

WILLIAM A. BURGEN

Deputy Sheriff
Colfax County, New Mexico

Twenty-four year old Gus Mentzer worked as barkeeper for a gambler named William "Billy" Burbridge who owned and operated the Bank Exchange Saloon* in Ratón, New Mexico. Burbridge fired Mentzer for drinking and carousing and Mentzer left town for a time. On the evening of June 26, 1882, he came back. A drunk Gus Mentzer, armed with two pistols provided by another gambler, named Turner, approached Deputy Sheriff Pete Dollman on the street in front of the Bank Exchange Saloon. He pulled one of the guns and jammed it against the deputy's ribs.

"Give up your gun," Mentzer demanded.

"Oh, no, I could not do that," Dollman replied.

"But you must!"

About then a citizen named Johnson got close enough to knock Mentzer's hand downward and his gun discharged harmlessly into the dusty street. Mentzer ran to the front door of the Bank Exchange Saloon. Deputy Dollman fired several shots in his direction, all of which missed except the one that struck a citizen named W. H. Harris who just happened to be hurrying along the sidewalk. Mentzer escaped into the saloon then fled out the back door.

Dollman and a group of citizens searched the town, but Mentzer was not to be found. At about 9:00 p.m. the young gunman appeared at the Bank Exchange Saloon and ordered a drink. Whether he got it or not is unrecorded. Deputy Dollman was present in the saloon and he and other citizens chased Mentzer into the street and began shooting at him. The fugitive fled toward the railroad depot where he shot and wounded J. H. Latimer in the leg and breast. He jumped aboard a railroad engine that had its steam up, but he couldn't make the giant vehicle move. Citizens S. H. Jackson and Hugh Eddleston approached the engine.

"There he is," Jackson shouted an instant before Mentzer shot and killed him. Eddleston was killed a few seconds later.

Deputy Dollman and another deputy, William Burgen, were then able to capture Mentzer whose guns were empty. They took the prisoner to the Little Brindle Saloon where he was left in the charge of Deputy Burgen behind a locked door. Burgen went about putting leg irons on the prisoner while Dollman went to the telegraph office to wire the bad news to Jackson's widow.

One of Mentzer's victims, Hugh Eddleston, had been a business partner of Justice of the Peace Harvey Moulton, and the judge soon arrived at the saloon where Mentzer was being held. He banged on the door, but Deputy Burgen would not let him in. Moulton kicked the door opened and entered, gun in hand.

"Give up the son of a ----- to be hung!" he ordered, according to a witness.

Burgen refused, citing his duty to protect the miscreant.

As Moulton made a grab for the prisoner, Burgen fired and the judge only lived long enough to fire a single shot into Burgen's stomach. Mentzer escaped and fled to the Williams and Frick butcher shop where Deputy Dollman arrested him again. The young killer begged Dollman to protect his life and the deputy said he'd do his best, but Dollman must of have known his efforts would be futile. The butcher, Williams, provided a rope and the crowd took Mentzer away from Dollman and told the killer to "say his prayers."

Someone threw the rope over a sign in front of the Raton Bank and the noose was put in place around Mentzer's neck. He "fought like a tiger" as citizens hoisted him up. Then a brace broke and the sign and Mentzer both tumbled to the board sidewalk. The crowd was not to be dissuaded. A young boy was boosted up and he placed the rope over the top of a sign post at the corner of Clark Avenue and First Street, and Mentzer was again strung-up. That time it worked. His body was left hanging until Tuesday morning. Later the same day a coroner's jury ruled that "Gus Mentzer came to his death by being hung by the neck by unknown parties."

Deputy Burgen, was taken to the offices of the Ratón Coal and Coking Company where he suffered great agony until he died at 10 o'clock on Tuesday morning. Not a great deal is known about Burgen. A local newspaper described him as an Irishman—a fine looking man, according to the editor—who lived in Canada for ten or twelve years before he arrived in Ratón in the spring of 1882. Colfax County Sheriff Allen C. Wallace appointed him deputy sheriff for the coal mining community of Blossburg, five miles northwest of Ratón, less than a week before Moulton killed him. Burgen was only present in Ratón on the day of the Mentzer affair because he'd come to town to visit with his brother who lived there. He was buried at Blossburg on June 28, 1882. "His funeral was largely attended."

The coroner's jury also passed judgment on the other four violent deaths. In the matter of William Burgen it reported thus:

> We, the Jury, find that William A. Burgen came to his death
> by a pistol shot wound received while in the exention [sic] of
> his duty, fired from a pistol in the hands of Harvey Moulton,
> Justice of the Peace.

The jury foreman was James Armstrong, who had witnessed the altercation and gunfight between Burgen and Moulton.

It is noteworthy that most of the participants in this unfortunate affair were in the saloon business. Deputy Sheriff Pete Dollman was a partner with S. H. Jackson in the Little Brindle Saloon (Jackson was also Dollman's brother-in-law). In fact, after the Gus Mentzer mess, Dollman resigned his job as deputy and entered the bar business full time. Hugh Eddleston and Harvey Moulton were partners in the Moulton House Saloon, and Billy Burbridge and Gus Mentzer were involved with the Bank Exchange Saloon. Burbridge sold out and left for San Francisco a short time after the killings.

Ratón's citizens were so irate at four killings, two woundings, and one lynching, in one night, that a mass meeting was held the very next evening. "Ten or twelve hundred" attended according to the local newspaper. A committee of eleven was named to prevent further disturbance. They issued a report that read in part:

> ...all professional gamblers, foodpads, thieves, cappers, dance
> hall men, bunko men, and all these [sic] who have no visible
> means of support, as well as all dance house girls and prostitutes
> generally, are hereby notified and publicly warned to leave this
> town within 48 hours from 12 o'clock at noon on the first day
> of July, 1882, and never return under penalty of incurring the
> just wrath of an indignant and outraged people.

It was never made clear why the gambler, Turner, provided Gus Mentzer with the guns he used to do his evil work. Turner was arrested in Las Vegas during the first week in July, 1882, and removed to Springer where he was tried on unspecified charges. The court fined him $20 and costs and set him free. A Ratón newspaper commented: "Turner will not be likely to show his elegant frame in Ratón again very soon."

* Some sources indicate that Burbridge and Mentzer were partners in the Bank Exchange Saloon.

Larry Ball, *Desert Lawmen, High Sheriffs of New Mexico and Arizona, 1846 -1912* University of New Mexico Press

Howard Bryan, "The Gus Mentzer Affair," *Robbers, Rogues, and Ruffians, True Tales of the Wild West*, Clear Light Publishers

Peter Hertzog, *Outlaws of New Mexico*, Sunstone Press, (This source incorrectly states that Mentzer went on his killing spree in Las Vegas, New Mexico, on June 28, 1882.)

Jacqueline Meketa, "Ratón's Black Comedy," *From Martyrs to Murderers, The Old Southwest's Saints, Sinners & Scalawags*, Yucca Tree Press

Robert J. Tórrez, *The Myth of the Hanging Tree*, University of New Mexico Press

Raton *Guard*, June 30 & July 7, 1882

DAN BUSTAMENTE

Deputy Sheriff
Valencia County, New Mexico

Deputy Bustamente died on May 25, 1898 in a gunfight with train robbers near Santa Rita in Socorro County. See *Frank X. Vigil*, page 316, for details.

ROBERT B. "BOB" BUTLER

Officer

Hobbs, New Mexico, Police Department

At age 68, Bob Butler served the Hobbs Police Department as parking control officer. At about 3:30 on Saturday afternoon, July 7, 1951, while making his rounds, Officer Butler stopped to visit with Phil Verner, owner of the K. C. Store on Broadway, and store clerk Ira Grantham. As the three men stood in the street talking, they observed brothers Speight Fondron Parks, 27, and Gene Afton Parks, 22, coming toward them. Both staggered along the street and appeared drunk. Officer Butler approached the men and when he put his hand on one of them the other one hit the elderly officer with his fist. In the fight that followed, Officer Butler was knocked down three times. At struggle's end, Speight Parks removed Butler's service revolver from its holster.

Butler and Grantham fled into the store. Speight Parks pursued them and began firing. Butler was shot first, three times, and fell dead a few feet inside the door and Grantham, 63, also shot three times, died further inside the store. Verner had entered the store when the altercation began on the street, and called the police station for help.

The Parks brothers fled. Hobbs policeman R. C. "Pinky" Hamlin captured Gene Parks almost immediately. Speight Parks managed to hijack a late model Ford and flee. He wrecked it and stole a second car from a Hobbs gas station. In all, he wrecked four cars and was in the process of stealing a fifth when Lea County Sheriff's Deputy Bruce McCallum and Hobbs Police Chief Ivan Reed accosted him. McCallum was armed with a 12-gauge pump shotgun.

"Raise your hands, Parks, and raise them empty!" the deputy shouted.

Parks did not respond, and McCallum repeated the order. Then Parks started to take aim with Butler's pistol and McCallum fired. A load of 00 buckshot hit the killer in the right arm and chest. He survived his injury.

After his capture, State Police officer Joe Aven asked Gene Parks if they meant to kill Butler.

"You're damned right we did. I'm glad the old S. O. B. is dead," Parks responded.

The press at the time reported that the Parks brothers were known dope addicts who were "hopped up" at the time Speight shot Butler and Grantham. Both brothers were tried for murder. Speight was convicted and sentenced to two life terms in prison. Gene was acquitted. Speight was stabbed to death by prisoner Alejandro Garcia about six months after he reached prison. Garcia was charged with voluntary manslaughter.

Officer Butler had worked as an officer for the Hobbs Police Department for about four years at the time of his death. His wife, Osie, six sons and two daughters survived him. His son Ned had previously served as mayor of Hobbs.

Albuquerque *Journal*, February 1, 1952
Hobbs *Daily Flare*, July 10, 1951
Hobbs *Daily News-Sun*, July 8, 1951
Hobbs Police Department
State Senator Joseph K. Harvey
Molly Dunaway (Daughter)

EMILIO CANDELARIA

Deputy Sheriff
Bernalillo County, New Mexico

On the evening of Wednesday, January 29, 1930 Federal Prohibition Agent C. U. Finley, two other agents and four Bernalillo County sheriff's deputies attempted to serve a search warrant on the ranch of Procopio Espinosa in the Sandia Mountains, near Sedillo, east of Albuquerque. The three agents entered the house leaving deputies Emilio Candelaria, Pablo Lujan, Abe Sour, and Ablencio Romero outside. As agent Finley read the warrant to Procopio Espinosa inside the house, Gregorio Espinosa, Procopio's brother, and several other men encountered the deputies hidden outside.

"There's one of them," Gregorio Espinosa yelled as Deputy Candelaria raised up from where he'd been laying on the ground. Gregorio fired his shotgun at the deputy, a blast of birdshot taking Candelaria in the face. Firing on both sides became general and Augustine Jaramillo—a nephew of Procopio and Gregorio Espinosa—received wounds in his leg and arm.

The agents inside the house thought they were trapped and they fled out the door and into nearby woods. Agent Finley left his two agents at the Espinosa ranch to help the deputies while he drove to the village of Barton, west of Sedillo, and called Bernalillo County Sheriff Philip Hubbell for help. In the meantime, federal agents and deputies back at the ranch managed to drag Deputy Candelaria into the safety of the woods where they all waited for help to arrive.

Sheriff Hubbell and the federal prohibition agent for New Mexico, Charles Sterns, arrived with about a dozen officers. They surrounded the house and demanded the surrender of those inside. The shooting of Deputy Candelaria seemed to have a dampening effect on the men in the Espinosa house, and they all surrendered without further gunfire or bloodshed.

No illegal booze was found during the raid, nor was a moonshine still. Officers said they could smell mash, however.

Deputy Candelaria, 33, died as he was being taken to a hospital in Albuquerque.

In addition to the Espinosas and Jaramillo, seven other men were also arrested and charged with murder even though Gregorio admitted firing the shot that killed the deputy.

A widow and ten-year-old son survived Deputy Emilio Candelaria, a veteran of World War I. Burial was made at the San Jose Cemetery in Albuquerque.

An Albuquerque newspaper reporter wrote this:

> When deputies approached the home of Candelaria's family on
> South Broadway to notify them of his death, they saw a dim
> light burning within, despite the late hour. It was from a lamp
> that the young officer's mother always left burning whenever he
> was out late. She lit it as usual Wednesday night, but it burned
> in vain."

Albuquerque *Journal*, January 30, 31, February 2, 4, 1930
Amarillo *Daily News*, January 31, 1930

RUBEN CARBAJAL

Deputy Sheriff
Doña Ana County, New Mexico

Deputy Ruben Carbajal, 31, died as a result of a single vehicle auto accident on August 20, 1990. Accident reports indicated that the vehicle being driven by the deputy, a Ford Bronco, was traveling south on State Road 185, at about 5:00 a.m. when a Chevrolet pickup entered from a side road and failed to yield to Carbajal's vehicle. The deputy swerved to his left to avoid a collision and crossed over to the northbound shoulder. He then overcorrected causing the Bronco to overturn onto its left side and skid for 132 feet before it rolled over three times, coming to rest on the left side. Deputy Carbajal was not wearing a seat belt and was thrown clear of the vehicle. He landed 42 feet from where his sheriff's unit came to rest. He was transported to Las Cruces Memorial Medical Center where he died just over two hours later. The odometer on the Bronco showed more than 135,000 miles.

Ruben Carbajal went to work for the Doña Ana County Sheriff's Department as a jailer in 1987. He became a deputy in March of 1988. Unmarried, Deputy Carbajal was survived by his parents, Ruben Sr., and Celia Carbajal and two sisters, Debbie Paz and Rosie Carbajal.

Albuquerque *Journal*, August 22, 1990
El Paso *Times*, August 23 & 28, 1990
Las Cruces *Sun-News*, August 22 & 23; September 21, 1990
Santa Fe *New Mexican*, August 22, 1990
State Police Reports

JAMES CARLYLE

Deputy Sheriff
Lincoln County, New Mexico

Jim Carlyle (sometimes spelled *Carlysle* or *Carlisle*) earned his living as a blacksmith at White Oaks, New Mexico, in the late fall of 1880. After William H. Bonney (Billy the Kid), Billy Wilson, Dave Rudabaugh and other outlaws fired shots at Deputy Sheriff James Redman on White Oak's main street, Carlyle, who also served as a Lincoln County deputy sheriff, took a leadership position in the 12-man posse that pursued the miscreants. The chase ended about 40 miles to the north at the Greathouse and Kuch ranch on the White Oaks-Las Vegas Road, near the present-day town of Corona. The ranch house, sometimes called Greathouse Tavern, was actually a saloon and way station for travelers. The outlaws had the better of the situation as a standoff developed; the outlaws inside where it was warm and the posse outside in the cold. Snow covered the ground and the temperature stood at below freezing.

A citizen named Joe Steck became an intermediary between the two groups. It was agreed that "Whiskey Jim" Greathouse—who acquired his nickname name by illegally selling liquor to Indians—would join the posse as a hostage if a representative of the law would enter the saloon and discuss the situation with William Bonney. Carlyle agreed and traded places with Greathouse. By late evening the deputy had not returned and the other possemen became concerned. They sent a note into the house saying that if Carlyle was not promptly released, they would shoot Greathouse. Shortly afterward, a shot was heard from outside and what happened next has been the source of debate from that day to this.

One theory is that Carlyle heard the shot and thinking his posse had killed Greathouse, he dived out a window to save his own life, only to be shot to death by Bonney and the outlaws. Bonney's version of events agreed that Carlyle jumped out of the window after the shot was fired, but Bonney claimed the deputy was actually shot and killed by members of his own posse who, not recognizing him, thought he was attacking them.

The posse withdrew after Carlyle was shot, leaving his body where it fell in the snow. Less than an hour later, the outlaws also fled the scene. Carlyle's body was frozen stiff when Joe Steck found it at daybreak. Another White Oaks posse, this one led by William Hudgens, burned the road-ranch to the ground on November 28, 1880.

It is not known who fired the shot that created the circumstances leading to Deputy Carlyle's death. Jim Greathouse was arrested in March 1881, and charged as an accessory to the murder of Jim Carlyle. He was released on bond two days later. In December 1881, after rustling some 40 head of cattle from Joel Fowler of Socorro, Fowler shot Greathouse to death in the San Mateo Mountains, west of Socorro. (Fowler, himself a criminal, was hanged for the murder of J. E. Cade at Socorro on January 23, 1884.)

Lincoln County Sheriff Pat Garrett killed William H. Bonney at Fort Sumner on July 14, 1881. Dave Rudabaugh was killed in Mexico in 1886. Billy Wilson was later convicted of counterfeiting and sentenced to Leavenworth Prison in Kansas, from which he escaped. President Grover Cleveland pardoned him in 1896 at the behest of Pat Garrett. One source says he later became sheriff of Terrell County, Texas. He was killed there, probably in 1918, by drunken cowboy.

Not much about Jim Carlyle is known for sure. He may have been born about 1860 in Trumbull County, Ohio. One source says that Carlyle and outlaw Billy Wilson were both from eastern Ohio where they attended school together. That may explain why Carlyle was willing to go into the ranch house in the first place.

Howard Bryan, *Robbers, Rouges and Ruffians, True Tales of the Wild West*, Clear Light
    Publishing
George Curry, 1861-1947, An Autobiography, University of New Mexico Press
Peter Hertzog, *Outlaws of New Mexico*, Sunstone Press
William A. Keleher, *Violence in Lincoln County, 1869-1881*, University of New Mexico
    Press
Leon Claire Metz, *The Shooters*, Mangan Books
Jay Robert Nash, *Encyclopedia of Western Lawmen & Outlaws*, Da Capo Press (This
    source incorrectly identifies Tarrell [sic] County as being in New Mexico.)
Dan L. Thrapp, *Encyclopedia of Frontier Biography*, University of Nebraska Press
Sammy Tice, *Texas County Sheriffs*, privately published

MACK R. CARMICHAEL

Sheriff
Mckinley County, New Mexico

Sheriff Mack Carmichael expected trouble. He assigned extra deputies to escort prisoners Eziquio Navarro and Victor Campos to the McKinley courthouse on Thursday morning, April 4, 1935. The prisoners were strikers and squatters—Communists, some said—whose prosecution for trespassing would attract a lot of sympathetic attention from others of the same ilk. Undersheriff Dee Roberts and deputies Lawrence E. "Bobcat" Wilson and Hoy Boggess encountered no problem getting the prisoners to Justice of the Peace William J. Bickel's Gallup courtroom.

A crowd began to gather on Coal Avenue outside the courthouse as the proceedings got underway inside. Justice Bickel, however, took no action against the accused men but continued the case until the following day to allow Navarro time to secure the services of legal counsel. Carmichael decided that rather than take his prisoners through the crowd outside the courtroom door, he'd take them the back way; out through the judge's chambers, down an alley from Third Street to Second Street and to the jail. The mob—75 to 300 strong, depending on who told the story—learned of the maneuver and thought Judge Bickel had railroaded Navarro and the sheriff was sneaking him back to jail. The J. P. was sometimes referred to as Bail-less Bickel.

A disorderly crowd confronted the sheriff and his men on Third Street and demanded the release of Navarro and Campos. A scuffle quickly followed and rioter Ignacio Velarde produced a gun and began firing. Sheriff Carmichael fell, blood gushing from his face and shoulder; shot dead and on the ground before he could draw his own gun. Dee Roberts quickly drew and fired. Velarde, 38, was hit and died instantly. Roberts also shot Solomon Esquibel, 37, who died eight days later.

Hoy Boggess, after lobbing a tear gas grenade, went down under the weight of four or five rioters, one of whom stabbed him with an ice pick. He lost his gun in the affray. Firing continued. Bobcat Wilson was hit in the chest. Boggess regained his feet, grabbed Wilson's gun and commenced firing. Roberts emptied his own pistol and three more rioters fell wounded. Navarro and Campos escaped.

Gallup police chief Kelsey Pressley and his officers moved in and the rioters broke and ran. After the gun smoke and tear gas cleared, Bobcat Wilson and Hoy Boggess were removed to the hospital. They recovered from their wounds. Dee Roberts immediately succeeded Mack Carmichael as McKinley County Sheriff and he went about rounding up the rioters.

In the days that followed, officers arrested about 150 people, 47 of them charged with murder under a statute which allowed such charges in cases where mob violence resulted in the death of a peace officer. Ten rioters remained charged with murder after a preliminary hearing before Judge Miguel A. Otero in Santa Fe.

Between the preliminary hearing and the trial, lawyers and representatives of some outside groups visited Gallup in an effort to gather evidence for the defense. In spite of a State Police escort by officer Earl Irish (who had previously served as chief of the New Mexico Motor Patrol), two New York lawyers were kidnapped, roughed up and threatened before they were released near Tohatchi, 25 miles north of Gallup. The outsiders demanded that Governor Clyde Tingley provide additional state police officers and help from the National Guard. Not everyone thought there was need for additional officers. Sheriff Roberts entertained the notion that the kidnapping was a hoax. A local resident said this:

> Well, if those birds didn't precisely kidnap themselves, they certainly laid themselves open to trouble. We don't care much for eastern dudes and their women telling us how bad we are. A few years ago, they'd have danced to a brace of pistols. As it was, all they got was a good scare, and it was probably coming to 'em.

No one was ever prosecuted for the "kidnapping" and the two "victims" returned to New York, no longer interested in defending the accused killers of Sheriff Carmichael.

Venue in the case was transferred from Gallup to Aztec in San Juan County, and Judge Otero was disqualified. The New Mexico Supreme Court appointed Judge James McGhee of Chaves County as trial judge and McGhee in turn appointed two New Mexico attorneys to defend the accused: Hugh Woodward, former U. S. Attorney, and John Simms, a Supreme Court Justice. Judge McGhee went around Aztec armed and accompanied by an armed bodyguard.

Finally, in October 1935, three of the rioters, Juan Ochoa, Manuel Avitia, and Leandro Velarde, were convicted of second-degree murder. Judge McGhee sentenced each of them to 45 to 60 years in prison. The convictions were appealed. The Supreme Court reversed Velarde's conviction. Ochoa and Avitia served short prison terms before they were pardoned and set free.

Mack R. Carmichael served as McKinley County undersheriff from 1931 to 1934 when he was elected sheriff. He was survived by his wife, Stella, and a son, Carl, 10.

Gallup *Independent*, April 4, 5, 15 & 17, 1935

Erna Fergusson, "New Mexico Tries Its Own," *Murder & Mystery in New Mexico*, Lightning Tree Press

Cpl. Sam Gomez, Gallup Police Department, correspondence, May 22, 1989

JOHN ARTHUR CARRILLO

Officer

Albuquerque, New Mexico, Police Department

It was near midnight on Saturday, February 21, 1987 when Officers John Carrillo, 27, and John Messimer, 23, responded to a domestic violence call in an affluent neighborhood in Albuquerque's far northeast heights. A female had called police and complained of being beaten at a residence occupied by Merrill Burrows Chamberlain, a physicist for Sandia Laboratories in Albuquerque. Chamberlain, 47 years old and divorced, told the officers there was no woman in his house and he invited them inside to look around. They followed him through the house and up the stairs to the second floor, toward the master bedroom. The officers didn't know the woman in question had taken refuge in a nearby residence.

Chamberlain suddenly grabbed a briefcase and stepped quickly into a nearby bathroom with the officers right behind him. The physicist pulled a nine-millimeter pistol from the case and opened fire. His first bullet struck John Carrillo in the left chest. The officer—who was not wearing a bulletproof vest—went down, his own pistol barely clear of its holster. Chamberlain ducked behind a low wall. Officer Messimer quickly pulled Carrillo out of the line of fire and began shooting at Chamberlain. He also made the dreaded radio call:

"Officer down! Shots fired!"

The two continued to exchange shots—Chamberlain fired eight times and Messimer seven—as other officers arrived. Officers outside the house convinced Chamberlain to throw his gun out the window and surrender. The scientist was taken into custody without further incident and charged with an open count of murder and four counts of assault with intent to commit a violent felony on a police officer.

Chamberlain claimed self-defense. He said he fired at the officers because he feared for his own life when he saw a gun in Carrillo's hand. Defense attorney Gary Mitchell claimed that officers Carrillo and Messimer violated several of Chamberlain's constitutional rights, and that those infringements pushed Chamberlain over the edge and caused him to react violently. Carrillo's tape recorder was on throughout the incident, however, and the recording refuted Chamberlain's allegations.

Chamberlain was first tried in 1988 and convicted of aggravated assault on a police officer, with intent to kill, for shooting at Officer Messimer and assault and battery on the woman who first called police. The jury, however, could not reach a verdict in the shooting death of Officer Carrillo. Chamberlain was tried again in November of 1989 and convicted of first-degree murder. He was sentenced to life in prison. Between November 1989 and August 1995, Chamberlian appealed his conviction five times. His arguments were rejected each time.

Officer John Messimer was awarded the medal of valor for pulling Carrillo out of the line of fire while he himself was being fired upon. The award is the Albuquerque Police Department's highest honor.

Officer John Carrillo was survived by his parents, Mr. and Mrs. Ben Carrillo, an infant son, Derek, two sisters Mary Ann McGraw and Cathy Jean Carrillo, and four brothers, Ben, Michael, Mark and George. George also serves as an Albuquerque police officer. The Northeast Albuquerque Police substation is dedicated to the memory of Officer John Arthur Carrillo.

Albuquerque *Journal*, February 23, 24 & 25, 1987; November 8, 16 & 22, 1989; September 27, 1991; August 1 & 16, 1995
Albuquerque *Tribune*, November 10, 1989
Albuquerque Police Department

JOE CARSON

Town Marshal
Las Vegas, New Mexico

In mid January 1880, four young toughs rode into Las Vegas, New Mexico and set about making drunken fools of themselves. A rumor circulated around town that they were horse and cattle rustlers looking for stock to steal; other gossip held that they were nothing more than young hot-bloods out for a good time. Whichever it was, they soon wore out their welcome.

If the gang had a leader, it was Thomas Jefferson House. He called Colorado home and used the alias Tom Henry. The other three were Anthony Lowe (alias Jim West), John Dorsey, and William "Big" Randall. All of them were drunk—and armed—in the Close and Patterson Saloon and Variety Hall on the evening of January 22. Marshal Joe Carson, alone, approached the four men and asked them to comply with a local ordinance that required them to check their guns with the bartender. History does not record what words were exchanged—one writer says Carson received "a barrage of profane insults"—but what happened next is pretty well documented. Tom Henry likely fired first, two of his bullets hitting Carson in the arms. The other three scofflaws commenced firing as the marshal went down. The marshal may have got off two shots—he carried two guns, one in a holster and one in his hip pocket—before he died with eight bullets in his upper body and one in his leg.

Present in the saloon at the time was deputy city marshal Dave Mather who joined the fracas and his aim was true. He quickly killed Big Randall with two bullets to the chest. He put two bullets into Jim West's body and another into Tom Henry's leg. When the smoke cleared, only Mather remained in the saloon, uninjured. Dorsey wasn't wounded, either, but he and Henry had managed to escape leaving the wounded Jim West behind. Reports at the time indicated that about 40 shots were exchanged in the period of a few seconds. (Some newspaper accounts failed to mention that Mather participated in the gunfight, but *someone* assisted the Marshal. Carson's wounds would have prevented him firing five or six shots.)

Henry and Dorsey didn't go far. Two weeks later they were seen at Mora, 30 miles north of Las Vegas. A seven-man posse set out after the killers. Joined along the way by Sheriff A. P. Branch of Mora County, they soon surrounded a farm-house where the outlaws were holed up. Henry wanted to fight it out but Dorsey talked him out of it based on a promise from the posse that the outlaws would be protected from mob violence back in Las Vegas.

Henry and Dorsey were back in Las Vegas, in jail, on the afternoon of February 6. Henry told a local newspaper reporter that the "fatal fuss" in which Joe Carson died was the result of drunkenness and he had no recollection of it. He seemed nonchalant and unconcerned about the seriousness of the crime he and his friends committed.

In the early morning hours of February 8, 1880, a large group of vigilantes, probably led by Dave Mather, took the three killers out of the jail—without any serious resistance—and led them to the water tower in the town plaza. What followed was as gruesome as any deed done by vigilantes in the annals of New Mexico history.

It started out civilized enough, as lynchings go. The condemned were asked if they had any final words.

West told the crowd his real name.

Dorsey said he had nothing to say and not a friend or relative in the world.

Tom Henry said this: "Boys, it's pretty rough to be hung, but I wish someone would write to my father and mother. I will stand the consequences and die like a man."

The wounded Jim West had been kept in jail rather than in the hospital since the night of Carson's murder. His condition had not improved. The mob decided to hang him first. Sick, bleeding and shivering in the winter cold, the young killer whimpered.

"Jim, be still and die like a man," Tom Henry said.

Strong hands pulled the rope and hung West, but the amateur executioners had neglected to tie his hands and he grasped the noose around his neck as his pants dropped around his thighs.

"Please button my pants," West gasped as he swung about.

Joe Carson's widow was in the crowd. She picked up a rifle and fired, probably at West first since he made the best target. Instantly, it seemed, everyone in the crowd with a gun began firing at the killers. West was riddled and hung dead from the noose. Dorsey was shot down and dying. So was Tom Henry. He crawled to the edge of the tower's platform, from which he would have been hung.

"Boys, for God's sake," he begged, "shoot me again. Shoot me in the head."

Someone obliged. All four of Marshal Joe Carson's killers were dead.

Joe Carson was 40 years old (one source says 43), married and the father of a 14 year old daughter. He was born near Knoxville, Tennessee, and previously resided in Sherman, Texas.

Howard Bryan, *Wildest of the Wild West, True Tales of a Frontier Town on The Santa Fe Trail*, Clear Light Publishers

Jack DeMattos, *Mysterious Gunfighter, The Story of Dave Mather*, The Early West

John Guttman, "Gunfighters & Lawmen," *Wild West*, December, 1994

Leon Claire Metz, *The Shooters*, Mangan Books

Richard Patterson, *Historical Atlas of the Outlaw West*, Johnson Books

Marc Simmons, *When Six-Guns Ruled, Outlaw Tales of the Southwest*, Ancient City Press

Dan L. Thrapp, *Encyclopedia of Frontier Biography*, University of Nebraska Press, 1988

GERMAINE CASEY

Officer
Rio Rancho, New Mexico, Police Department

On August 27, 2007, along with about 70 officers from the Albuquerque Police Department, the Bernalillo County Sheriff's Department, and New Mexico State Police, Rio Rancho Police Officer Germaine Casey, a motorcycle officer, was assigned to a motorcade which escorted United States President George W. Bush from the Albuquerque Sunport to a lunch gathering in the North Valley, and then back to Air Force One. While on the return leg of the trip, after reaching the Sunport, Officer Casey's motorcycle struck a curb and he was ejected from the vehicle and slammed into a tree. Fellow officers were able to render what help they could almost immediately. Officer Casey was transported to the University of New Mexico Hospital where he died at approximately 3:30 p.m.

Germaine Casey was the first Rio Rancho police officer to be killed in the line of duty. The department was created in 1981.

A graduate of Rich Central High School in Olympia Fields, Illinois, Casey played minor league baseball with the Atlanta Braves organization. He and his family moved to Albuquerque in 2002 and he joined the University of New Mexico Police Department soon after that. He moved to the Rio Rancho Police Department two years later. He was survived by his wife, Lisa, and two children, Melissa, 17, and Mitchell, 14.

President Bush personally offered his condolences to Mrs. Casey and her children. "I am deeply saddened by his death and extraordinarily grateful for his protection. It is a high calling to choose to serve and protect your fellow citizens, and I will always be indebted to Officer Casey's service," the President said.

Casey, 40, was well regarded in the community. A sign placed on Quantum Road, near the Rio Rancho Police Department, summed it up this way: "It's not the way that he died that made him a hero. It's the way that he lived. Thank you Officer Casey."

Albuquerque *Tribune*, August 28 & 31, 2007
Rio Rancho *Observer*, August 30 & September 2, 2007

LUIS CASTILLO

Chief
Jal, New Mexico, Police Department

The Jal Police Department participated in a drug interdiction program on the evening of August 2, 2001, and that included, based upon his own authority, Chief Luis Castillo. A part of the program involved stepped-up patrols of roads leading into and out of the community. Chief Castillo received a radio call from Officer Larry Burns requesting assistance in searching a vehicle he'd just stopped. As the Chief hurried to back up Officer Burns, he lost control of his police car which left the roadway and rolled over. Officer Adam Montez arrived at the scene only moments later. Chief Castillo was transported to a hospital in Kermit, Texas, were he was pronounced dead just after midnight.

Luis M. Castillo was 48 at the time of his death. His wife, Rosa Maria, and three adult children survived him. He served 18 years with the Jal Police Department. He had received numerous commendations from area law enforcement agencies. More than 1,000 people attended his funeral (Jal has a population of fewer than 2,000 people).

Hobbs Police Chief Tony Knott praised Chief Castillo's dedication by pointing out that as chief, Castillo was not required to be out conducting patrol duty. "Here he is, the chief of police, and he's out working late at night. You don't get much more dedicated than that."

"[Chief Castillo] affected all of us here in a positive way," said Gerald Anderson, a Jal resident.

Albuquerque *Journal*, August 4, 2001
Hobbs *News-Sun*, August 7, 2001

MACKIE C de BACA

Patrolman
New Mexico State Police

Patrolman C de Baca, 31, died in late 1944, killed in action while serving in the U. S. Army in Germany during World War II. He had previously participated in the D-Day invasion of France and he'd been awarded the Bronze Star for gallantry in action near St. Barthelmy, France, in August, 1944. His citation read in part:

"...[F]or heroic service in connection with military operations against an enemy of the United States. His heroic action was instrumental in coordinating the movements of units during a critical period. [His] skill and devotion to duty reflect credit upon himself and the military service...."

A native of Clayton, Patrolman C de Baca joined the State Police in 1937 and remained an active officer until he was drafted into the Army in 1941. His wife, Lucy-Alice, and his parents, Mr. and Mrs. Fulgencio C de Baca of Clayton, survived him.

New Mexico State Police
The Roadrunner (New Mexico State Police Association, Vol. 3, No. 2, Summer, 1992)

PHILIP H. CHACON

Officer
Albuquerque, New Mexico, Police Department

On Wednesday evening, September 10, 1980, Albuquerque Policeman and Community Liaison Officer Phil Chacon was off-duty and working on a project at the Shelter for Domestic Violence when two children who lived at the shelter told him the nearby Kinney Shoe Store on East Central Avenue was being robbed. Unarmed and dressed in civilian clothing, Officer Chacon jumped on his personal motorcycle and took up pursuit of the bandits. He was shot and killed near a doughnut shop at the southeast corner of Wyoming and Central Avenue.

Officer Chacon had previously been successful in arresting criminals while off-duty. On two occasions, he arrested burglary suspects while on his lunch hour. Albuquerque Police Chief Bob Stover joked at the time that he was going to give Phil Chacon an eight hour lunch period. Chacon was named officer of the month for November 1977.

As a member of the chief's community liaison office, Officer Chacon was well known and liked in various organizations. He served as president of the Parent-Teacher Association for San Felipe de Neri Catholic elementary school, which his children attended. He was a member of the San Felipe Old Town Community Association. He founded "Walk With a Cop" and raised money for the Sickle Cell Council of Albuquerque, the Muscular Dystrophy Association and the Salvation Army. Officer Chacon also did "Officer Bill" presentations at local schools.

"He was recognized with several awards, which included plaques, trophies, and certificates. These can go unrecognized, however, because nothing meant more to him than his own personal satisfaction of helping out," his daughter Denise wrote of him.

One man, Van Bering Robinson, was arrested, tried and convicted of killing Officer Chacon. He received a life sentence. The State Supreme Court, however, reversed the conviction. The Court held that improper questioning of a witness prejudiced the jury. Robinson was acquitted at a second trial. No one else was ever prosecuted for the crime. Robinson, however, continued a life of crime. Since

1981, he has been convicted of the federal offenses of cocaine distribution and illegal purchase of food stamps, and state charges of distributing a controlled substance and aggravated assault on a peace officer with a deadly weapon. In December, 1999, Robinson was sentenced to 5½ years in prison as a habitual offender after pleading guilty to cocaine possession and evidence tampering. Auto theft charges were dismissed as a part of a plea bargain.

A seven year veteran of the Albuquerque Police Department, Officer Chacon was survived by his wife, Rita, a daughter, Denise, and son Robert. The Southeast Albuquerque Police Substation is dedicated to the memory of Officer Philip Chacon.

Albuquerque *Journal*, September 11, 12, 13, 16 & 25, 1980; March 2, 1990; December 11, 1999
Denise Chacon, (Daughter)
Street Beat, The Official Magazine for Albuquerque Police Officers and the Community
Albuquerque Police Department

ANDRES CHAVEZ

Deputy Sheriff
Valencia County, New Mexico

On Saturday night, January 6, 1934, Deputy Sheriff Andres Chavez was on duty in Jarales, four miles south of Belen, charged with keeping the peace at dance being held there. A disturbance began in the dance hall and the individuals involved moved the altercation outside. Deputy Chavez went outside to prevent the fight and was shot four times—once in the abdomen and three times in the leg. Before he died, he told Sheriff Abelicio Sanchez that another deputy, Diego Trujillo, shot him.

After an investigation conducted by Sheriff Sanchez and Undersheriff Romulo Aragon, Trujillo and a second deputy, Edmundo* Lovato, were arrested. Also charged with shooting the deputy were Matias Chavez and Tomas Garcia.

"All four of the men were armed and all fired shots," the sheriff said. He added that no additional arrests were expected. The four were released on $8,000 bond each.

Trial of the four was scheduled for March 1934, but a problem was encountered when attorneys were unable to find a jury of 12 out of a venire of 24 names. A second venire of 51 was demanded by Judge Harry P. Owen. A jury was finally seated and at the conclusion of the trial, Diego Trujillo, Edmundo Lovato and Tomas Garcia were convicted of second degree murder. Matias Chavez was acquitted. The New Mexico Supreme Court subsequently granted the three men a new trial which took place in December 1934. The jury deliberated for nine hours before notifying the court that its members were unable to agree upon a verdict. Judge Owen dismissed the jury. Nothing indicates that they were tried again.

Deputy Chavez, a resident of Belen, was survived by two minor children.

* Sources vary on Lovato's first name. One identifies him as Reymundo, another simply Mundo.

Albuquerque *Journal*, January 8, 9, & 10; and December 6, 1934

LEO CHAVEZ

Deputy Sheriff/Lieutenant
Valencia County, New Mexico

Lt. Leo Chavez, 36, was killed on the evening of December 12, 1986, when the department vehicle he was driving was involved in an accident. As chairman of the program, he was collecting Toys From Cops to Tots at the time of his death.

A lifelong resident of the Albuquerque area, Lt. Chavez was survived by his wife, Linda, and two sons, Lawrence and Leo. He was buried at Mt. Calvary Cemetery in Albuquerque.

Albuquerque *Journal*, December 14, 1986
Lawrence Romero, Valencia County Sheriff, correspondence, February 23, 1987

VICTORIA "VICKIE" CHAVEZ

Community Service Officer
Farmington, New Mexico, Police Department

A part of Vickie Chavez's job involved checking residences of vacationing Farmington residents. The chore was called "close patrol." That's what she was doing at a little after 11:00 o'clock on the morning of July 9, 1992 when she stopped at the Ogden residence on West 27th Street. She radioed the dispatcher.

"I need an officer to 87 [meet] with me here. I think there's someone here that isn't supposed to be here." She repeated the message. Then she screamed into her microphone, "He's got a gun!" That was her last radio transmission.

When Farmington police officer Raymond Nelson arrived on the scene only minutes later, he found Officer Chavez in the front seat of her city car, shot in the head, neck and left hand with a shotgun. Officer Nelson saw four empty shotgun shells on the ground near the car. Officer Chavez was dead.

Kevin Ogden, 33, was captured by New Mexico State Police Patrolman Gary Ross about an hour after the shooting. He surrendered without resistance. He'd been staying at his mother's home against her wishes. At the time of the shooting, authorities held a warrant for Ogden's arrest for failure to appear for a competency hearing. Officers speculated that Ogden shot Chavez because he thought she was there to serve the warrant. Charged with first degree murder and tried in November 1994, Ogden received a life sentence. He'd previously served prison time for embezzlement.

Vickie Chavez, 39, was the first female New Mexico peace officer to be killed in the line of duty. More than 700 people attended her funeral, including officers from 30 jurisdictions in New Mexico, Colorado and Arizona, the U. S. Border Patrol, and the Navajo Tribal Police. Her funeral was conducted with full law enforcement honors.

She was survived by her husband, Ben, and two daughters, Dannette, 13, and Amber, 16.

Albuquerque *Journal*, July 15, 1992, March 23, 1993 & November 1, 1994

Farmington Police Department Offense Report

Richard Melton, Chief (Ret.), Farmington Police Department

New Mexico Department of Corrections

R. L. Stockard, Captain (Ret.), New Mexico State Police, conversation, January 30, 1996

Gregg Willis, Sergeant, Farmington Police Department

JAMES M. CHASE

Deputy Sheriff
Torrence County, New Mexico

Details of this affair are somewhat sketchy. A young cowboy identified as Jap L. Clark was arrested, tried and convicted of horse stealing, probably in late 1904. He did not take his conviction quietly and swore vengeance upon those who had testified against him, including Deputy Sheriff James Chase. The court sentenced Clark to one year in prison, but the cowboy appealed to the Territorial Supreme Court and was released on a $3,000 bond in the spring of 1905.

J. C. Gilbert was another of the witnesses against Clark, and he wrote a letter describing the affray which occurred in April 1905.

> "Jap Clark and W. A. McKean came to this town [Torrance] yesterday for the purpose of killing Chase and myself. They tried to shoot me first, but were prevented by bystanders. Chase and I were over to the [railroad] depot when they found him and began to pick a racket. He told them he did not want to fight and they followed him about two hundred yards when Clark shot at him. He [Chase] then began shooting and they both emptied their six shooters. McKean was holding a man with his gun to keep him from helping Chase, or, rather prevent him from doing anything. After the pistols were shot empty, Clark and McKean ran to a saloon nearby and got their rifles and began shooting at Chase. When about the third or fourth shot had been fired, Chase fell. He died in twenty minutes after he was shot."

A physician who examined Chase's body confirmed that the deputy was shot in the back. There was some debate as to who fired the fatal shot. Some witnesses reported that McKean did it. Other witnesses—McKean's friends in the saloon—alleged that he was not armed throughout the entire affair.

The two shooters escaped from the scene in a buckboard while Gilbert fired at them with his rifle. A report reached Torrance that Clark was hit in the leg, but that may have been in error. Officers at Capitan, New Mexico, arrested Clark and transferred him back to Torrance where he was taken into custody by Sheriff C. y Sanchez y Valdez who in turn took the Clark and McKean to the territorial prison at Santa Fe. Chaves County Sheriff K. S. Woodruff of Roswell, who held a warrant to return Clark to prison on the horse stealing charge, accompanied the Torrance County sheriff on the train trip. They were so promptly moved to the Santa Fe prison because the Torrance County jail was considered unsafe. Torrance County had been created only two years before.*

Newspaper sources do not show the final disposition of the case against Clark, and nothing of a personal nature is known about Deputy James Chase.

*The town of Torrance was never the county seat of Torrance County, although the community boasted a population of a thousand or so and had its own post office from 1902 to 1907. (First county seat was at Progresso, southeast of Willard, before it was moved to Estancia in 1905.)

Dallas (Texas) *Morning News*, April 13, 1905
Robert Julyan, *The Place Names of New Mexico*, University of New Mexico Press
Las Vegas (New Mexico) *Optic*, April 11, 1905
Santa Fe *New Mexican*, March 6, 1906

JAMES EDWARD "JIMMY" CLARK

Captain
New Mexico State Police

On Monday evening, September 19, 1960, Captain Jimmy Clark attended a meeting at Cannon Air Force Base, west of Clovis. He was headed for home at about 10:30 p.m. when he approached a double-track railroad crossing not far from U. S. Highway 60-84. He didn't have a clear view of the crossing because of a farmhouse and buildings and some tall sunflowers. His patrol car collided with a westbound freight train traveling at about 60 miles per hour. A railroad car dragged Clark's police unit along the railroad tracks for 142 feet before it was tossed aside. Investigators reported that Captain Clark died instantly upon impact.

Jimmy Clark, 55, was a native of Bonham, Texas. He joined the State Police in 1937 and was assigned to the Clovis area in 1943. He was promoted to captain in 1951. His wife, Christine, two sons, Gene and James, and two daughters, Carolyn and Cathryn survived him. Captain Clark was buried at Clovis.

Clovis *News-Journal*, February 22, 1981
New Mexico State Police records
Roadrunner (New Mexico State Police Association, Vol. 3, No. 2, Summer, 1992)

KELLY FAY CLARK

Deputy Sheriff
Sierra County, New Mexico

Early on the afternoon of March 4, 1999, Sierra County Deputy Sheriff Kelly Clark left the courthouse in Truth or Consequences with prisoner Michael A. Archuleta, 21, bound for Western New Mexico Correctional Facility at Grants. At about 3:50 p.m., seven or so miles east of Grants, Archuleta was able to assault Deputy Clark, take her gun and shoot her in the head, killing her instantly.

After the shooting, Deputy Clark's patrol unit veered across Interstate Route 40 and slammed head on into an eastbound semi-truck. Archuleta survived the crash and then car-jacked an eastbound auto driven by a Presbyterian minister from Grants. The fugitive released the minister a few miles from the scene of the killing and continued east to a gasoline station at nine-mile hill, west of Albuquerque, where he was captured by Bernalillo County authorities.

Michael Archuleta was charged with one open count of murder, two counts of assault with intent to commit a violent felony, escape, disarming a peace officer, kidnapping, armed robbery, and auto theft. Authorities ordered him housed at the state prison in Santa Fe pending trial. On July 21, Thirteenth Judicial District Attorney Mike Runnels announced that he would seek the death penalty for Archuleta. However, before the case went to trial in August 2000, the death penalty was taken off the table in exchange for Archuleta's plea of guilty to first degree murder, and several other felony crimes. Judge Joseph F. Arite sentenced Archuleta to life in prison, plus 31 years on the other charges; the sentences to be served consecutively. The sentences amount to at least 45 years imprisonment. As to his plea, Archuleta said, "I'm not going to get anything better."

Deputy Clark, 38, was first employed by Sierra County in the detention facility in 1990. In 1991, she was promoted to deputy sheriff. A single mother, she was well regarded by area law enforcement personnel and the community. Peace officers and citizens alike expressed sorrow at the untimely loss of the dedicated and hardworking officer. An estimated 1500 people attended a memorial service held in Deputy Clark's honor on the evening of Wednesday, March 10, and her funeral procession the following day included 16 motorcycle police officers, more than 100 marked police cars, and many additional unmarked law enforcement vehicles.

Kelly Fay Clark was the first Sierra County deputy sheriff to be killed in the line of duty, and the second female officer killed in New Mexico. Her daughter, Lindsey Hauser, survived her. Deputy Clark was engaged to marry State Police Officer Santiago Hernandez at the time of her death.

Albuquerque Journal, March 5, 6 & 12; July 21; December 2, 1999, August 15, 2000
Desert Journal (Truth or Consequences), March 5 & 12, 1999
Las Cruces Sun-News, March 11, 1999
Sierra County Sentinel, March 10 & 17, 1999
Sierra County Sheriff Terry Byers
Truth or Consequences Herald, March 19, 1999

J. M. "JIM" CLIFTON

Deputy Sheriff
Lea County, New Mexico

Deputy Sheriff Jim Clifton and a citizen named D. A. Jones sat drinking coffee in Bullard's Cafe in Tatum, New Mexico, on the morning of February 24, 1932, when Clifton got a telephone call. The sheriff's office advised the deputy to be on the look-out for two or three men who had just robbed the Dean Hardware Store in Lovington. The robbers were believed to be heading toward Tatum. Only minutes later, Clifton saw a car fitting the description, going north.

Clifton took up pursuit and stopped the car two or three miles south of the community of Crossroads. The deputy got out of his car as two men got out of the suspect car.

"I'd like to talk to you boys," Clifton said.

One of the men, an Oklahoma bank robber named Walter Carlocke, 22, produced a .41 caliber revolver. Clifton was able to take it away from him, but not before the second outlaw, John O'Dell, 23, shot the deputy, several times, with a .38 caliber revolver. Bullets struck the deputy's left shoulder and arm and one took him in the stomach passing nearly all the way through his body. Bleeding and reeling, Clifton drew his own gun and fired with telling effect. He shot Carlocke once in the heart and O'Dell, twice in the chest. Both men died at the scene.

Clifton managed to get back into his car and drive himself to the schoolhouse in Crossroads. A teacher there, seeing how badly wounded the deputy was, drove him to the Crossroads Store where local folks provided what emergency treatment they could. Doctors from Tatum and Lovington rushed to the scene. An airplane from Roswell was ordered but no one bothered to tell the pilot what his chore would be. He showed up in an open cockpit, two-seater, plane. Clifton was moved by automobile to Tatum where a "cabin plane" picked him up about dark that evening for a flight to a hospital in Lubbock, Texas, nearly 100 miles away. Deputy Clifton died at 9:45 p.m.

Medical authorities said that even if Clifton had received comprehensive medical attention from the very beginning, he likely could not have been saved.

His wounds were too severe.

As is often the case, rumors abounded that Clifton stopped the wrong men. One newspaper account read:

> Carlocke was wanted in Waurika, Okla., for bank robbery, officers said, and O'Dell was tentatively identified as an escaped convict from the Oklahoma State penitentiary. Neither were implicated in the robbery of the hardware store, officers said, after an investigation.

These allegations were supported by the fact that no loot was found at the scene of the shooting. Some folks believed a third man was involved, and a third gun *was* found in the outlaw's car. Some years later Clifton's sister received information that a convict in the Huntsville, Texas prison admitted that he was the third man present when Carlocke and O'Dell were killed. He said he remained concealed until Clifton drove away from the scene and then took the loot and hid in some sand hills nearby. He later made his way cross-country, 30 or so miles, to the highway near Elida. He hitched a ride north to Portales and made good his escape.

Folks around Tatum didn't care about any such questions. An estimated 1,000 people attended Deputy Clifton's funeral.

The Largest Concourse of People In the History of Town

> Jim Clifton...was a born officer, who knew not fear; a man who has many times looked death in the face without flinching; a man who has been instrumental in making this county a place that is shunned by criminals, and [he] wiped off the books two of the most desperate characters that have ever visited this section....

> In his passing, law and order in New Mexico have lost a champion; in his passing a place has been made vacant that cannot be filled, for there was but one Jim Clifton—the mould [*sic*] in which he was cast has been broken, and the like of him, in these parts, will never be duplicated. We knew him. We liked him. Even those who felt the weight of his authority, respected him, and stood with bowed heads, sorrowing, when they found that his earthly career was over....

It was a terrific blow—a few hours before he was strong and vigorous; a few hours before he smiled, he laughed, then the crashing of heavy pistols, and his race was run. We grieve with the sorrowing wife, we sympathize with the weeping mother, and we bow our head with the grieving father, brothers and sisters.

Deputy Jim Clifton was buried at the Tatum Cemetery.

As a footnote to this sad story, Clovis, New Mexico, law officers had received a tip several days before Clifton's death that Carlocke and O'Dell were going to meet a third man in a local hotel around the time Clifton stopped them along a road 90 miles away. The exact purpose of that meeting was never learned, but Clovis officers had the hotel staked out in hopes of capturing the two wanted men. Officers had been advised that the outlaws would be armed and dangerous.

Albuquerque *Journal* February 25, 1932
Clovis *Evening News Journal*, February 25, 1932
Lea County newspapers, assorted, undated, and unidentified
Lea County Sheriff's Department
Lovington *Daily Leader*, May 10, 1990
Santa Fe *New Mexican*, February 25, 1932

GERALD EUGENE "JERRY" CLINE

Patrolman

Albuquerque, New Mexico, Police Department

The weather was cold and clear at 11:37 on Thursday evening, February 24, 1983, when Officer Jerry Cline was dispatched to a man-with-a-gun call at the Tewa Lodge on east Central Avenue in Albuquerque. A passing motorist had telephoned police and reported a man carrying a rifle near the motel. The officer pulled his car into an alley just off Alvarado Drive and got out. He walked around the corner to check out motel units. The door to room 24 stood open and from inside, out of the dark, a single shot was fired from a .30-30 rifle. The bullet struck Officer Cline in the chest. He died at the scene.

The offender, Joel Lee Compton, 29, fled across Alvarado Drive toward Kap's Coffee Shop. Albuquerque police officer Geraldine Ferrara, 22, one of the first back-up officers to arrive on the scene, arrested the killer in the coffee shop parking lot. Witnesses reported that Compton discarded his rifle and fell to the ground when he saw Officer Ferrara draw her gun. "I give up!" he yelled.

Officer Ferrara pointed her gun at Compton's head. "Move and you're dead," she said.

Compton had a history of mental problems and previous arrests in Texas for larceny, possession of synthetic narcotics, possession of marijuana and passing worthless checks. At the time he killed Officer Cline, Compton was wanted in Hill County, Texas, for possession of synthetic narcotics and in Dallas County for possession of a deadly weapon, resisting arrest and probation violation. Compton was charged with first degree murder and in September 1983, he was convicted and sentenced to death. In November 1986, Governor Toney Anaya commuted Compton's sentence—along with the sentences of four other murderers—to life in prison.

Officer Cline, 35, was born and raised in Albuquerque. He was in the first graduating class at Del Norte High School in 1966. After completing a BS degree in psychology and sociology at Eastern New Mexico University in 1971, he entered the Albuquerque Police Academy. He was named Officer of the Month in July 1977. Cline was survived by his wife, Yolanda, children Mendi, Cindy and G. T., his parents, Charlie and Melba, brothers Jimmy and Rusty, and brother-in-law, Albuquerque Police Officer Thomas Haralson Jr.

More than 1500 people attended the officer's funeral. The Albuquerque *Journal* said this:

> The sheer number of people who attended slain Policeman Gerald Cline's funeral...were a testimony to the man. A quiet, unassuming fellow, Cline would have been embarrassed by the huge turnout and elaborate service....
>
> A color guard and some 300 policemen from around the city and state attended, paying tribute to a kind, community-minded peace officer. A 13-year veteran of the Police Department, Cline put a lot into his job and into his life.... In addition to being a good cop, he coached Little League baseball, was involved in his church and often took street kids into his home.
>
> It's policemen such as Gerald Cline the community will miss the most.

The Albuquerque Police Department North Valley Substation is named in honor of Gerald E. Cline.

Albuquerque *Journal*, February 26, 1983, March 1 & 5, 1993
Albuquerque *Tribune*, February 25, 1983
Yolanda H. Cline, correspondence, March 23, 1990
Albuquerque Police Department

J. V. COGDILL

Deputy Sheriff
Union County, New Mexico

The *Union County Leader* reported the sad story:

> The quiet little village of Grenville was startled Saturday night [October 23, 1937] when Raymond Baum, a young ranch hand, walked into the community dance hall about 1 o'clock in the morning and threw down on the dance floor his own bloody revolver and then another one that he said belonged to Deputy Sheriff J. V. Cogdill. In a braggardt [*sic*] and dramatic manner he commanded "Some of you S of Bs take me to the county jail at Clayton for I have just killed old man Cogdill." The dance broke up and the dance manager and a friend hustled Baum into a car and started for the county seat. Immediately a search for the officer was started and in a short while his dead body was found near Baum's flivver car on a side street at the rear of the Central Hotel.... At first it was presumed Baum had shot and killed the officer but the nearness to the hotel caused...(some) doubt.... Later investigations disclosed that Cogdill had been stomped to death. The head and face were terribly mutilated.

It is believed Baum took an hour or so to decide his course after he realized what he had done. The victim's body was cold and the blood on his face had dried when he was found. As only a few minutes elapsed from the time Baum made his announcement at the dance hall until the body was found it is believed Baum took the time to decide whether to flee or give himself up.

There is also conjecture as to how it came that the officer was at the car owned by Baum. As Baum had shown a disposition to make trouble at the dance it seemed reasonable to suppose the officer took Baum in charge and led him to his car and ordered him to go home. This Baum resented and made his attack.... Fearing the officer might be able to reach for and use his gun there in the darkness his fear knew no bounds until he had committed one of the most brutal murders in the annals of crime.... The balance of the story will be written by the grim officers of the law and then the curtain for Raymond Baum.

District Attorney V. A. Doggett charged Baum, 20 years old, with first degree murder on the following Monday. Baum entered a plea of not guilty claiming that he'd been drunk at the time and had no recollection of anything that had happened. He was ordered held without bond.

Baum was tried and convicted of second degree murder in March of 1938, and sentenced to 90 to 99 years in prison. Two other men, Dale Cherry and Charles Oldham, were tried in September, 1938 for aiding and abetting in the murder of Deputy Cogdill. Cherry was acquitted and the jury could not reach agreement regarding Oldham. Raymond Baum was released from prison in November 1946 and pardoned and restored to citizenship in December 1952.

Born in North Carolina in 1869, J. V. Cogdill moved to Texas at a young age and then to New Mexico in 1910. He became a Union County deputy sheriff in 1915. His wife, Mamie, and children Elbert, Myrtle and J. V. Jr. survived him. He was interred at Grenville.

Albuquerque *Journal*, October 25, 1937
Clayton *News*, March 16, 1938
Linda Lovin, granddaughter, correspondence, November 15, 1999
New Mexico State Penitentiary records
Union County *Leader*, October 28, 1937; September 15, 1938

DAVID COKER

Patrolman
New Mexico State Police

Officer David Coker used a stopwatch to check traffic for speeders on Interstate 40 near Santa Rosa on Sunday, November 18, 1979. Sometime around 12:15 p.m. he stopped an eastbound red and black Corvette with California plates about seven and a half miles west of town. Officer Coker was in his patrol car, using the radio to conduct an NCIC check, when the Corvette's driver, David Perry Blackmore, 34, approached the police car and pulled a gun on the officer. Blackmore ordered Coker remove his pistol from its holster, unload it, and to get out of his car. The officer complied. Witnesses reported seeing Officer Coker about 15 feet from his car, and down the embankment at the side of the road, with Blackmore pointing a gun at him.

Coker had a backup gun concealed inside his jacket and he began removing the garment to get to it. The officer was able to pull the gun and fire as Blackmore also fired. Coker's bullet hit Blackmore in the gun-hand and upper right chest, but Blackmore's bullet struck the officer in the forehead, just above the right eye, killing him instantly.

Blackmore staggered to the front of the police car where he dropped his gun and collapsed on the ground. He was groping around for his gun when a passing motorist stopped and kicked the weapon away. The motorist then used the officer's police radio to call for help. Blackmore died on the way to the hospital.

Investigators learned later that no wants or warrants were outstanding for Blackmore, a resident of Santa Monica, California, and the Corvette he was driving was not stolen. Blackmore had stolen a credit card from his roommate and forged his signature on a gas credit slip. Beyond that, no reason for the shooting was ever discovered.

Officer David Coker, 31 at the time of his death, was commissioned as a State Police officer on October 1, 1975, just over four years before he was killed. He served a year in the Santa Fe District before being assigned to Santa Rosa in 1976. His wife, Faye, and his parents, Mr. and Mrs. Harvey Coker of Tucumcari survived him. Officer Coker was killed on his father's birthday. He is buried at the Terrace Grove Cemetery in Belen.

Albuquerque *Journal*, November 19 & 22, 1979
Levi Chavez, former Santa Rosa police officer, conversation, August 1995
New Mexico State Police Annual, 1985
Roadrunner (New Mexico State Police Association, Vol. 3, No. 2, Summer, 1992)

JASPER CORN

Deputy Sheriff
Lincoln County, New Mexico

In early 1884 Nicholas Aragon and another man, both from San Miguel County, stole some horses along the Rio Hondo in Lincoln County and removed them to a canyon near Anton Chico on the Rio Pecos, south of Las Vegas. Lincoln County authorities learned where the horses were hidden and Deputy Sheriff Jim Brent and a posse soon recovered the animals, captured Aragon and his friend, and jailed them in Lincoln. Aragon escaped from jail on May 28. In October 1884, Sheriff John Poe learned that Aragon was back in his old haunts around Gallinas Springs and Anton Chico in San Miguel County. Sheriff Poe told Deputy Sheriff Jasper Corn of Roswell to take as many men as he needed to arrest the horse thief.

Corn, 24, took only one man: his brother-in-law, Bill Holloman (Holliman?). They soon learned that Aragon regularly visited a particular woman near Anton Chico and they approached her house. The outlaw saw Deputy Corn coming and dashed out the back door, running for his horse which stood saddled and waiting some distance away, beyond a stone wall. Corn, from horseback, opened fire with his pistol as his mount galloped toward Aragon. Aragon, using the stone wall for cover, returned fire with a Winchester rifle. His first shot struck Corn's horse in the neck, knocking it down, and the deputy with it. Even though Corn was pinned to the ground, his leg caught under the horse and badly broken, he continued the fight until his gun was empty. Aragon took his time, then, aimed carefully, and shot Corn in the stomach. Aragon mounted his horse and escaped.* The deputy was taken to Coyote Springs by wagon, and medical help was summoned, but too late. Corn died thirty-six hours later without ever receiving treatment.

Aragon hid out for a few months and then returned to Anton Chico. In January 1885, Sheriff Poe led a posse made up of Jim Brent, Johnny Hurley, Barney Mason, Billy Bufer and Jim Abercrombie in search of the killer. A little investigation led the posse to a house where Aragon was believed to be hiding. Two women said they were alone in the house; that Aragon was not there. Sheriff Poe assigned Deputy Hurley—who spoke fluent Spanish—to take the women into the kitchen and interrogate them carefully while the remainder of the posse surrounded the house. After a while one of the women admitted that Aragon was in the house. She said the fugitive was heavily armed and ready to fight. In his haste to tell the sheriff that Aragon was there, Hurley allowed himself to be silhouetted in the kitchen door.

"We've got him! He's in there!" Hurley called out to Sheriff Poe.

"Johnny, get out from in front of the door or he'll kill you," Poe yelled just as Aragon fired.

"Are you hit, Johnny?" Poe asked.

"Yes. Gut shot."

Hurley staggered back into the kitchen and lay down before the fire. The women made him as comfortable as possible. He died 36 hours later just as Corn survived for 36 hours after Aragon shot him in the stomach (see page 148).

In the meantime, gunfire became general between Aragon inside the house, and the posse outside. Though wounded in three places—in the head and leg— the outlaw managed to hold off his pursuers for sixty hours. Aragon didn't surrender until the sheriff from Las Vegas, Hilario Romero, arrived and promised the outlaw he would not be harmed.

Sheriff Poe and Deputy Brent took Aragon to Santa Fe and lodged him in jail there.** Aragon was tried during the summer of 1885 and acquitted on charges of murdering Jasper Corn. Aragon's argument was that he didn't know Corn was a deputy, and that Corn fired first. In the fall of 1885, a Colfax County jury found Aragon guilty of second-degree murder for killing Johnny Hurley and gave him a life sentence. He actually served about ten years before he was released and returned to Anton Chico where he died of natural causes many years later. ***

Jasper Corn was the brother of Martin Corn who migrated from Kerr County Texas and settled in the Pecos Valley in the late 1870s. Martin Corn was the father of 20 children and the Corn family remains prominent in Chaves County yet today. One chronicler of the times described Jasper Corn "...as brave as the bravest."

* One source asserts that Aragon escaped from the scene on foot.

** One source says Aragon was held in the Territorial Penitentiary, but that is unlikely since the New Mexico prison didn't open until August, 1885. Another source indicates that Aragon was taken to Las Vegas and jailed there.

*** One source holds that Aragon was acquitted of killing Hurley and convicted of killing Corn. The story as told Lily Klasner [see below], who was alive at the time, seems most creditable.

George Curry, 1861-1947, An Autobiography , University of New Mexico Press
Fred Harrison, *Hell Holes and Hangings* Clarendon Press

Lily Klasner, *My Girlhood Among Outlaws*, University of Arizona Press

Carole Larson, *Forgotten Frontier*, University of New Mexico Press, (This source identifies William Holliman as married to Zilpha Corn, Martin Corn's sister. Judge Smith Lea in Lily Klasner's book [see above] identified Bill Holliman as Jasper Corn's brother-in-law. It is logical to assume that Martin and Jasper Corn were brothers. The Corns are an important Chaves County family.)

"Sophie Poe's Scrapbook," news clipping, publication and date not noted

James D. Shinkle, *Martin V. Corn, Early Roswell Pioneer*, publisher unknown

John P. Wilson, *Merchants, Guns & Money, The Story of Lincoln county and Its Wars*, Museum of New Mexico Press

Lincoln *Golden Era*, February 5, 1885, October 1, 1885

Santa Fe *Daily New Mexican*, July 16 & 17, 1885

CHARLES CUNNINGHAM

Deputy Sheriff
Valencia County, New Mexico

The affair began at about 7:00 a.m. on Saturday, March 1, 1930. A 19 year old named Bonifacio Torres had been declared incorrigible by the court, upon a report made by his mother, Mrs. Juan Torres. Valencia County Sheriff Ignacio Aragon, a deputy named Baca and Belen City Marshal Daniel Sanchez went to the home of young Torres' grandmother, near Jarales, where the boy had been staying. The first encounter seemed amiable enough, and Torres asked whether he would be sent to reform school or the penitentiary. One of the officers replied that he didn't know, but possibly to neither. Torres then asked if he could get his gloves from the bedroom before they left. The officers agreed. Suddenly, shots were fired and Marshal Sanchez was hit in the thigh and hand. He fell to the floor as Aragon and Baca sought to get out of the line of fire. Torres ran to a window and, taking careful aim, shot the Sheriff in the back as the lawman sought cover. Sanchez managed to get out of the house and Baca was unscathed. He took the wounded men to Belen for medical treatment.

Deputies Dennis and Joe Gabaldon and Charles Cunningham, returned to scene of the shooting, intent on arresting Torres. They saw no activity and entered the house, where they found no one. As they stood looking around, Torres, hiding in the attic, shot Deputy Cunningham by aiming through a hole in the ceiling intended to accommodate a stove pipe. The bullet hit the deputy in the shoulder and ranged downward into his body. Torres managed to get out of the attic and on to the roof before Dennis Gabaldon could get a shot at him. Torres fired at officers again, as they left the area, but missed. Gabaldon returned fire, but also missed.

By 10:00 a.m. an estimated 20 police officers from several departments in the area, and 75 or so citizens surrounded the house. Estimates are that by afternoon, 300 people were present. Gunfire was exchanged by officers and young Torres, with no one injured. Virtually all of the windows were shot out of the house, and efforts to use tear gas were not successful because it dissipated too quickly to be effective. An effort to use dynamite also failed when only a small hole in the adobe wall resulted from the blast. At last, late in the afternoon, officers decided that it was necessary to burn the structure to force Torres out. They could not risk giving him a chance to escape in the coming darkness.

At a little after 5:00 p.m., using gasoline and a gas soaked burlap bag, officers managed to set house on fire. Smoke from the burning floor and furniture poured out the windows, but Torres managed to get into a room not burning and close the door. He put off the inevitable for a few minutes. Officers moved up close to the house to prevent escape in all directions. Suddenly, Torres smashed through a window, splintering the frame and breaking what glass remained, and landed on the ground. He raised both hands and officers initially thought he meant to surrender; but his hands came down quickly and each contained a pistol. He began firing as he ran toward an open field, and officers returned fire. Only one bullet struck Torres, and that was a rifle ball to the heart. He died within a few minutes. Hardly a dashing figure, young Torres was clad in bib-overalls, heavy work shoes and an ancient woman's coat, trimmed with imitation fur. He seemed to smile as he died.

Deputy Cunningham died two days later, while Sheriff Aragon, after a long period of convalescence, recovered. Marshal Sanchez's wounds proved to be minor by comparison.

Nothing of a personal nature is known about Deputy Cunningham.

Note: The above account is taken from the Albuquerque *Journal* for Sunday, March 2, 1930. An Associated Press story dated March 1, indicates that Bonifacio "Bonnie" Torres was 21 years of age at the time of his death. This story spells the young man's name *Torrez*. The AP story also indicates that Torres was drunk and disturbing the peace immediately before the officers attempted to arrest him.

Albuquerque *Journal*, March 2, 3, & 4, 1930
Dallas (Texas) *Morning News*, March 4, 1930
Las Vegas (New Mexico) *Optic*, March 1 & 3, 1930

LEONARD EUGENE DANIEL

Officer
Eunice, New Mexico, Police Department

In the early morning hours of January 27, 1953, Eunice police officer Leonard Eugene Daniel was stricken and died as he attempted to arrest a man outside a bar in downtown Eunice. A Lea County Coroner's jury ruled on January 29, 1953, that "the deceased came to his death by reason of a Coronary Occlussion [*sic*], brought about [by] reason of over exertion and excitement from attempting to make an arrest in line of duty [*sic*]."

Officer Daniel had been a member of the Eunice Police Department for about three months at the time of his death. He had previously been employed by the nearby Snyder Ranch. He was survived by his wife, Mary, and one son, Muriel. He was interred in the Eunice Cemetery.

Hobbs *News Sun*, January 28, 1953
Lovington *Leader*, January 30, 1952
David L. Minton, Correspondence, November 17, 2007

OSCAR DAVIS

Chief

Raton, New Mexico, Police Department

Newton Brigance (AKA Clyde Norman), 28, and his brother, Oscar, 22, arrived in Ratón from Kansas at about eight o'clock on the morning of Friday, April 6, 1923 in a Nash touring car. A couple of hours later they drove to Trinadad, Colorado, where they purchased whiskey from a bootlegger. They returned to Ratón about five p.m. and ate supper. The brothers then picked up five girls, ranging in age from 13 to 16, on Second Street, just to take them for a ride.

Newton's erratic driving got the attention of local officers, but he wouldn't stop for them. At the corner of Second Street and Park Avenue, Chief Davis was able to step onto the car's running board and he ordered Newton to drive to the police station. The driver turned away from police headquarters, pulled out a gun and ordered the officer off his car. Davis grabbed at Newton's gun with one hand and reached for the car's ignition switch with the other. Newton fired twice, both bullets hitting Chief Davis in the chest, near the heart. Doctors said later that either would have been almost instantly fatal.

Newton slowed enough that the girls could get out of the car and then sped away. Officer W. T. Markham took up pursuit of the Brigance brothers, firing at them with his pistol until it was empty, without effect. Oscar Brignance fired back, also without effect. Officer Ben Pooler also pursued the fleeing car but didn't fire for fear of hitting Officer Markham. At the railroad crossing, Second Street made a sharp turn, but the Nash was traveling too fast to make the curve. It rolled over completely, twice. Neither of the Brigance brothers were injured and were able to escape from the scene.

Dozens of deputies, police officers and armed citizens took up the search for the killers. All roads were guarded and the hills around the town were searched. Two bloodhounds arrived from Santa Fe, but because of high winds they were unable to pick up a scent. During the course of the manhunt, one citizen, Lee Davis (no relation to the chief) was shot by Deputy Sheriff T. J. Crumley when he failed to stop at the deputy's command. Davis said he couldn't hear the command because of the high wind. His wound was painful but not fatal. Two other officers, Emmett Adair and J. A. Black, were seriously injured when their motorcycle and sidecar overturned on a mountain road during the search.

Then on Sunday afternoon, April 8, at about six o'clock, Deputy Sheriff F. R.

Durgeloh encountered two men near Maxwell. He wasn't armed but questioned them. They claimed to have arrived on the railroad from Trinidad. Durgeloh returned to Maxwell and rounded up an armed posse. It took about an hour and a half for the posse, Deputy Tom Farmer in particular, to find the killers hiding in a cave along the bank of the Red River. The Brigance brothers were returned to Ratón and locked up. Sheriff W. J. Linwood placed them under heavy guard to prevent any mob violence since feelings in the community were at a "fever heat."

Both suspects made statements which they later refused to sign. Norman Brigance concluded his by saying this:

"We had both been drinking and were pretty full."

Newton was tried for murder in December 1923 and sentenced to hang. Oscar pleaded guilty to charges of assault with intent to kill and was sentenced to four to five years in prison. The New Mexico Supreme Court overturned Newton's conviction in January 1926. He was later sentenced to 99 years in prison.

Oscar Davis was born the eldest of five children in Canyon City, Colorado, but was raised in Ratón from about age five and was educated there. His wife, Maud, and one son, Clifford, survived him. He had been chief of police for several months at the time of his death.

His funeral was one of the largest in Ratón history. All business houses closed for the service, as did the high school.

Albuquerque *Morning Journal*, April 7, 8, 9 & 10, 1923; January 7, 1929
Ratón *Range*, Tuesday, April 10, 1923
Ratón *Reporter*, Tuesday, April 10, 1923
Lt. William Kuehl, New Mexico State Police, June 7, 1991
Mike J. Pappas, *Raton, History Mystery and More*, Coda Publications
Robert Torrez, New Mexico State Historian, August 30, 1991

RAY DAVIS

Deputy Sheriff/Detective
Bernalillo County, New Mexico

In the early morning hours of November 23, 1968, Bernalillo County Sheriff's Deputy and Detective Ray Davis, 24, was assigned to show State Police Officer Jim Wilson Albuquerque's high burglary districts. When Officer Wilson was dispatched to an accident just before 3:00 a.m., Davis accompanied him.

En route to the scene, with emergency equipment operating, the state car swerved to avoid a collision with another car, struck a mailbox and dropped off a six-foot embankment. Davis was pinned in the car but was later transported to the Bataan Memorial Methodist Hospital. He died there on Monday afternoon, November 25. Officer Wilson escaped serious injury.

Deputy Davis had been employed by the Sheriff's Department for three years and had been a detective for about eight months. "He was a good man who knew how to take orders," Sheriff's Captain Santos Baca said. "He wanted to make a career of detective work. He was the type who would follow a case through until it was solved."

Ray Davis was survived by his parents, Mr. & Mrs. J. O. Davis, brother Frank and sister Patty, all of Albuquerque where the officer was born and raised. He was a member of the Presbyterian Church. The Sheriff's Department provided an honor guard for Deputy Davis' funeral.

Albuquerque *Journal*, November 26, 1968
Albuquerque *Tribune*, November 26, 1968
James L. Wilson, correspondence, 1990

JAMES LESLIE "LES" DOW

Sheriff
Eddy County, New Mexico

The newspaper article read:
Yesterday evening, [February 18, 1897] about 6:45 p.m., Sheriff J. L. Dow was assassinated on Fox street in Eddy [now called Carlsbad].

He was coming from the bank building, and when almost in front of The Argus [newspaper] office was shot by one of two men who were concealed in the doorway and who had evidently been waiting for him. Two shots were fired, only one taking effect. The ball entered the left corner of the mouth, shattered the jawbone and passed out at the back of the neck.

The pistol was held quite close and his face was severely powder burned. Immediately after the shooting the parties ran past the post office and turned down into the alley.

Mr. Dow staggered across the street ditch, finally sinking down in front of the E. K. restaurant, from where he was carried into Blackmore's drug-store, his wound dressed and later removed to his home.

It was not thought at the time that the wound was fatal, but he only survived till early this morning, dying about 7 o'clock. While nothing positive has been announced, it is thought the men were recognized by Mr. Dow, and are also known to the officers, and that arrests will follow very soon.

Sheriff James Leslie "Les" Dow, 37, had only been in office seven weeks at the time of his death.

David Lyle Kemp, 35, a Texas killer, rustler and gambler was elected Eddy County's first Sheriff in 1891. He was also a personal and political foe of Sheriff Les Dow. Kemp, during his term in office, according to some sources, functioned in the best interests of his outlaw friends and Eddy County became "quite rowdy." Dow, a former Chaves County deputy sheriff, deputy U. S. Marshal and range detective, had a strong record in support of law and order.

Observers of events at the time were convinced that Kemp and a second man, Will Kennon, killed Sheriff Dow. Eddy Town Constable Dee Harkey claimed that Kemp admitted the murder to him, but Harkey didn't like Dow any better than Kemp did and he helped Kemp avoid a posse led by Dow's Deputy, Bob Armstrong. Harkey arrested Kemp later that night and held him at his own house rather than the local jail for fear he'd be lynched. Kemp was later tried at Roswell.

Harkey wrote in his autobiography that Kemp paid a man named Bill Smith $50.00 to give perjured testimony. Smith swore the shooting was a matter of self-defense. He testified that Dow called Kemp a "damn son-of-a-bitch" and pulled his gun first. Kemp was acquitted. Harkey also said this: "Dave Kemp and Les Dow were both considered dangerous men, and Les's reputation helped Dave in his defense. After the trial, Dave left a note on [Bill] Smith's door to leave the country, and Smith did so."

As for the person of Dave Kemp, history offers a mixed report. Harkey and some others paint the picture above. Others paint a more attractive picture. Kemp remained a resident of Eddy for 15 or so years after Dow's murder, and he remained in the saloon and cattle business. He neither smoked nor drank alcohol. A local newspaper noted that his only vice was that he constantly chewed gum. Kemp was not involved in another violent affair for the remainder of his life. A report circulated that his own sister killed him, but that was not so; he died of a heart attack on January 4, 1935 in his residence in Lipscomb County in the Texas Panhandle.

Dow, a Texan by nativity and a saloonkeeper by trade, was survived by his wife of 14 years, Molly, and two sons, Hiram and Robert. He is buried at Carlsbad. Hiram Dow became an attorney and served as both Mayor of Roswell and Lieutenant Governor of New Mexico under the second administration of Governor Clyde Tingley (1937-1938).

Pecos Valley *Argus*, Friday, February 19, 1897

Larry D. Ball, *Desert Lawmen, The High Sheriffs of New Mexico and Arizona 1846–1912*, University of New Mexico Press

Don Bullis, *Duels, Gunfights & Shoot-Outs: Wild Tales from the Land of Enchantment*, Rio Grande Books

George Curry, 1861-1947, An Autobiography, University of New Mexico Press

Elvis E. Fleming, *Captain Joseph C. Lea*, Yucca Tree Press

A. M. Gibson, *The Life and Death of Colonel Albert Jennings Fountain*, University of Oklahoma Press

Dee Harkey, *Mean as Hell*, University of New Mexico Press (it should be noted that Harkey's autobiography is self-serving and inaccurate at the very least; and downright dishonest at most.)

Bill O'Neal, *Encyclopedia of Western Gunfighters*, University of Oklahoma Press

Bill O'Neal, "They Called Him MISTER Kemp," *True West*," April 1991

RUFUS J. "RUFE" DUNNAHOO
Deputy Sheriff
Chaves County, New Mexico

Chaves County Sheriff John Peck, his chief deputy, Rufe Dunnahoo, and a second deputy, Dwight Hebrst, drove to the tenant farm of Gilford Welch, near Greenfield, on Sunday, August 2, 1931, to look for some items reportedly stolen from an automobile which had been wrecked between Hagerman and Dexter. When they arrived they first met Charles Appleby, owner of the farm, and as they talked with him, Welch emerged from the house. Sheriff Peck explained why they were there and Welch said they were free to look around. Sheriff Peck began a search around the outside of the house while Deputy Hebrst looked into some nearby outbuildings. Deputy Dunnahoo went into the house and shortly emerged carrying an auto license plate and bracket.

"Well, we have found the plate and you might as well come clean and tell us where the other articles are hidden," Dunnahoo said to Welch.

Welch invited the other officers into the house to look around. "I will go in and help you search," he said.

As they entered a bedroom, Welch produced a pistol from behind a dresser and said, "I'll kill both of you."

"Why, man, you can't afford to do anything like that," Peck said. "This case does not amount to anything." The sheriff related what happened next. "I saw that the man would not listen to reason and I nodded to Dunnahoo to come up from behind. I grabbed one arm and at the same time Rufe grappled with him from the other side. We were attempting to take the gun away from him and in the mix-up the three of us fell on a bed in the corner of the room. In some manner Welch must of [*sic*] gotten his right arm loose and the [fatal] shot was fired."

Investigation revealed that Dunnahoo was shot as he lay on the bed, the bullet ranging upward from his neck and into his brain. The deputy had not attempted to draw is own gun and Sheriff Peck was not armed. Neither officer considered the situation dangerous, even after Welch pulled his gun, Peck said later.

Sheriff Peck escaped from the house and ran to his car where he'd left his gun. Welch fired at the sheriff repeatedly, until his gun, a .380 automatic, was empty. Then Peck fired and Welch returned fire, having reloaded his gun in the meantime. None of the shots took effect. Welch backed toward the door of the house. Peck demanded that he be allowed inside to see what could be done for Dunnahoo.

"Don't you try to go into that house, or I will kill you," Welch said, then he fled out a rear door and ran across a cotton patch to a cornfield. As Welch raced across the cotton patch Peck fired at him a number of times.

Welch reached the Hagerman-Dexter road only to be met by Sheriff Peck who'd headed him off. Welch turned around and raced back toward his house, with the sheriff in hot pursuit. Back inside the house, his wife and stepdaughter pleaded with him to surrender. By that time, several armed men arrived on the scene and surrounded the house. Welch sent out a note saying that he would surrender to a deputy sheriff named Jim Williamson, and no one else. Williamson arrived from Hagerman and took Welch into custody without further ado.

Welch, still angry, said, "I killed Dunnahoo because he made me mad when he started to search my home." He said he would have killed Sheriff Peck, too, if he had not run out of ammunition. But as Sheriff Peck and Deputy Williamson took the killer to Roswell, he seemed to realize the enormity of his crime. "Take me out to the side of the road and kill me," he said. "I'm a good man. Just kill me."

There were folks around who were willing to do just that. Historian Elvis Fleming reported that one well-armed citizen approached the sheriff's car and said, "If you will get out, I will end this case right here!" The sheriff declined. The local newspaper reported, "Feelings ran high in Roswell…where Rufus J. Dunnahoo was well and favorably known."

Fifty-two year old Rufe Dunnahoo had lived 51 of his years in Roswell. His wife Mary, and two children, Alex of Roswell and Mrs. Edgar Peters of Clovis survived him. He had served as deputy sheriff, police officer and constable in Roswell and Chaves County for twenty years. He was interred at South Park Cemetery in Roswell.

"He was known as an efficient, courageous and faithful officer and yesterday his life was snuffed out while he was acting in the line of duty," The Roswell *Daily Record* eulogized.

At his arraignment on the morning of August 3, Welch pleaded guilty to the murder of Rufe Dunnahoo. His plea, according to the law, was not accepted and he was remanded to custody. On October 16, 1931, it took a jury two hours and fifteen minutes to convict Welch of second degree murder. Judge Miguel A. Otero sentenced him to 40 to 90 years in prison. In September, 1933, the State Supreme Court reversed Judge Otero based on the fact that Dunnahoo had entered Welch's house without a warrant, thus giving Welch the right to arm and defend himself. Welch pleaded guilty to a charge of involuntary manslaughter and on October 10, 1934 Judge James McGhee sentenced him to four to five years in prison.

As a footnote to this story, Deputy Jim Williamson, 72, was shot and seriously wounded the following April (1932) after he arrested two robbers at Lake Arthur. One of the two produced a gun and shot the officer as both escaped his custody.

Elvis E. Fleming, Archivist, Historical Center for Southeast New Mexico, Roswell, correspondence, June 24 & July 15, 1996, and "Chaves County Deputy Sheriff Rufus J. Dunnahoo, 1879-1931: Killed in the Line of Duty," June 2, 1998

Funeral Record, Dunnahoo, Rufus J.

Lubbock *Morning Avalanche*, April 19, 1932

Roswell *Daily Record*, August 3, 4 & 7; September 1; October 10 & 17, 1931

EDWARD J. FARR

Sheriff
Huerfano County, Colorado

At about 10:30 on the evening of July 11, 1899, a gang of bandits made up of Sam Ketchum,* Harvey Logan and Elza Lay stopped the Colorado and Southern passenger train near two cinder cones called Twin Mountain, about five miles south of Folsum in Union County, New Mexico. Train number 1 was on its regular run from Denver to Fort Worth. The thieves blew the safe in the express car and made good their escape. The railroad claimed the thieves got nothing, but other accounts at the time reported that the thieves made off with about $70,000. Logan and Lay were both regular members of Butch Cassidy's Wild Bunch, but Cassidy did not participate in the Twin Mountain robbery.

W. H. Reno, a special agent for the railroad, accompanied by Sheriff Ed Farr of Huerfano County, Colorado, soon arrived in Cimarron, New Mexico. On Sunday, July 16, officers learned that three men who fit the descriptions of the robbers had been seen entering Turkey (or Turkey Creek, according to some) Canyon, about eight miles north of Cimarron. Reno and Farr organized a posse that included Henry N. Love, and Perfecto Cordova of Springer, F. H. Smith of New York (who went along for "the fun of it"), and others.** At about 5:15 that afternoon, the posse came upon the outlaw camp.

Bullets began flying at once. Lay was hit first but remained able to return fire. Ketchum, hit in the arm, was put out of action. Logan laid down a withering fire. He had the advantage of using smokeless gunpowder which made it difficult for the lawmen to see where the bullets were coming from. Sheriff Farr took a bullet in the wrist. He calmly bandaged the wound with his handkerchief and continued the fight. Smith was hit in the calf of his leg and Farr was hit again, this time in the chest. He fell on top of Smith. "I'm done for," he said, and died. Love was badly wounded in the thigh. Firing died down, then. It was nearly 6:00 p.m. and beginning to rain. Early news reports indicated that one of the bandits had been killed in the fight, but that was in error. The posse remained in Turkey Canyon throughout the rainy night as all three outlaws managed to escape.***

Sam Ketchum, his upper arm badly shattered by a bullet, made it to the Ute Creek headquarters of the Lambert ranch, about three miles west of Turkey Canyon. Ketchum told cowboys there he'd been shot in a hunting accident. They had not heard of the gun battle and believed him. A ranch hand in Cimarron for supplies the next day learned of the gunfight and told authorities that a wounded man had appeared at the ranch. W. H. Reno and others arrested Ketchum later that day without incident. Transferred to the Territorial Prison at Santa Fe, Ketchum's arm was amputated, but that didn't save him. He died of blood poisoning on July 24, 1899.

Logan and Lay rode all night and all the next day putting as much distance between themselves and Turkey Canyon as possible. Large posses searched the mountains for the outlaws, but they were severely hampered by almost continuous rain. One source says Logan left Lay with a man named Red Weaver who nursed the outlaw back to health. Another source says Logan paid a young Hispanic family a large sum of money to minister to Lay's wounds. Whichever it was, Lay recovered and joined Logan at the Virgil Lusk Ranch, near Eddy (now Carlsbad), in mid August.

Lusk managed to get word to Eddy County Sheriff Cicero Stewart that the outlaws were at his place. The sheriff and two deputies, J. D. Cantrell and Rufus Thomas, hurried to the ranch. In a brief gunfight, Lusk, Thomas and Lay were all wounded and Lay was captured. Under the name McGinnis, Lay was convicted of second-degree murder and sentenced to life in prison for killing Sheriff Farr. On July 1, 1905, Governor Miguel A. Otero commuted the sentence to ten years. Elza Lay was released on January 10, 1906. (Legend holds that he lived an honest and upright life thereafter.)

Harvey Logan, also known as Kid Curry, was considered one of the most violent members of the Wild Bunch. He was never prosecuted for the murder of Sheriff Farr although he was arrested in Knoxville, Tennessee in 1901. He escaped from jail there and made his way back to the West. Logan committed suicide in July 1903, near Glenwood Springs, Colorado, after a train robbery near Parachute, rather than submit to arrest.

Posseman Henry Love died of his wound on July 20, 1899 (see page 189).

Edward Farr was born at Kerrville, Texas and moved first to New Mexico, and then Walsenburg, Colorado, about 1887. He was elected sheriff of Huerfano County in 1898. A special train took his body from Trinidad to Walsenburg for burial on July 20, 1899.

* Sam Ketchum, about 45, was the older brother of Tom Ketchum who was

one of several New Mexico outlaws who used the name "Black Jack."

** Different sources include different posse members. One source says Deputy U. S. Marshal Wilson Elliott was a part of the posse, and in fact led it. Two other sources fail to list Elliott as a posse member. Two sources list Miguel Lopez and a Captain Thacker as posse members, while a third omits them. One source says the posse was seven men strong, another says eight. The first news reports named six possemen. Some writers seem to confuse the posse which fought in Turkey Canyon with posses which took up pursuit of the bandits afterwards.

*** There arose a dispute after the battle as to who did what. U. S. Marshal Creighton Foraker claimed that Deputy Marshal Elliott was in charge at Turkey Canyon. Other reports said that Sheriff Farr had discretionary authority, and W. H. Reno claimed he was personally in charge. The dispute got so acrimonious that Foraker claimed that Reno deserted the posse when the first shots were fired. There were also hard feelings because Sheriff Farr's body remained at Turkey Canyon, in the rain, over night.

Howard Bryan, "The Black Jack Gangs: The Ketchum Brothers," *Robbers, Rogues and Ruffians, True Tales of the Wild West*, Clear Light Publishers

Charles Kelly, *The Outlaw Trail, A History of Butch Cassidy and His Wild Bunch*, Bonanza Books

Bill O'Neal, *Encyclopedia of Western Gunfighters*, University of Oklahoma Press (This source incorrectly identifies Tom "Black Jack" Ketchum as a participant in the Twin Mountain train robbery of July 11, 1899. Tom Ketchum, alone, attempted to rob the same train on August 16, 1899. Tom Ketchum was hanged at Clayton, New Mexico, on April 26, 1901, the only man ever executed in New Mexico for train robbery.)

Miguel A. Otero, *My Nine Years As Governor of the Territory of New Mexico, 1897-1906*, University of New Mexico Press

Santa Fe *New Mexican*, July 12, 17, 18, 19, 20, 21 & 25; August 16, 1899

Dan L. Thrapp, *Encyclopedia of Frontier Biography*, University of Nebraska Press

WINSONFRED A. FILFRED

Officer
Navajo Department of Law Enforcement

On April 2, 1999, at a little after 11:00 a.m., Officer Filfred, 22, was dispatched to a structure fire at the intersection of U.S. Route 160 and Arizona State Road 98—Shonto Junction—on the Navajo Reservation. The weather was particularly bad that day; rain mixed with snow, fog, and ice covered roads. Officer Filfred was severely injured when his westbound police vehicle collided head-on with an eastbound recreational vehicle. He was transported to Tuba City medical facilities where he died late that afternoon.

Officer Filfred joined the Navajo Police in October, 1997. He attended the New Mexico Law Enforcement Academy and was certified as a peace officer on February 26, 1998. His wife survived him.

Navajo Division of Public Safety, Kayenta Police District, Crime Report, April 4, 1999

New Mexico Department of Public Safety Training Center, Notice of Termination, April 5, 1999

WARREN GRAY FLESHMAN

Security Police Officer
United States Atomic Energy Commission

On February 11, 1950, Officer Warren Fleshman, along with Officer Robert Francis Purcell, 30, (see page 237) returned to New Mexico from the East Coast carrying "national security assets." The airplane in which they traveled crashed west of Albuquerque, killing both officers and the pilot, Hugh Williams, 31, of Albuquerque.

A great deal of mystery surrounded the accident. A news blackout was initiated immediately after the crash for national security reasons. But even when the Atomic Energy Commission (AEC) did release information the following day, no clue was provided regarding the cause of the crash. Indeed, the reason for the crash has never been explained. It is known that Williams refueled the Beechcraft in Tucumcari and then flew west. He landed at an emergency airstrip in the Estancia Valley, east of the Sandia and Monzano Mountains, and called Albuquerque for weather information. Williams then flew on to Albuquerque and buzzed his own home, which he always did when returning from a flight. He radioed the tower and reported that he had the airport in sight. He was not heard from again. The plane was found about two hours later, five miles west and several miles north of the airport, well out of normal air traffic patterns.

All national security assets the two men carried were either accounted for or recovered.

Warren Fleshman, a World War II veteran, was a bachelor who lived in a dormitory at Los Alamos. His parents and a brother who resided in Watonga, Oklahoma survived him. An AEC honor guard escorted his body there for burial.

Albuquerque *Journal*, February 11 & 12, 1950
Albuquerque *Tribune*, June 13, 1957
Certificates of Death, State of New Mexico, February 12, 1950
Allen M. Osborn, Albuquerque, correspondence
The TSD News, May 17, 1996

ALBERT J. FOUNTAIN

Prosecutor

Southeastern New Mexico Stock Growers Association

Two gangs of cattle thieves were extremely active in southern New Mexico during the 1890s. Eli "Slick" Miller led one group, the so-called Socorro gang. Oliver Lee is believed to have led the other, known as the Tularosa gang. By the end of 1894, through the efforts of Col. Albert J. Fountain and his investigators, Ben Williams and Les Dow, the Socorro gang was out of business and Slick Miller was serving a 10 year prison sentence. Fountain then turned his attention to the Tularosa gang.

By late in 1895, Dow and Williams had amassed a considerable body of evidence against Oliver Lee and William McNew. In January 1896, Colonel Fountain, traveling with his eight-year-old son, Henry, went to the town of Lincoln to present his evidence to a grand jury meeting there. Among 32 indictments handed down during that session of the jury, two were returned against Lee and McNew for larceny of cattle and defacing brands (January 21).

On Thursday, January 30, Col. Fountain and young Henry loaded a buckboard and left Lincoln headed for home in Las Cruces more than 100 miles away. They stopped for the first night at Mescalero, 18 miles from Lincoln. The second day they made La Luz, north of present day Alamogordo. On Saturday, morning they set out on the last long leg of the trip, past the White Sands and Chalk Hills and over the San Andreas Mountains at San Augustine Pass and into Las Cruces.

At mid morning the Fountains met Santos Alvarado, a stagecoach driver, who told the Colonel he'd seen three riders along the road, but they'd galloped off to the east before he could recognize them. In the afternoon, about three miles from the Chalk Hills, they met Saturnino Barela, another stage driver. Col. Fountain and Barela talked about the three riders they could both see on the horizon about a mile away. Barela suggested that the Fountains return to Luna's Well with him and spend the night at the stage station, and then ride into Las Cruces with the stagecoach the next morning. The Colonel declined. He said that Henry had a cold and needed the attention of his mother. Saturnino Barela is the last person known to have seen the Fountains alive.

On Sunday evening, February 1, Barela called at the Fountain house in Las Cruces and asked if the Colonel and Henry had arrived. He said he'd seen a place near the Chalk Hills where a wagon had swerved off the road and he was concerned for the Fountain's welfare. Two of the Colonel's sons, Jack and Albert, quickly gathered a search party and rode hard for the Chalk Hills. Their group was followed a few hours later by a second, larger, posse.

At dawn's light, Captain Thomas Brannigan, Chief of the Mescalero Apache Scouts, began the most thorough kind of search. He found spent cartridges and a large pool of blood and personal effects belonging to young Henry Fountain, covered with blood. He also led the posse when the Colonel's buckboard was located some 12 miles east of the main Tularosa-Las Cruces Road. All of the Fountain's possessions had been plundered and the Colonel's papers scattered about. A trail led east, toward Dog Canyon and Oliver Lee's ranch. Before a small detachment of possemen could follow the trail, they reached a point where a large herd of cattle had been driven across the prairie, erasing any horse tracks. Another group of possemen found one of the team of horses known to have been pulling the Fountain's buckboard. A considerable amount of dried blood covered its left side. A posseman named Carl Clauson found another set of tracks, those of a large, shod, horse and he followed them to Oliver Lee's southern ranch headquarters at Wildy Well. Clauson visited with Lee there and Lee declined to help in the search. He said the Fountains meant nothing to him.

No trace of Albert Jennings or Henry Fountain was ever found.

After a considerable investigation which involved Doña Ana County Sheriff Pat Garrett, and the Pinkerton Detective Agency, among others; months of political chicanery; and a gunfight which cost Deputy Sheriff Kent Kearney his life (see page 161), Oliver Lee, Bill McNew and Jim Gilliland were charged with the murders of the Fountains. In late May and early June 1899, Lee and Gilliland were tried at Hillsboro, Sierra County, New Mexico, for the murder of young Henry Fountain. Thomas Catron, who would become New Mexico's first U. S. Senator, prosecuted the case, and Albert Bacon Fall, who would become New Mexico's second U. S. Senator, defended Lee and Gilliland. The trial took 18 days and the jury took just seven minutes to acquit both defendants. No one else was ever prosecuted for the crimes.

In later years, Jim Gilliland was heard to boast on several occasions, "...if the bodies had to be found before a murder could be proved, no one would ever be convicted."

George Curry who served as New Mexico territorial governor (1907-10) and New Mexico's first congressman after statehood (1912-13) expressed another point of view. He was personally acquainted with all the players in this drama. He said this of Oliver Lee: "He might kill in self-defense or in defense of his property, but murder, personally or through hired assassins, was wholly out of character; and the idea of his having any part in the murder of an innocent child was simply beyond belief."

Colonel Albert Jennings Fountain was a prominent man in southern New Mexico and west Texas during the last half of the 19th century. As a military officer, he fought against Texas Confederates, Apache Indians, and outlaws of every stripe. As a lawyer/prosecutor, he was relentless in pursuit of criminals of all kinds. "I don't want to live in a place," he said, "where I have to carry a gun all the time."

Fifty-eight years old at the time of his death, Colonel Fountain had been married to the former Mariana Pérez for 33 years. They were the parents of nine children.

Larry D. Ball, *Desert Lawmen, The High Sheriffs of New Mexico and Arizona, 1846-1912*, University of New Mexico Press

George Curry, 1861-1947, An Autobiography, University of New Mexico Press

Erna Fergusson, "The Mystery of the White Sands," *Murder & Mystery in New Mexico*, Lightning Tree Press

A. M. Gibson, *The Life and Death of Colonel Albert Jennings Fountain*, University of Oklahoma Press

William A. Keleher, *The Fabulous Frontier*, University of New Mexico Press

Leon Metz, *Pat Garrett, The Story of a Western Lawman*, The University of Oklahoma Press

LUCIANO B. GALLEGOS

Sheriff
Union County, New Mexico

The book, *History of Clayton and Union County, New Mexico*, makes the following terse statement:

> Luciano B. Gallegos, respected sheriff of the county, was killed accidently in the jail where he lived. He was cleaning a rifle which fell to the floor and discharged killing him instantly.

An Albuquerque newspaper reported the incident thus:

> Sheriff Gallegos, of Union County, accidentally shot himself on Friday night while engaged in guarding prisoners, dying in a few hours.

Sheriff Gallegos was elected to office on November 9, 1896, and took office on January 1, 1897. He died on April 5, 1897 after serving just over three months in office. The Union County Commission appointed Emiterio Gallegos to succeed Luciano B. Gallegos in office.

Nothing of personal nature is recorded concerning Sheriff Gallegos.

Albuquerque *Weekly News*, April 10, 1897
Goldianne Thompson, *History of Clayton and Union County, New Mexico*, Monitor
       Publishing Company
Lee Johnson, Sheriff of Union County, October 22, 1999
Union County Commission minutes (undated)

ANGELIC S. GARCIA

Deputy Sheriff
Bernalillo County, New Mexico

Deputy Angelic Garcia was assigned to the graveyard shift in Albuquerque's North Valley shortly after midnight on Sunday, March 4, 2001. She was dispatched to assist another deputy who had been sent to a bar fight which possibly involved a gun. Near the corner of Fourth Street and Ranchitos Road, as she sped to the scene, she lost control of her patrol vehicle and slammed into a tree. She was pronounced dead at the University of New Mexico Hospital a short time later. She was not wearing her seat belt at the time of the accident.

A 1993 graduate of Rio Grande High School, Deputy Garcia, 26, was an avid softball player. She attended the University of New Mexico for three and one half years before she dropped out to join the Sheriff's Department in 1997. Her parents, Michael and Vivian Garcia, and a brother, Michael, survived her. She was interred at Mt. Calvary Cemetery.

"She was a real morale booster to the people around her," Sheriff Joe Bowdich said. "She was top producer in her squad."

Albuquerque *Journal*, March 3, 5, 6, & 7, 2001

NASH PHILLIP GARCIA

Patrolman
New Mexico State Police

State Police Officer Nash Garcia sat in his parked police car along U. S. Route 66 about 20 miles east of Grants on Friday, April 11, 1952; he may have been doing paperwork. A pickup sped past him. Then it turned around and sped by him again, being operated erratically. The officer took up pursuit.

Garcia followed as the truck turned off the highway about 18 miles east of Grants and drove south on dirt roads across Acoma Pueblo Indian Reservation land for about 19 miles at which point it stopped. As Officer Garcia slowed and drove up to the pickup, two subjects opened fire from ambush with .30 caliber rifles; one from about 100 yards and the other from about 50 feet.* They fired nine shots into the police car and Nash Garcia. The officer managed to open the car's door and then fell out onto the ground, severely wounded. The offenders then beat him about the head with gun-butts to make certain he was dead. They loaded his body into the police car and drove another six miles into reservation land, to a spot near Sandstone Mesa where they abandoned it. They returned the following day, filled the car with juniper brush and set it afire.

Officer Garcia wasn't missed until Sunday morning when he failed to respond to a call from headquarters. State Police Chief Joe Roach said it wasn't unusual for the officer to be out of contact for a day or so, especially if he was working on the reservation. Concern for Garcia's safety increased when officers contacted his wife and she said she had not heard from him, either. His work, she said, sometimes kept him away from home for several days at a time.

A search and an investigation were initiated. It didn't take long. A local cowboy and several other witnesses told investigators they saw Garcia in pursuit of a pickup driven by one of the Felipe brothers: Willie, 31, or Gabriel, 28. On Sunday evening, State Police officers Dick Lewis and Joe Fernandez went to Willie Felipe's house on the Acoma reservation. Felipe offered no resistance and told the officers what he and his brother had done.

"I knew they'd get me," Willie Felipe said later to an Albuquerque *Journal* reporter. "They always get them."

The next morning Willie led a seven-vehicle caravan of officers and other searchers to Sandstone Mesa. They found "…a few pitifully small pieces of charred bone in a pile of ashes on the floor [of the car]."

On Monday evening, April 14, Albuquerque motorcycle policeman Robert Olona, Nash Garcia's cousin, arrested Gabriel Felipe on North First Street in Albuquerque. Gabriel offered no resistance when taken into custody. He maintained that he took no part in the killing. He asserted that he actually tried to stop Willie from shooting the State Policeman. Officers found Garcia's service revolver in a suitcase in Gabriel Felipe's hotel room along with another gun which belonged to the suspect.

In the fall of 1952 the Felipe brothers were tried, convicted and originally sentenced to death. They appealed on the basis that they were drunk and insane at the time the crime was committed. In March 1953, U. S. District Court Judge Carl Hatch found them both sane and competent and sentenced them to life in federal prison. Gabriel served 19 years and Willie served 20 years. They were released in the 1970s.**

Nash Garcia was the first member of the New Mexico State Police to be murdered in the line of duty. Two officers, Walter Taber in 1937 (page 305) and Delbert Bugg in 1946 (page 31), were previously killed in motorcycle accidents. A third State Police officer, William Speight, died as he tried to reach a radio tower near Cloudcroft in February of 1949 (page 295). Two State Police officers—Mackie C de Baca (page 54) and José Francisco Quintana (page 238)—were killed while serving the U. S. Armed Forces during World War II. The State Police Department was created in 1935.

Nash Garcia, 38, was born in Torreon and reared in Albuquerque. He served two years as a Bernalillo County Sheriff's Deputy before he joined the State Police in June of 1944. He was first assigned to the Albuquerque area, promoted to captain in June 1948, and placed in command of the district. When Joe Roach was named State Police Chief in 1950, he ordered Garcia demoted to the rank of patrolman (his pay was $284 per month). Garcia requested reassignment to the Grants area where he worked for nearly a year before his death. Nash Garcia was survived by his wife, Martha, and three daughters; Yvonne, 13, Yolanda, 11, and Yvette, 7.

* One source indicates that only one rifle was used.

** It was rumored in the Grants area that one of the brothers died, or was killed, in prison.

Albuquerque *Journal*, April 14 & 15; September 27 & December 13, 1952; March 4, 1953
The Roadrunner, (New Mexico State Police Association, Vol. 3, No. 2, Summer, 1992)
State Police Records

RALPH GARCIA

Corrections Officer
Guadalupe County Correctional Facility

The time was about 6:30 p.m. on August 31, 1999. The place was the Guadalupe County Correctional Facility, just south of Santa Rosa, New Mexico. Two inmates began scuffling in the prison gymnasium and in the course of the altercation, one of them was stabbed. Prison guards moved in immediately and ordered all prisoners back into their cells for a lockdown. Many prisoners refused to cooperate and an insurrection seemed to be building.

About then, Corrections Officer Ralph Garcia entered Pod "E" which contained cells for about 60 prisoners plus a common area. The door closed and locked behind him. Garcia was immediately set upon by a group of prisoners, numbering nine or ten. He was stabbed repeatedly before two other guards were able to enter the pod and attempt to pull him to safety.

Ralph Garcia died of his wounds.

Wide-spread disorder in the prison followed, and officials said later that they lost control for about three hours. They were able to restore order by about 11:30 that evening. No prisoners were able to escape and no other injuries were reported.

A Tucumcari resident, Ralph Garcia, 42, spent most of his life doing ranch work, but ranch profits had fallen and he took a job at the prison to earn extra money about six months before he was killed. He was survived by his wife, Rachel, sons Jason, 18, Justin, 12, and daughter Monique, 15.

Frank Gutierrez, commander of the Tucumcari VFW described Garcia as a respected member of the community. "He was an awesome cowboy. That was his life. He had a lot of goodness in him."

"He didn't deserve what he got," his wife, Rachael, said. "He was a good man. He loved his kids. He loved me very much and I loved him…. He didn't have much experience with it [prison work], but he knew what he was doing. He always said that in order for it to work, the corrections officer had to have respect for the inmate, and the inmate had to have respect for the corrections officer." In a newspaper piece published in March 2005, Mrs. Garcia stated her opposition to the death penalty for her husband's killers, along with her opposition to the death penalty in general. "My husband would have wanted ... this as much as I do."

Among those suspected of participating in Garcia's murder were:

Reis Lopez, 22, serving life for murder
Danny Sanchez, AKA "Piasso", 22, serving 20 years for attempted murder
Robert Young, AKA "Diablo", 22, serving 18 years for attempted murder
Robert Gallegos, 23, serving six years for armed robbery
John Montano, 22, serving 18 months for aggravated battery.

Albuquerque *Journal*, September 2 & 8; October 8, 1999; December 2, 2000
Albuquerque *Tribune*, October 8, 1999; December 12, 2000
Criminal Justice Newsletter, September 10, 1999
Roswell *Daily Record*, September 2, 1999

MANUEL GARCIA Y GRIEGO

Constable
Ranchos De Albuquerque, New Mexico

A local newspaper reported the incident thus:

> Murder. It is our painful duty to report that Manuel Garcia y Griego, constable of the precinct of Ranchos de Albuquerque, was murdered night before last [Wednesday, June 24, 1868] in that precinct. The body was found in the road near Blas Lucero's house, early yesterday morning by the teamsters of Pablo Barela's train when coming to this place. He had been out on horseback that evening summoning the people to work on the acequia yesterday, and was shot through the side of the breast, when near the place where the body was found, and had a cut of a knife in the temple. His horse and revolver were stolen. Diego Lucero, a *coyote* who was confined in jail in the default of payment of a fine for carrying deadly weapons, and who broke jail a few days ago, is suspected of the commission of this murder, as he is said to have threatened to kill the deceased and others who testified against him. Deceased has left a wife and seven young children, as well as a large circle of other relatives and friends to mourn his loss. Yesterday a party of citizens of Ranchos de Albuquerque started in pursuit of Diego Lucero.

No additional information regarding this unfortunate event has been located.

Semi-Weekly Review (Albuquerque), Friday, June 26, 1868.

PATRICK FLOYD GARRETT

Sheriff

Lincoln & Doña Ana Counties, New Mexico

On the morning of February 29, 1908, former Sheriff Pat Garrett left his ranch home near Bear Canyon on the east slope of the Organ Mountains. Driving a buckboard and accompanied by Carl Adamson, an alleged business associate, he headed for Las Cruces. They were soon joined by Jesse Wayne Brazel who rode along-side the buckboard on horseback. The three of them passed through the village of Organ and continued west down the long grade toward the Rio Grande. Near a spot called Alameda Arroyo, Garrett stopped the wagon and got down to urinate. The old lawman had just unbuttoned his trousers when he was shot, first in the back of the head and then through the body. He died on the spot without touching his own gun.

A great deal of controversy surrounded the later life of Pat Garrett. He had fallen on hard times, financially, and was involved in a controversy over a herd of goats grazing on his ranch land. The goats belonged to Wayne Brazel. Carl Adamson was allegedly involved in negotiations to purchase the animals through a third party, Jim Miller, his brother-in-law. Miller, known as "Killin' Jim" or "Deacon Jim" was believed to have killed 20 to 40 men in Texas, depending on who told the story.

Immediately after the murder, Wayne Brazel rode into Las Cruces and surrendered himself to Doña Ana County Deputy Sheriff Felipe Lucero. He claimed he shot and killed Garrett in self-defense. Brazel was tried for murder in April 1909. He argued that Garrett's reputation was so fearsome that he was justified in shooting him in the back. The jury must have agreed. Brazel was acquitted. It should be noted that the Territorial Attorney General's office did an abysmal job of prosecuting Brazel. Adamson, the only eyewitness, was not even called to testify.

The Garrett family generally believed that Adamson actually did the killing but many historians are of the opinion that Jim Miller killed the old sheriff by shooting him with a rifle from ambush. A case could be made that a local rancher did the killing, or in the alternative, paid Miller and Adamson to do it, and Brazel to take the blame. Fred Fornoff, captain of the New Mexico Mounted Police, examined the crime scene and did not believe that Brazel's story made sense. Fornoff could not, however, produce enough hard evidence to point to any other assailant. No one else was ever prosecuted for killing Pat Garrett.

Jesse Wayne Brazel came to a mysterious end. In the fall of 1909, after he was acquitted of killing Garrett, he acquired a homestead west of Lordsburg. He married and had a son. His wife died six months after giving birth. In 1914 Jesse Wayne Brazel disappeared and was never heard from again. A search conducted at the behest of his son about 20 years later revealed that Brazel may have migrated to South America where he was killed.

Jim Miller, along with three others, was hanged by a lynch mob at Ada, Oklahoma, on April 19, 1909, for the murder of A. A. "Gus" Bobbitt, a former deputy U. S. Marshal for the Indian Territory, who Miller killed from ambush with a shotgun. Rumors circulated at the time that Miller confessed to killing Garrett just before he was strung-up. A jailer who was present at the lynching, however, reported that Miller made no mention of Garrett.

"I ought to know," Walter Gayne said. "I hung him."

In addition to the years Pat Garrett served as sheriff in both Lincoln and Doña Ana counties, 1880-81 and 1897-1900 respectively, he also served brief stints as Ranger (paid by Texas cattle interests), Deputy U. S. Marshal and Collector of Customs at El Paso. He had not served as an active lawman for some years at the time of his death. Garrett is best known, of course, for killing William H. Bonney—Billy the Kid—at Fort Sumner in July, 1881.*

Garrett, 58, was survived by his wife, Apolinaria, and seven children: Patrick Jr., Anna, Dudley, Oscar, Pauline, Jarvis, and Elizabeth. A daughter, Ida, preceded him in death. He is buried in Las Cruces.

* William H. Bonney—Billy the Kid—participated in the killings of at least five New Mexico peace officers between 1878 and 1881: Lincoln County Sheriff William Brady; Lincoln County deputies George Hindman, James Carlisle and J. W. Bell; and Doña Ana County Deputy Bob Olinger.

Larry D. Ball, *Desert Lawmen: The High Sheriffs of New Mexico and Arizona, 1846-1912*, University of New Mexico Press
Richard Benke, Albuquerque *Journal*, February 19, 1995
Don Bullis, "The Murder of Pat Garrett," *Rio Rancho Observer*, October 5,1988
William A. Keleher, *The Fabulous Frontier*, University of New Mexico Press, 1962
John J. Lipsey, *The Life of Pat F. Garrett and the Taming of the Border Outlaw*, The Filter Press

Leon C. Metz, *Pat Garrett, The Story of a Western Lawman*, University of Oklahoma Press

Frank Richard Prassel, *The Western Peace Officer, A Legacy of Law and Order*, University of Oklahoma Press

Colin Rickards, *Sheriff Pat Garrett's Last Days*, Sunstone Press

Pete Ross, "Some Prominent New Mexicans May Have Been Accessories to the Murder of Pat Garrett," *True West*, December 2001 (Ross was a New Mexico Peace Officer, see page 254.)

HOSKIE GENE

Acting Sergeant
Navajo Tribal Police

Acting Sergeant Hoskie Gene, as a Navajo Tribal policeman, was a certified New Mexico peace officer. At about 1:00 a.m. on Saturday, January 6, 1996, he responded to a call from the Bryant Trading Post at Shonto, 45 miles northeast of Tuba City, Arizona. Sgt. Gene learned that someone had attempted to break into the store and he began a search of the area for the culprits. No other officers were available to assist him. At 1:17 a.m. he contacted the dispatcher at Kayenta and reported that he would be out of the police car with two suspicious people. That was his last communication.

A second unit was dispatched to the area and officers later found Sgt. Gene's body along a remote roadway. He'd been hit on the back of the head and strangled to death; his car, gun and ammunition stolen.

Two suspects wrecked Gene's police car several miles from where his body was found. They were arrested at about 10:00 a.m. the same day. Two others were arrested on Saturday evening. All were from Shonto.

"They were in the community," FBI agent Dennis White said. "Police officers know everyone out there."

Two of the suspects were juveniles, and the disposition of charges against them is unknown. Vincent Cling, 21, was charged with first-degree murder. In August 1997, a jury found him guilty of second-degree murder. He could have received a life sentence but Federal Judge Paul Rosenblatt handed down a sentence of fifteen years after a plea from the defendant. "I feel sorry for the officer and his family. I am filled with pain when I think about it. It was wrong what I did and it saddens me still," he wrote to the judge. He was also ordered to pay about $26,000 restitution to the Gene family. Jervis Cling, 23, was sentenced to three years probation in a plea bargain.

Sgt. Hoskie Gene, 35, was married and the father of five teenagers. He was an 11-year veteran of the Navajo Tribal Police Department and he often worked nights to earn extra money. He'd been appointed acting sergeant shortly before he died. More than 700 mourners attended his funeral at Piñon, Arizona.

Albuquerque *Journal*, January 8 & 14, 1996; August 27, 1997
Captain Leonard Butler, Acting Chief, Navajo Tribal Police Department, March 15, 1996

GREGORY ANTHONY GEOFFRION

Inspector
New Mexico Transportation Department

On November 4, 1997 at about 6:00 p.m., Inspector Greg Geoffrion, 35, drove north on Interstate 25, near the Budagher's exit between Albuquerque and Santa Fe, he noticed a car parked alongside the road with all of its doors and trunk lid opened. He called the Sandoval County Sheriff's Department for assistance and stopped to investigate. Deputy Sheriff Kevin Perno soon arrived on the scene. The law enforcement vehicles were positioned to protect the car, narrowing the traffic lanes considerably. A woman walked toward the abandoned vehicle and the officers ordered her to stop. Instead she ran across the highway. Officer Geoffrion pursued and caught up with her, but was hit by a northbound vehicle as he did so. The car knocked him into a traffic lane and a second car ran over his legs. Deputy Perno pulled Geoffrion to safety and called for help.

During his hospitalization, nearly 200 employees of the Tax and Revenue Department and the Motor Transportation Division donated blood and provided moral support to the family. Inspector Geoffrion died at about 4:00 p.m. on November 11, 1997. Unmarried, Geoffrion was survived by his mother, Cordelia Geoffrion of Las Vegas, New Mexico, six sisters and one brother.

Albuquerque *Journal*, November 12 & 20, 1997
New Mexico State Police Report, November 21, 1997

RICHARD GOMEZ

Patrolman
New Mexico State Police

Officer Richard Gomez confronted Modesto Martinez, 60, at a small store in Coyote, Rio Arriba County, New Mexico, at about 2:30 on Thursday afternoon, April 17, 1980. The officer warned the older man about driving away from the store in his intoxicated condition. About a half an hour later, Officer Gomez stopped Martinez in his pickup truck on State Road 96 west of Coyote. As Gomez stood talking to Martinez, he motioned for a passing motorist, Urban Morfin, to stop and witness the conversation. As Morfin watched, Martinez shot Gomez with a .22 caliber pistol.

Land-grant activist leader Reyes López Tijerina happened by only minutes after the shooting. Tijerina attempted CPR on Gomez and at 3:08 p.m. notified the State Police dispatcher using Gomez's State Police radio. An ambulance and a State Police officer were immediately dispatched. Help reached the scene at approximately 3:50. The officer had been shot in the upper chest. His heart stopped beating before he reached the hospital in Española. Doctors spent an hour trying to revive him but it was too late. He was pronounced dead at 5:15 p.m.

Officers responding to the scene found Modesto Martinez sitting in his pickup parked in front of the officer's police car. Martinez, a native of Coyote and a sheepherder by trade, offered no resistance. He was charged with first degree murder. He was eventually convicted of voluntary manslaughter and on March 13, 1981 he was sentenced to 13 years in prison.

A native of Hatch, New Mexico, Richard Gomez was 31 at the time of his death. He was assigned to Gallina after he completed the State Police training academy on December 1, 1970, and there he met and married Bernice Chavez. The couple had two children. In 1977, he spent nearly a year as an undercover officer, and was then reassigned to the Truth or Consequences State Police office. In 1979, at his own request, he was transferred back to Gallina.

So many people—more than 500 including 150 police officers—attended

Richard Gomez's funeral that the service was held in the gymnasium of Coronado High School in Gallina. The officer was buried in the Gallina cemetery.

Santa Fe *New Mexican*, April 21 & 22, 1980; March 13, 1981
New Mexico State Police Records
New Mexico State Police *Annual*, 1985
The Roadrunner, New Mexico State Police Association, Vol. 3, No. 2, Summer, 1992

JOSÉ MARÍA "JOE" GONZALES

Night Marshal
Santa Rosa, New Mexico

The newspaper account read:

> Victim of a knife-attack without forewarning, Joe M. Gonzales, former sheriff of Guadalupe County, was almost instantly killed early last Sunday morning as he sat talking to friends in the Medley Lounge.
>
> Earlier in the evening Gonzales, who was recently appointed night marshal, and Abel Sanchez, night marshal, had taken one Delfido Duran to his home across the tracks, rather than place him under arrest, for allegedly disturbing the peace. Returning about 1:45 a.m. Duran is said to have stealthily entered the lounge, and without warning, plunged a hunting knife into the left side of Gonzales' neck, the knife going through the wind-pipe and severing the jugular vein and almost coming out on the right side of the neck above the collar bone.
>
> Gonzales got up from the chair, where he had been sitting with his back to the entrance, and walked across the room, almost reaching the telephone before he slumped to the floor, dead.

Delfido "Fito" Duran tried to run; tried to escape from the Medley Lounge after he killed Officer Gonzales, but deputy marshal Abel Sanchez and another officer named Antonio Chavez were able to restrain and disarm him. They took the suspect to the jail at the courthouse but before they could get him into a cell, he broke free and ran toward the railroad depot. Both officers fired their guns at Duran, but he kept on running. An employee of the Medley Lounge, Joe Jackson, arrived about then and took up foot pursuit and Sheriff Fred Chavez, in his automobile, managed to head off Duran before he reached the depot. Jackson and

Sheriff Chavez took the suspect back into custody and returned him to the jail. He was later transferred to the jail in Las Vegas for his own protection.

Duran was convicted of murdering Marshal Gonzales and sentenced to 95 to 99 years in the state prison. He served about two years in the penitentiary at Santa Fe, and then eight years at the prison farm at Los Lunas before he developed cancer and was released. He died soon after leaving prison. Gonzales family members believed that Duran was released before his death because he was an army veteran who had been a prisoner of war during World War II.

Joe Gonzales, a sober and well-respected man, was elected Guadalupe County sheriff in 1944. He served two terms and left office on December 31, 1948. On February 1, 1949, he was appointed Santa Rosa night marshal. He was killed 13 days later.

José María Gonzales was born on May 4, 1900 at Cabra Springs, New Mexico, the youngest of six children born to Martin de J. Gonzales and Albinita Vargas De Gonzales. His wife, Josefita, and three daughters, Mrs. Jim Ortega of Kismet, Kansas, Helen and Mary Francis, and one son, George, survived him.

Mary Francis later wrote:

THE VIOLIN

My father's violin has been stored away
Never been touched since that sad day
When tragedy struck, That left a scar
So long ago and I still cry
Time has lessened the hurt I feel
But my heart will never heal
For he was young and full of life
He started playing when he was five
And every day when I awake
I hear that music he used to play
The forty nine years, that he was here
Will live in our hearts from year to year
The road to Heaven was open wide
For he was just too young to die.

Santa Rosa *Communicator*, February 27, 1986
Santa Rosa *News*, February, 18, 1949
Mary Frances (Gonzales) Via, correspondence, June 4 & August 3, 1990

O. C. GRAY

Officer/Biologist
New Mexico Game And Fish Department

The winter of 1959-60 was a hard one. The New Mexico Department of Game and Fish undertook an operation to airdrop hay to antelope starving in deep snow in San Miguel County. Officer Austin Roberts (page 248) piloted a Game and Fish Department airplane when it crashed on January 4, 1960, between Trujillo and Maes, near State Road 104, east of Las Vegas. Roberts and his passenger, O. C. Gray, also a Game and Fish Officer, were killed.

Ocie Gray, nicknamed "Little Big Man," was born in Floydada, Texas, April 12, 1929. He was raised on a ranch near Magdalena, New Mexico. He served a tour with the military in Korea. At the time of his death, he'd been with the Game and Fish Department for seven months. Unmarried, Officer Gray was survived by his parents.

Albuquerque *Journal*, January 5, 1960
Ms. Jerry Montgomery, Public Affairs staff, New Mexico Department of Game and
    Fish, correspondence, December 5, 1989

BENJAMIN LOWELL GREEN

Deputy Sheriff
Grant County, New Mexico

On Saturday morning, February 28, 1981, at about 7 o'clock, Grant County Sheriff's Deputies Ben Green and George Reed responded to a complaint of a prowler with a rifle at Pinos Altos, north of Silver City. As they searched around the residence, Mark T. St. Claire, armed with a .303 British Enfield rifle, hid in some trees nearby. From that vantage point he ambushed and shot Deputy Green. The bullet struck the deputy in the shoulder; dead-center in his departmental shoulder patch, it passed completely through Green's body. Deputy Reed returned fire and called for help. He remained at Green's side until an ambulance arrived and Green was transported to Hillcrest General Hospital. The bullet had caused serious internal damage that resulted in massive bleeding. By 9:00 a. m. Saturday, a call for blood donors went out, and the response was "extensive." That notwithstanding, Deputy Green died on the operating table on Saturday afternoon.

The search for the killer extended into four counties. Roadblocks were established and a helicopter from the U. S. Customs Department was called in. Peace officers from many departments participated. St. Claire, however, was very familiar with the area around Pinos Altos and Silver City and he was able to avoid the searchers. He kidnapped a citizen who drove him to a point near Clifton, Arizona, about 65 miles west of Silver City, at gunpoint. St. Claire was arrested near Clifton as he walked along a rural road.

St. Claire was convicted of first degree murder on September 25, 1981, and sentenced to life in prison. On January 7, 1985, along with four other inmates, he escaped from the medium security correctional facility at Los Lunas. He was captured the following month in Canada.

Deputy Green, 38, a native of Grant County was a resident of Central, New Mexico. His wife Carolyn, two daughters, Kelly Joe and Pamela, and two sons, Kenneth and Scott, all of Albuquerque, and three stepchildren survived him. He had previously been employed by the University of New Mexico and the Venice (Florida) Police Departments.

116

A Past Master of the Hurley Masonic Lodge No. 55, Ben Green was buried at the Masonic Cemetery with military honors on March 3.

Grant County Sheriff James Palacios said Ben Green was "... a good officer. He was highly thought of and respected not only by his peers but the public. He will be greatly missed."

Grant County Sheriff's Department records
Terry Humble, "The Murder of Ben Green," July 13, 2003
New Mexico Department of Corrections records
Santa Fe *New Mexican*, February 12, 1985
Silver City *Enterprise*, March 5 & 12, 1981

VICENTE GUERRO

Posseman
Valencia County, New Mexico

    Vicente Guerro was killed in a gunfight with train robbers in May of 1898. See "Frank X. Vigil" on page 316 for details.

LEOPOLDO C. "LEO" GURULE

Deputy Sheriff
Santa Fe County, New Mexico

Deputy Leo Gurule received a radio call from the Santa Fe County Sheriff's dispatcher at about one minute past 6:00 p.m. on Saturday, June 7, 1980. The deputy was assigned to handle a domestic dispute at the Villitas de Santa Fe mobile home park on Airport Road southwest of Santa Fe. He arrived on the scene a few minutes later. He'd no more than parked when the female resident of trailer number 35, Carol Roybal, ran up to his car, crying hysterically.

"He's got a rifle," she screamed. "He's going to kill you!"

"Get out of here right now!" Deputy Gurule ordered the woman. He began backing his car away from space 35.

The deputy's next radio transmission to the dispatcher was, "I've been shot! I've been shot! Please hurry."

Deputy Sheriff Harold Ulibarri arrived at the scene within minutes of the shooting. He found Leo Gurule lying on the ground beside the left door of his car, badly wounded suffering from a bullet wound to the chest. Deputy Ulibarri also found the body of Joe Roybal, 20, in the doorway of trailer 35, dead from a self-inflicted bullet wound to the head. Near him lay the .308 hunting rifle he'd used to shoot Deputy Gurule before he took his own life.

A State Police investigation concluded that the incident was a murder-suicide, but that didn't bring to an end the controversy surrounding the matter. There existed a standing Sheriff's Department policy that deputies respond to domestic dispute calls in pairs, never alone. As a matter of practice, however, it was not uncommon for officers to handle such calls without backup. One deputy and two Santa Fe police officers reported that they heard Deputy Gurule request assistance before he arrived at the scene, and the request was denied. Other department officials denied that Deputy Gurule made a call before he was shot. The dispute was compounded by the fact that Deputy Gurule had been given a termination letter by Sheriff Eddie Escudero on Friday,

June 6; the day before he died. Gurule's last day on the job would have been June 20.

A grand jury investigation into Deputy Gurule's death was conducted and several days of testimony by those on both sides of the dispute were heard. No charges resulted from the grand jury probe, but indications were clear that Leo Gurule had been terminated from the sheriff's department for political reasons, and not because of any work-related problems. He had been commended in the past for his work in law enforcement and he was well regarded by his fellow officers in the sheriff's department and other law enforcement agencies.

In May of 1982, the Santa Fe county commission voted to rename Valle Lindo Park on County Road 48 as Leo Gurule Park. The commission also retired Gurule's badge number, 9. In December, 1984, the new Santa Fe County Detention Center was dedicated to the memory of Leo Gurule.

Deputy Gurule, a six year veteran of the sheriff's department, had previously served as a Santa Fe city policeman and a Los Angeles County (California) deputy sheriff. He was survived by his wife, Beverly, and three children, Terrance, 13, Robin, 9, and Robert, 5.

In 1984, his widow joined the Santa Fe Police Department. She said, "A fantastic officer was lost to the community [when Leo was killed]. I wanted to do my best to make up for that loss." She subsequently married Paul Lennen, also a Santa Fe Police officer. Bev Lennen rose through the ranks to the position of Chief of Police and served in that capacity from 2003 to 2006.

Santa Fe *New Mexican*, June 8, 9, 10, 11, 13, 15, 19, 20, & 21, 1980; May 4,1982;
      December 31, 1984; May 29, 1990; February 25, 2006
Santa Fe County Sheriff's Department records

THOMAS HALL

Deputy Sheriff
Grant County, New Mexico

Tom Hall lived in the mining town of Pinos Altos, seven miles northeast of Silver City in Grant County, New Mexico. He'd married a local Hispanic woman and together they had five children. Grant County Sheriff James B. Woods hired Hall as a deputy in 1883. The local press regarded Hall as "... an honest, fearless and capable officer."

On Tuesday, March 16, 1886, Deputy Hall took a ride from Silver City to Pinos Altos. He may have been on personal business, but it's more likely he was on the lookout for a group of rustlers and bandits who'd kidnapped a 15 year old girl named Reyes Alvarez in the Santa Rita Mountains, east of Silver City, on the previous Friday. In their flight, the outlaws had killed a citizen named Santiago Aguilar and they'd been seen in the San Jose-Ivanhoe area east of Silver City and also on a trail about three miles northeast of town.

Hall approached the junction of the Pinos Altos and Fort Bayard roads on his return trip. It was nearing dark when he overtook a party of riders, including a young girl. He rode along with them for some distance and asked some probing questions about who they were and where they lived. One of the riders dropped back, pulled his gun, and shot Deputy Hall from behind. The first bullet knocked him from his horse and as he ran for his life, the outlaw shot him again. Severely wounded with a bullet through the body and a shattered right arm, Hall was not found lying along the road until about 10:00 p.m. He was weak from loss of blood and exposure but doctors did the best they could to save his life. They were not successful, however, and Deputy Tom Hall died about 1:00 a.m. on Wednesday, March 17, 1886. All he'd been able to say was that he could not identify the man who shot him.

On Thursday, March 18th, young Miss Alvarez was discovered at the residence of a Mrs. Fessler in Silver City. She'd been there since the evening Tom Hall was shot but kept her presence a secret because she feared the man who'd kidnapped her and killed the deputy. She said she managed to escape when the outlaw, identified only as Pilar, shot Deputy Hall. She hid in some brush alongside the road and made her way into town later in the evening. A coroner's jury could find no contradictions in her story. A posse set out in search of Pilar.

But Pilar was not to be found. Many crimes and depredations in and around Grant County were laid at his feet, but he seemed impervious to capture. The fact was that he'd left Grant County shortly after he killed Tom Hall. He headed north, then west, and found work as a sheepherder near Flagstaff, Arizona. In December of 1887, Grant County authorities learned that Pilar was in jail in Flagstaff. He made no secret of who he was and claimed he shot Deputy Hall in self-defense. Pilar was returned to Silver City to stand trial.

Pilar's trial took place on Wednesday, June 6, 1888. It took three hours from the time the first juror was questioned until the jury returned a verdict. Pilar continued to claim that Hall fired first. He also claimed that he had not kidnapped Miss Alverez, but had "... won her away with love." Her testimony refuted those assertions. And those who found Hall along the road testified that the officer's gun had not been fired. Moreover, Pilar's court-appointed attorney, J. M. Ginn, "... could not say anything in favor of the defendant." Pilar was convicted of first-degree murder and sentenced to hang.

Known as both Pilar Saiz and Pilar Perez, he was executed as Pilar Perez at 9:58 a.m. on July 6, 1888 at Silver City. The local newspaper said: "Thus the law is vindicated and the death of Thomas Hall is avenged by the hanging of one of the most desperate young murderers ever known in the southwest."

Larry D. Ball, Desert Lawmen, *The High Sheriffs of New Mexico and Arizona, 1846-1912*, University of New Mexico Press

West Gilbreath, *Death on the Gallows: The Story of Legal Hangings in New Mexico, 1847-1923*, High-Lonesome Books

Jacqueline Meketa, "The Bandido and the Señorita," *From Martyrs To Murderers, The Old Southwest's Saints, Sinners & Scalawags*, Yucca Tree Press

Silver City *Enterprise* March 19, 1886; January 21, September 30 & December 3, 1887; June 8 & July 6, 1888

Robert J. Torrez, New Mexico State Historian, "Executions in Territorial New Mexico," 1989

THOMAS H. HALL

Deputy Sheriff
Luna County, New Mexico

When the Mexican Revolution began in 1910, many North Americans went south to fight on the side of the rebels under Francisco I. Madero. Among them were brothers John and Reynold Greer and their friend Irvin Frazier*. The three of them participated in the March 1911 battle at Casas Grandes in northern Chihuahua during which rebel forces were defeated by Federal troops. In the course of the fighting, John Greer received serious bullet wounds to his head and body and was left behind on the battlefield as the rebels retreated. Irvin Frazier rode to his aid. Firing his rifle until it was empty, Frazier was able to hold off advancing soldiers long enough to get Greer on to his horse, and the two rode to safety. They soon crossed the border into the United States and Frazier remained with Greer in a mountain cabin until the wounded man recovered from his wounds. Greer promised Frazier that he would repay the favor, with his own life if necessary.

In November of the same year, John Greer was given an opportunity to make good on his pledge.

Irvin Frazier, using the name John Gates, was arrested for burglary and held in the Luna County, New Mexico, jail at Deming. He got word to his friend, John Greer, that he needed help in escaping. On the night of November 7, 1911, a masked man climbed over the wall at the jail and held Sheriff Dwight B. Stephens and two deputies at gunpoint as he stole their guns and freed Frazier. A third man, also masked, waited with three horses outside the wall. They all made it safely away from the jail.

Sheriff Stephens and a posse made of deputies Tom Hall, A. L. Smithers, Johnnie James and W. C. Simpson took up pursuit. The chase took eight days during which the outlaws were able to provision themselves by robbing ranch houses along the way. Finally, late on the afternoon of November 18, the posse caught up with the outlaws at an adobe house on the VXT ranch in the Black Mountains of Socorro County. As the posse surrounded the house, the outlaws mounted their horses and rode out, single file, as if to meet the officers. Suddenly, at a distance of fifty or so yards, they stopped and quickly dismounted, drawing guns as they did so, as if in a military maneuver. Then they opened fire, shooting both deputies Hall and Smithers. Smithers fell dead in his tracks, shot through the body, and Hall was able to empty his Winchester rifle before he, too, fell mortally wounded from a bullet in the head. The killers remounted and attempted to flee.

Sheriff Stephens who had taken a position on the opposite side of the house, hurried into the fight. He shot John Greer as bullets hit all around him, and both Reynold Greer and Irvin Frazier again jumped from their horses and fled into an arroyo on foot, firing as they went. Deputy Simpson arrived on the scene and opened fire on Frazier with some success, and, though wounded, the outlaw made good his escape, as did Reynold Greer. John Greer, 19, died at the scene of the fight.

Sheriff Stephens and what remained of his posse abandoned the chase and took the three bodies to the railroad at Engle, 85 miles to the east.

A few weeks later, a man using the name John Gates, hungry and desperate, attempted to pawn a pistol in El Paso, Texas. Engraved on the butt of the weapon was the name of the man from whom Luna County Sheriff Dwight Stephens had acquired it. Gates was shortly arrested and identified as Irvin Frazier. He was promptly returned to Socorro where he was tried for the murders of Tom Hall and A. L. Smithers, convicted and sentenced to hang.

During his time in the state penitentiary awaiting execution, he was able to smuggle out a letter to Reynold Greer in which he detailed the best way for Reynold to rescue him as he was being transferred from Santa Fe to the gallows in Socorro. His suggestion was that Greer board the train in Albuquerque and set up a trap at La Joya. Officers learned of the letter and took appropriate measures, but no effort was made to deliver Frazier. Reynold Greer was never captured.

Captain Fred Fornoff of the New Mexico Mounted Police, Socorro County Sheriff Emil James, Eddy County Sheriff Miles Cicero Stewart and 15 or so additional deputies, armed with rifles and shotguns, transferred Frazier and another killer, Francisco Grando, from Santa Fe to Socorro in the early morning hours of April 25, 1913. Along the way, Frazier told Sheriff Stewart that he hadn't killed either of the Luna County deputies. He said both officers were down before he ever fired a shot. The condemned men were taken to the courthouse and held there briefly before they were removed to a gallows which amounted to a trapdoor placed in the floor of a second story room in the jail. Frazier asked for a drink of whiskey. Fornoff refused. His final words were, "Get that noose tight, boys. Have as little pain to this as possible."

At exactly 5:42 a.m., the trapdoor dropped open and Frazier came to the end of his rope. A doctor declared him dead 12 minutes later. He was 26 years old.

The *Deming Headlight* eulogized deputies Hall and Smithers in this way:

> Thos. H. Hall and E. L. Smithers [*sic*], as truly heroes as ever
> went forth in the defense of law and justice have died a martyr's

death. A home in Deming is desolate. A wife and mother's heart is bleeding at every pore. Five orphan children, four manly sons and a noble daughter are bowed in grief and go forth into the world to battle without the counsel, and strong protecting arm of a father.

Sheriff Dwight Stephens was himself killed by jail escapees in February of 1916 (page 298).

* One source shows Frazier's first name as "Ivory". Most news accounts of the day show it as Irvin

Albuquerque *Morning Journal*, November 20, 1911, April 25, 26, 1913
Associated Press, April 25, 1913
Deming *Headlight*, November 24, 1911
West Gilbreath, *Death on the Gallows*, High-Lonesome Books

JOSEPH ANTHONY "JOE" HARRIS

Deputy/Sergeant
Sandoval County, New Mexico, Sheriff's Department

Sgt. Joe Harris was a part of a concerted effort to put an end to a series of burglaries and assaults that had occurred in the Jemez and Naciamento Mountains of northern Sandoval County, New Mexico. Someone had been victimizing local residents and vacation home owners for as long as ten years, and his actions became more aggressive by the spring and summer of 2009. The criminal had been dubbed "The Cookie Bandit"* for his habit of stealing food as well as liquor, clothing, and other items useful in living in the mountains. The name does not imply anything humorous about his crimes. He had confronted and threatened residents, and he had started severely vandalizing cabins as well as robbing them.

One of the tactics used by the Sheriff's Department was placing deputies in various cabins overnight in hopes of catching the burglar in the act. Sgt. Harris and his partner, Deputy Theresa Moriarty, were in a cabin in the Jemez Mountains when the bandit broke in during the early morning hours of July 16, 2009. When the officers confronted him, he violently resisted and a fight followed in which the two officers, after a considerable struggle, managed to get handcuffs on him. Unfortunately, they failed to notice, in the heat of the struggle, that he had a .357 magnum pistol concealed at the back of his waistband. He managed to get it out and fire, the bullet striking Harris in the groin and hand. Harris returned fire and the thief died at the scene with two bullets in the head.

Sgt. Joe Harris died a few hours later at University of New Mexico Hospital in Albuquerque to which he had been airlifted.

Subsequent investigation revealed that the Cookie Bandit was a life-long criminal named Joseph Henry Burgess, 62. A native of New Jersey, Burgess had fled to Canada to avoid the draft during the Viet Nam War, and while there, in British Columbia, in 1972, he is believed to have murdered Ann Durrant and Leif Carlsson. Since Burgess was something of a religious fanatic, investigators suspected that he killed the couple because he believed that they were behaving in a sinful way: cohabitating. Canadian authorities identified Burgess as a suspect

126

in the murders, but were never able to capture him. He is believed to have spent some time in California before he settled for a life in the mountains of northern New Mexico. One police officer suggested that he lived like an animal in the mountains. Investigating officers believe Burgess also killed David Lloyd Eley, a resident of the Jemez area who was reported to be missing in 2007.** Burgess may have used Eley's gun to kill Sgt. Harris.

Joe Harris was born in South Ozone Park, Brooklyn, New York, and grew up on Long Island. He and his family moved to New Mexico in the late 1970s, and he graduated from Cibola High School. He joined the Rio Rancho Police Department in 1984 and soon became involved in community relations programs: DARE, GREAT, Neighborhood Watch, McGruff the Crime Dog, Citizen's Police Academy, and others, while he also performed regular patrol duties. He served 20 years with Rio Rancho DPS before he retired and later joined the Sandoval County Sheriff's Department.

An estimated 2,000 citizens and police officers attended a memorial service for Joe Harris held at the Santa Ana Star Center in Rio Rancho. He was interred at the Vista Verde Memorial Park in Rio Rancho.

* One news source referred to the thief as the "Milk and Cookie Bandit."
** The report was made in 2006, according to one news source.

Albuquerque *Journal*, July 17, 18, 20, 21, 22, 23, 24, 2009
Jemez *Thunder*, August 1, 2009
Memorial Service Obituary, July 21, 2009
Rio Rancho *Observer*, July 19, 23, 26, 2009
David Smoker, Jemez resident, conversations, summer 2009

JAMES F. HAYNES

Deputy Sheriff
Otero County, New Mexico

It was Saturday afternoon, February 3, 1934, and the streets of Tularosa, New Mexico were busy with shoppers and other visitors to town. Deputy Sheriff James Haynes received a report that a young mounted cowboy named Jim King had attempted to ride-down two women on Main Street. The officer found the young man and tried to arrest him, but rather than submit, he rode the officer down with his horse. Deputy Haynes was knocked to the ground and trampled. He suffered "concussion of the brain" and died about an hour later.

Tularosa night marshal Robert Scroggin, with the help of volunteers, arrested King after a considerable struggle. Feelings ran high against the cowboy and Sheriff W. A. Denley had him placed in a separate cell in the Otero County jail at Alamogordo.

King, for his part, admitted being drunk, but maintained that that he did not attempt to ride anyone down. He also said, "Old man Haynes had no right to stop me."

The cowboy was charged with first-degree murder. In June, 1934 a district court jury acquitted him. Defense witnesses swore that King tried to steer his horse to the side of the officer.

Deputy James Haynes, 63, had many years experience as a peace officer, previously serving as Tularosa town marshal. A widower, he was survived by several adult children, among them James Haynes, Jr., foreman of the Hereford Ranch at Three Rivers, New Mexico, and Mrs. John Carroll of Alamogordo.

Alamogordo *Daily News*, June 28, 1934
Albuquerque *Journal*, February 5, 6, 7, 8, 1934

TRAVIS HAYNES

Special Deputy Sheriff
Quay County, New Mexico

On Tuesday, May 2, 1972, at a few minutes before eight o'clock in the morning, Special Deputy Travis Haynes received a telephone call at his store in Ragland, about 25 miles south of Tucumcari. The call came from the Bill Upton ranch and requested that Haynes drive over to assist two motorists who'd had car trouble. The deputy obliged just as he'd responded to many other calls over the years. He picked up one of the men at the ranch house and drove him to where his car was parked, about a half mile away. A witness said later that there seemed to be a flurry of activity and then all three men drove away in Haynes' car.

At a little after 10:00 o'clock that morning, Mrs. Haynes called the Tucumcari Police and reported that she hadn't heard from her husband for about two hours. A search was mounted immediately by the sheriff's department, the Tucumcari Police Department, the State Police and the District Attorney's office.

Between 1:30 and 2:00 p.m., District Attorney Norman Runyan, investigator Paul Quintana and Tucumcari Police Chief Bronson Moore found Deputy Haynes near a telephone line station about eight miles south of the Upton ranch and four miles north of the community of Taiban. He'd been shot once in the head, but remained alive, and conscious. Haynes was transported first to a Clovis hospital and then on to Lubbock Methodist Hospital.

At just before 3:00 o'clock that afternoon, State Police Officer William Mascarenas saw a car traveling south on U. S. Route 54 at a high rate of speed. It matched the description of Travis Haynes car. Mascarenas took up pursuit at speeds reaching 125 miles per hour. At a point about ten miles north of Carrizozo, the car suddenly stopped and the two men inside, Larry Coatney, 20, and Kermit A. Frame, 35, surrendered without incident. Two loaded guns were found in the car.

Coatney and Frame had escaped from the Kansas State Prison at Lansing on April 27. Coatney was serving a two to ten year sentence for burglary and larceny and Frame was doing twenty to forty years for robbery. The car they were driving when Haynes approached them near the Upton ranch had been stolen in Stratford, Texas. Both were convicted of armed robbery after shooting Deputy Haynes and stealing his car and sentenced to ten to fifty years in prison. In May of 1990, Coatney failed to return to Camp Sierra Blanca after an unescorted furlough. He was captured two days later in Coffeeville, Kansas. Frame was released from New Mexico custody in October 1980.

Travis Haynes never recovered from his wound. He remained an invalid for what remained of his life. He died in February, 1984, at Abilene, Texas. He had served as a special deputy in Quay County for about twenty-five years under several sheriffs. His wife, Lue, and two children, Raymond and Nancy survived him.

Tucumcari *Daily News*, May 3 & 4, 1972
Quay County *Sun*, February 18, 1984 & May 18, 1988
Marilyn Parker, Quay County *Sun*, correspondence, November 21, 1989
New Mexico Department of Corrections records

J. H. "JAY" HEARD

Inspector
United States Customs Service

The pickup truck Customs Inspector Jay Heard was driving when he was shot to death by Claude Gatlin on June 3, 1932 near the Mexican border.

In the early 1930s, Claude Gatlin* was named foreman of the Little Hatchet ranch in the bootheel region of southwestern New Mexico. Among other livestock Gatlin found at the ranch was a flock of turkeys which belonged to his predecessor, Tom Berkely, and J. H. "Jay" Heard who was the inspector in charge of the Hachita station of the U. S. Customs Service.** The birds were a nuisance to Gatlin because they roosted in the ranch tack shed and left their droppings all over saddles, bridles, and other horse riding equipment. Gatlin sent word to Inspector Heard to come and get the turkeys. Heard seems to have ignored the request.

After a period of time and further annoyance, Gatlin crated up the birds and hauled them into the community of Hachita where Jay Heard lived. He proceeded to dump them over a fence into Heard's front yard. The inspector heard the racket and confronted Gatlin, and a fight soon followed. Legend holds that Heard administered to Gatlin a sound thrashing.

"Next time I see you," Gatlin said as he left Heard's house, "I'll kill you."

Gatlin's tenure as ranch foreman at the Little Hatchet was short-lived and he was soon fired for drunkenness. He went to stay on a ranch owned by Tom Boles in the Animas Mountains on the Mexican border. Whiskey may have been the common thread in the relationship between Gatlin and Boles as Boles held his own reputation for drinking and drunkenness.***

At about the same time Inspector Heard developed reason to suspect that cattle and horses were being smuggled into the United States from Mexico across the Boles ranch. On Tuesday, June 3, 1932, Heard and another inspector, A. J. "Andy" McKinney, set out to investigate and interview Boles. Gatlin saw them as they drove up to the ranch headquarters in a Ford pickup. He quickly secured an automatic rifle and hid around the corner of the house. As the officers unknowingly approached the house, Gatlin stepped into the open, rifle in hand.

"What are you doing here, Heard?" Gatlin demanded.

Before the officer could respond, Gatlin opened fire. He fired four times, and all four bullets penetrated the windshield of the truck and hit Heard, two in the chest, one in the jaw and one shot away the thumb on the inspector's right hand. Even so, Heard was able to draw his own gun and get off two shots, but both went into the dirt. Inspector McKinney pulled his gun and started in pursuit of Gatlin, but the killer dashed into the house where he used Tom Boles' wife and another woman as shields. Gatlin dared the officers to shoot at him, or to try to enter the house. McKinney and Boles agreed that it would be suicide to try, and in any event, one of the women might well be injured or killed if more shots were fired. They determined that the best immediate course of action was to seek medical help for Inspector Heard. They took him by automobile to Hachita where they put him aboard a passenger train bound for El Paso. One source indicates that Heard died on the train; another that he died in the hospital.

Inspector McKinney notified peace officers from Hachita to Cloverdale in southern Hidalgo County to be on the lookout for Gatlin, and he organized a posse and returned to the Boles ranch to take up a search for the killer. As word of the shooting spread up and down the Animas Valley, other posses were mounted and took up pursuit. They scoured the rugged and desolate country along the Mexican border for miles in either direction for several days. Gatlin made good his escape and was never captured and prosecuted for the crime.

Gatlin did not completely disappear from history, however. He remained in Mexico, living a "squalid" life, according to one source, and returning to the United States periodically on thieving raids. He also seems to have kept up with his drinking ways. He died from exposure one night, drunk, in a snow bank, in northern Mexico.

Jay Heard was 51 years old when he died. He'd been a Customs Inspector for about ten years, five of which he'd spent in Hachita. A wife and son, two brothers and a sister survived him.

* One source identifies this subject as Claude Gatliff. Probably a typographical error.

** J. H. Heard was a mounted Customs rider. These officers were sometimes called outriders. One source incorrectly refers to him as a Border Patrol Officer.

*** In February 1937, Tom Boles, while drunk, shot up the town of Hachita. Deputy Sheriff John Hall shot him in the arm when he 'menaced' the officer. The bullet broke the cattleman's arm and he was later charged with resisting an officer, flourishing a deadly weapon and discharging firearms within a settlement.

Albuquerque *Journal,* May 3, 1932

Deming *Graphic,* May 5, 1932

El Paso *Times,* May 3, 1932

George Hilliard, *Adios Hachita, Stories of a New Mexico Town,* High-Lonesome Books

Roger Payne, Deputy Chief, New Mexico State Police (Ret.)

Silver City *Daily Press,* February 22, 1937

ROBERT HEDMAN

Deputy Sheriff
Otero County, New Mexico

The call came into the Otero County Sheriff's Department as a domestic disturbance near Cloudcroft. One source reported that a gunshot had been heard. The time was Saturday evening, December 18, 2004. Deputies Robert Hedman and Billy Anders responded to the residence where they confronted Earl Flippen, 38, who refused them entry into the house. The officers found it suspicious that a hatchback automobile was backed up to the front door of the house. Blood stains on the porch floor were also suspicious. Deputy Hedman went to the rear of the building while Deputy Anders went to his car to put in a call for assistance from backup officers. Anders heard a gunshot and soon confronted Flippen, who was armed with a .357 caliber magnum revolver. Anders shot Flippen, who died at the scene.* Deputy Hedman, 53, was found at the back of the house, dead from a single shot to the head.

Subsequent investigation revealed that Flippen's pregnant girlfriend, Deborah Rhoudes, 30, was dead of a gunshot wound. Her body was concealed in a closet. Her three year old daughter was found injured but alive. It was also discovered that Flippen had been burglarizing residences in the area, and in fact used stolen items to furnish the house that became the scene of the crime.

Deputy Hedman was a native of upstate New York. He'd worked for several law enforcement agencies in southern New Mexico, including the Alamogordo Department of Public Safety, Tularosa Police, and the Lincoln County Sheriff's Department, before he joined the Otero County Sheriff's Department. He was survived by his wife Cheryl, two adult children and two stepchildren. Cheryl managed the Alamo Rosa Restaurant and Truck Stop between Alamogordo and Tularosa. Deputy Hedman often helped out on his days off. He was also in the process of building a home in Cloudcroft.

"He was a good guy," Sheriff John Blansett noted, "very dedicated. He'd take the shirt off his back for you; anything you needed."

* On August 2, 2005, Deputy Billy Anders entered a plea of guilty to the

charge of voluntary manslaughter for killing Earl Flippen. Evidence indicated that Anders shot Flippen after the killer had been wounded and restrained in handcuffs. Anders served a short prison sentence.

Albuquerque *Journal*, December 19, 20, 21, 2004
Albuquerque *Tribune*, December 20, 2004
Santa Fe *New Mexican*, August 2, 2005

E. D. HENRY

Deputy Town Marshal
Albuquerque, New Mexico

Deputy Henry was killed in a gunfight with outlaws in November, 1886. See "Robert McGuire," page 206 for details.

BEN HERRERA

Officer

Farmington, New Mexico Police Department

On March 31, 1962, at just after 8:00 p.m., Officers Ben Herrera and Eddie Herrington were dispatched to a convenience store to meet with Mrs. Wallace McCroskey. She told the officers that her husband, drunk and armed with a .308 rifle, had threatened to kill his family. She provided the officers with a description of the car Wallace McCroskey was driving, an older model green Plymouth station wagon. She said that if he wasn't at home, he'd be at the residence of a friend in a mobile home park called Peace Acres.

The officers, along with animal control officer Harmon Gravlee, 55, who lived in the area, drove to the McCroskey residence. They found no one there. By 8:20 they located the Plymouth parked near two mobile homes in Peace Acres. Herrera and Herrington approached one of the trailer homes while Gravlee remained in his city car. McCroskey stepped out of the other trailer, his rifle in hand.

"Put 'em up and drop them guns or I'll blow your heads off!" he commanded.

Herrington noted that McCroskey didn't have his rifle pointed at either officer. He darted behind one of the trailers and ran around it hoping to get into position to shoot at McCroskey. When he found a position where he could survey the scene, McCroskey was behind Officer Herrera and Herrington had no clear line of fire. He heard McCroskey say, "Tell your buddy to come back here or I will blow your head off."

Herrington stepped from cover and stood beside Herrera. A neighbor made a noise that distracted McCroskey and both officers took the opportunity to attack the gunman. Herrington grabbed the rifle and McCroskey grabbed Herrera's gun from its holster and shot Herrera in the chest. Herrington thought the shot had been fired from the rifle and continued trying to wrest it free from McCroskey. McCroskey then shot Herrington in the hip and the two men fell to the ground, struggling. McCroskey shot Herrington again, in the leg.

Animal control officer Gravlee used his police radio to call for help when the struggle began. Then he ran to the scene and joined the fray. He dragged a struggling McCroskey off the wounded Officer Herrington. Gravlee found some clothesline rope and used it to bind McCroskey's hands until other help arrived. Officers discovered then that McCroskey's rifle was not loaded.

Officer Herrera was pronounced dead on arrival at the San Juan Hospital. Officer Herrington, 27, shot a total of three times, survived his wounds.

Wallace McCroskey, 49, initially committed to the State Hospital at Las Vegas, pleaded guilty to second degree murder and attempted murder on April 12, 1967. He was sentenced to three years to life in prison on the former charge and one to 10 years on the latter, the sentences to run concurrently.

Ben Herrera, 38, a teacher by education, began his law enforcement career working for the Farmington Police Department during the summer of 1961. He returned to the Blanco School as principal in the fall of the year but resigned to become a full time night police officer in January of 1962. Even then, he continued to teach at Sacred Heart Elementary School. Officer Herrera was a veteran of World War II. After his death, the Farmington Knights of Columbus established the annual Ben Herrera award for outstanding citizenship.

The officer was survived by his wife, Connie, and six children: Deborah, Valarie, Beata, Stan, Mark and Matthew. The oldest of the children was in her father's fourth grade class at Sacred Heart School.

Farmington *Daily Times*, April 1, 2, & 3, 1962; January 22, 1967
Farmington Police Department, Offense Report, March 31, 1962
Harmon B. Gravlee, Statement, March 31, 1962

RALPH R. HIGGINBOTHAM

Deputy Sheriff
Doña Ana County, New Mexico

On Memorial Day, 1952 (May 30) Doña Ana County Deputy Ralph Higginbotham and Hatch town marshal Guy Dunivan* were standing on the street in Hatch when they noted a speeding car approaching. They waved the car to the curb. As the officers approached, the car's driver opened fire with a .45 caliber semi-automatic pistol. Higginbotham was hit in the neck and arm and knocked down; he died a few hours later. Marshal Dunivan was hit in the shoulder, but survived. In spite of their wounds, both officers returned fire, each emptying his revolver. The killer made good his escape, and suffered only minor wounds from flying glass.

Five young men, one of them Marshal Dunivan's brother, Jack, formed an impromptu posse. They commandeered Dunivan's police car and pursued a 1947 Plymouth convertible occupied by the shooter. The posse was able to follow the fugitive because recent rainfall had left the dirt roads wet and the tire tracks were clear. They located the car near Caballo Dam several hours after the shooting. The suspect fled on foot as they approached. They shouted for him to stop but he continued his flight until posseman Billy Jack Clear fired a shot toward the man's feet. He surrendered then without further ado. Other members of the posse were Bob Miller, Pewee Bernolo and Ken Clear. Officers later counted six .38 caliber bullet holes in the Plymouth.

Arrested and charged with murder was James Oliver Morgan, 55, of El Paso. He was later convicted of killing Higginbotham and sentenced to life in prison.

Deputy Higginbotham, 32, was survived by his wife and three small children. One of his daughters, Paula, had a successful career with the Santa Fe Police Department.

* Guy Dunivan joined the New Mexico State Police in 1955. He retired as a captain in 1985 and died in May 1995.

Albuquerque *Journal*, May 31, June 1 & 2, 1952

Doña Ana County Sheriff's Department
El Paso *Times*, May 16, 1984
The Roadrunner (New Mexico State Police Association), Winter 1995
Santa Fe *New Mexican*, May 29, 1990
Lt. Paula Ulibarri (daughter)

GEORGE HINDMAN

Deputy Sheriff
Lincoln County, New Mexico

Lincoln County Deputy Sheriff George Hindman was shot to death from ambush on the street in the town of Lincoln, New Mexico, on Monday, April 1, 1878. See Sheriff William Brady, page 27, for details.

George Hindman arrived in Lincoln County in 1875. He came from Texas as part owner of a cattle herd. He sold out his share before the herd moved on to Arizona and for a time he farmed along the Rio Feliz and worked for a family named Casey. He was described as "a good, quiet, inoffensive person."

William A. Keleher, *Violence in Lincoln County, 1869-1881*, University of New Mexico Press

Lily Klasner, *My Girlhood Among Outlaws*, University of Arizona Press

Donald R. Lavish, *Sheriff William Brady, Tragic Hero of the Lincoln County War*, Sunstone Press

Robert M. Utley, *High Noon in Lincoln, Violence on the Western Frontier*, University of New Mexico Press

John P. Wilson, Merchants, *Guns & Money, The Story of Lincoln County and Its Wars*, Museum of New Mexico Press

MELVIN LEE HODGES

Motorcycle Officer
Carlsbad, New Mexico Police Department

Officer Hodges was severely injured at about 8:30 a.m. on May 7, 1962, when the police motorcycle he was riding collided with an automobile at the intersection of Muscatel Avenue and the Carlsbad-Hobbs Highway. A witness reported seeing both the officer and his motorcycle flung into the air by the collision. Officer Hodges was dead on arrival at St. Francis Hospital. He had been employed by the Carlsbad Police Department for three months at the time of his death.

A native of Arkansas, Hodges had previously served as a police officer in Arroyo Grande, California. His wife, Patricia Carol, and a fourteen-month-old son survived him.

Police Chief Luther Daniels said he believed Hodges to be the first Carlsbad officer killed in the line of duty. He said the officer was hard working and well liked by the department.

Carlsbad *Current Argus*, June 7, 1962

LOWELL D. HOWARD

Officer/Pilot
New Mexico State Police

Monday morning, August 6, 1984. State Police Officer and pilot Lowell Howard, along with Patrolman David Smith (page 290) who served as spotter, conducted an airborne check for speeding motorists on U. S. Highway 550 just east of Farmington. After about an hour, Howard concluded the effort and turned the Cessna R172E west toward the Farmington airport. No one knows for sure why Howard turned the plane back to the east at low level—some believe to further observe traffic or to take some other enforcement action—but it hit a power line and nose-dived onto Route 550 just inside the Farmington city limits. The plane flipped onto its back and burst into flames. Both officers died in the crash and both bodies were badly burned.

Stationed in Santa Fe, Officer Howard was in Farmington to conduct traffic checks. In his last radio contact with the Farmington State Police dispatcher he reported that air conditions were bumpy and he recommended against an afternoon traffic surveillance operation. The plane itself was well maintained and equipped with modern avionics equipment. Howard was rated as a fixed-wing instructor pilot with single and multiple engine aircraft, and as a helicopter pilot. He had been a licensed pilot since 1977.

Lowell Howard was born in Clovis, New Mexico, and graduated from high school in Ft. Sumner in 1965. He attended Lubbock Christian College. He'd previously worked in law enforcement with the DeBaca County Sheriff's Department and the Ft. Sumner police. He joined the State Police in 1978 and served in the Uniform Division in Santa Fe for about a year before being reassigned to the Aircraft Division. The officer was survived by his wife, Patsy, and two sons, Scott and Randy. He was buried at Ft. Sumner. One report indicated that the funeral procession was four miles long.

Officer Lowell Howard was the first State Police pilot to be killed in an on-duty airplane crash; pilots Wayne Allison (page 4) and Andy Tingwall (page 307), have been killed on duty in the years since.

Albuquerque *Journal*, August 7, 1984

Farmington *Daily Times*, August 6, 7, 8 & 10, 1984

The Roadrunner (New Mexico State Police Association, Vol. 3, No. 2, Summer, 1992)

GLEN HUBER

Patrolman
New Mexico State Police

Between 4:00 and 4:30 on the afternoon of Saturday, January 26, 1991, State Police Officer Glen Huber and other officers were dispatched to a residence between Española and Chimayo just off State Road 76 in Rio Arriba County. Shots had already been fired but Huber had no way of knowing just how bad the situation was; no way of knowing that Deputy Sheriff Jerry Martinez was already dead, shot twice in the head.

Huber stopped well away from the scene to give himself an opportunity to size-up the area and the situation before taking any action. At a range of about 200 yards, Ricky Abeyta shot Glen Huber in the side of the head with a 7 millimeter rifle. The officer died instantly as he sat in his State Police car, his radio microphone in his hand.

Also shot to death by Ricky Abeyta that afternoon were:

Ignacita Sandoval, 36, Abeyta's live-in girlfriend
Maryellen Sandoval, 19, Ignacita's daughter
Marcario Gonzales, 18, Maryellen's boy friend
Justin Gonzales, five months, son of Maryellen and Marcario
Cheryl Rendon, 24, Ignacita's sister.

Shot in the buttocks and back, Eloy Sandoval, 13, Ignacita's son, survived his injuries. Another of Ignacita's sisters, Celina Gonzales, and her niece, Nikki Rendon, 3, (the daughter of Cheryl Rendon), escaped injury by fleeing out a window.

Members of Ignacita's family had gathered that Saturday afternoon to help Ignacita move out of Abeyta's mobile home. Earlier in the day, Deputy Martinez had gone to the residence to serve a restraining order on Abeyta who had fired three shots at Ignacita and Celina on the previous Wednesday. The deputy didn't find Abeyta and departed before 4:00 p.m.

Abeyta arrived on the scene soon after Deputy Martinez left. According to witnesses, he said, "*¡Con esto pagan!*" (With this I pay you back!) Then he began shooting at Ignacita and her family.

Deputy Martinez returned as the initial shooting ended. Abeyta confronted the deputy at gunpoint, and, according to witnesses, shot the deputy twice in the head at close range. He killed Officer Huber when he arrived a few minutes later.

Other officers began arriving then, and Abeyta managed to escape. Roadblocks were established and scores of officers took up the search for the fugitive. A helicopter equipped with night vision equipment was brought in. The fugitive evaded capture throughout the night and the next day. Then, at about 9:30 on Sunday evening, State Police officers received word that Ricky Abeyta, along with some of his family members, were at the State Police office in Albuquerque. The killer wished to surrender. Captain James O. Jennings, Sgt. Gary Smith and Officer Danny Lichtenberger took Abeyta into custody without incident. Abeyta expressed concern that if he continued to run and hide, he would not be taken alive by police officers when they found him. Abeyta asked that he not be hurt and that he not be handcuffed. Jennings assured him that he would not be hurt, but also assured him that he *would* be cuffed.

Tried for his crimes in November, 1991, Ricky Abeyta was convicted on four counts of first degree murder (for killing Glen Huber, Ignacita Sandoval, Maryellen Sandoval, and Cheryl Renden); two counts of second degree murder (for killing Jerry Martinez and Marcario Gonzales); and one count of involuntary manslaughter (for killing Justin Gonzales). He was acquitted of attempted murder for shooting Eloy Sandoval. Combined, and served consecutively, Abeyta's sentences totaled 146 years.

Glen Huber was born in Boulder, Colorado, and raised in Roswell and Santa Fe, New Mexico. He graduated from Santa Fe High School in 1973. He also graduated from the New Mexico Military Institute in 1975 and then from New Mexico State University in 1977. He served four years in the U. S. Army, honorably discharged with the rank of first lieutenant. He joined the State Police in 1981 and resigned in 1986 to become town marshal in Pecos, New Mexico. He returned to the State Police in 1988 and was a senior patrolman at the time of his death.

Officer Huber was survived by a daughter from his first marriage as well as a daughter from his second marriage. He also had two stepdaughters. He was buried at the National Cemetery in Santa Fe with full military and police honors. His funeral procession was ten miles long.

Albuquerque *Journal*, January 27 & 28; August 1, 1991; January 26, 1006

New Mexico Department of Corrections, records
James O. Jennings, Deputy Chief, New Mexico State Police, interview, August, 1995
The Roadrunner (New Mexico State Police Association, Vol. 3, No. 2, Summer, 1992)

JOHN HURLEY

Deputy Sheriff
Lincoln County, New Mexico

John Hurley, 37, was killed in a gunfight with outlaw Nicholas Aragon in January of 1885. For details see "Jasper Corn," page 76.

Deputy Hurley was at various times a Lincoln County cowboy, small farmer, and saloonkeeper at Fort Stanton. He served as deputy under several Lincoln County sheriffs.

George Curry, 1861-1947, An Autobiography, University of New Mexico Press
Fred Harrison, *Hell Holes and Hangings*, Clarendon Press
Lily Klasner, *My Girlhood Among Outlaws*, University of Arizona Press, 1972
Carole Larson, *Forgotten Frontier*, University of New Mexico Press
John P. Wilson, *Merchants, Guns & Money, The Story of Lincoln county and Its Wars*, Museum of New Mexico Press
Golden Era, Lincoln, February 5, 1885, October 1, 1885
Santa Fe *New Mexican*, July 16 & 17, 1885

ANTONIO "TONY" JARAMILLO

Patrolman
New Mexico State Police

January 31, 1965. The two car accident at the corner of Third Street and Corona Avenue in Santa Rosa was minor. State Police Officer Tony Jaramillo was busy measuring skid marks when a car struck him and carried him about 70 feet. The officer sustained a compound fracture of the right leg, a broken left ankle, a brain concussion and an injury caused by the car's hood ornament. He was transported to Presbyterian Hospital in Albuquerque where he died on February 2.

The 19-year-old driver of the car that struck Officer Jaramillo was arrested and charged with manslaughter. He pleaded no contest and was sentenced to prison for from one to five years.

Antonio Jaramillo, 25, was born in Encino and graduated from high school there. He served four years in the Air Force before he joined the State Police in 1964. His wife Josephine, two sons, J. Anthony and Vicente Joseph, and two daughters, Rosaina and Debra Ann survived him. He was a member of the Knights of Columbus. Officer Jaramillo is buried at Encino.

Albuquerque *Journal*, February 2, 1965
The Roadrunner (New Mexico State Police Association, Vol. 3, No. 2, Summer, 1992)

W. L. JERRELL

Deputy Sheriff
Doña Ana County, New Mexico

An unusual set of circumstances led to the demise of Doña Ana County Deputy W. L. Jerrell in February 1884.

On New Year's eve, 1883, two men dressed in the style of miners dismounted their horses and walked into Barncastle's Store in the town of Doña Ana, north of Las Cruces. They produced pistols and robbed the store of several hundred dollars. (They overlooked a safe that contained somewhere between $1,000 and $5,000.) The robbers tied up store owner John Barncastle and warned him, upon pain of death, not to stir until they were out of sight.

A posse quickly organized and took up pursuit of the bandits. Barncastle, a prominent merchant, offered an initial reward of $100 for the capture of the thieves. Neither pursuit nor reward resulted in an arrest. By January 26, a local newspaper reported the reward offered at $1,000 and one of the outlaws had been identified as George Hester. A man by the name of Walters had gone after the robbers. (It was agreed that expenses incurred in capturing the outlaws would come out of the reward.) Walters wired back to Las Cruces that he'd traced Hester to Seven Rivers in southeast New Mexico, but that he needed more money to continue the pursuit. H. C. Harding was sent with additional funds and assigned to assist Walters. Word got back to Barncastle that Harding went to El Paso where he pawned a pistol and overcoat the storekeeper had loaned him and gambled away the expense money.

In the meantime, word reached Las Cruces that George Hester had left Seven Rivers headed south to Fort Concho, near San Angelo, Texas. W. L. Jerrell, a billiard hall owner, volunteered to go after the outlaw and Doña Ana County Sheriff Guadalupe Ascarate appointed him deputy. By early February, Jerrell had reached San Angelo and apparently met with no success in locating Hester. On the morning of February 5, Jerrell boarded a stagecoach bound for Abilene, Texas. Also aboard the coach was Sgt. L. S. Turnbo of the Frontier Battalion of the Texas Rangers.

A few miles outside San Angelo, the coach met another stagecoach coming from Abilene. Its driver reported that he'd been robbed just a few miles back. The driver of Jerrell's coach elected to continue his run. Jerrell and Turnbo—the only two passengers who were armed—drew their guns and held them at the ready in the event of hold-up. Soon a gunshot was heard and the stage was ordered to stop. Jerrell immediately fired at one of the robbers who shot back. Turnbo also opened fire and a bandit clasped his hands to his stomach and fell to the ground. The horses bolted and the stage raced away from the scene of the robbery as the outlaws fired at the vehicle. Several bullets pierced the coach and two of them hit Jerrell, one in the back and one in the shoulder, breaking his collarbone. The coach returned to San Angelo where Deputy Jerrell died later the same day.

The officer was initially buried in San Angelo, but later exhumed and returned to Las Cruces. The city of San Angelo paid all transportation and burial costs for Deputy Jerrell.

History does not record that George Hester was ever captured and prosecuted for the Barncastle robbery; nor does it record that the stage robbers who killed W. L. Jerrell were ever captured and punished.

No account of Deputy Jerrell's death reports his age, although he was described as a young man. He was married and the father of three. His brother-in-law, James H. White, was elected sheriff of El Paso County, Texas in November 1884 and served until 1890.

Local newspapers described W. L. Jerrell thus: "[He was] a man of nerve and brave as a lion."

Mesilla News, January 5 to 16, 1884

Larry D. Ball, *Desert Lawmen, The High Sheriffs of New Mexico and Arizona, 1846-1912*, University of New Mexico Press

Lt. West Gilbreath, "Just a Little Bit of History," Doña County Sheriff's Department *Employee Newsletter*.

Frances T. Ingmire *Texas Rangers, Frontier Battalion, Minute Men, Commanding Officers, 1847-1900*, Ingmire Publications

Sammy Tice, *Texas County Sheriffs*, privately published

LOUIS FRANKLIN JEWETT JR.

Correctional Officer
New Mexico Department Of Corrections

Things seemed normal enough in the New Mexico State Penitentiary at Santa Fe on the evening of February 26, 1981. In Cellblock 3—the area reserved for the most dangerous prisoners—inmate Jesse Trujillo, 21, serving life for murder, was taking a shower in a lower tier. At about 8:00 p.m., another inmate, Richard "Ricky" Garcia, 25, serving 30 to 115 years for armed robbery, asked Correctional Officer Louis Jewett, if he could return some books and pick up a radio. Jewett let him in. A third inmate, Bobby C. Garcia, 35, also known as "Barbershop," serving 10 to 50 years for robbery and battery, was picking up trash in the area. Without warning Jesse Trujillo and Ricky Garcia attacked Bobby Garcia with prison-made shanks (knives).

Jewett and other officers attempted to intervene but the inmates threatened them with their weapons while they continued to stab Bobby Garcia. Jewett saw an opening and grabbed Jesse Trujillo and pinned his arms to his sides at which time Ricky Garcia stabbed the officer in the back. Jewett fell to the floor. Trujillo and Ricky Garcia then backed away from the other officers at the scene. Bobby Garcia, stabbed countless times in the upper body died of a stab wound to the heart at a Santa Fe hospital about two hours later.

Louis Jewett died about five weeks later, on April 4, from complications resulting from the stab wound.

Ricky Garcia emphatically denied that he intended to harm Officer Jewett. He freely admitted that he was out to get Bobby Garcia but, he claimed, Jewett just got in the way. Other correctional officers, however, clearly remembered Ricky Garcia deliberately stabbing Officer Jewett. Trujillo and Ricky Garcia were subsequently tried and convicted of two counts each of first-degree murder. They remain imprisoned.

Louis Jewett, 38, was certified as a corrections officer after completing the Corrections Department Academy on October 10, 1980, less than five months before he was critically injured. For the previous 15 years he'd worked as an optician in Junction City, Kansas, and Albuquerque, New Mexico. He also served in the U. S. Army as a paratrooper. As a Corrections Officer I, his salary was $885.00 per month.

His wife, Sylvia, a son, John Louis, III, and a daughter, Cindy Eileen, all of Santa Fe, survived him.

Albuquerque *Journal*, February 27 & 28; April 5, 1981
New Mexico Department of Corrections Records
New Mexico State Police Reports
Adolph Saenz, *Politics of a Prison Riot*, Rhombus Publishing

BUD JOHNSON

Deputy Sheriff
Eddy County, New Mexico

Trouble over water rights had been brewing for some time around the community of Hope in the northwest corner of Eddy County. In particular a man by the name of Joe Taylor had beaten the daylights out of one L. E. Pratt as the latter worked in an irrigation ditch. Mr. Pratt, about 60 years old and a man described as honest and hard-working, but somewhat imperious, reacted by carrying a shotgun and guarding the head gate at a ditch on his property. Some said he was taking more than his allocated share of water.

A warrant was issued for the arrest of Pratt for carrying firearms. On Wednesday, May 25, 1898, at about 8:00 o'clock in the morning, Deputy Sheriff Bud Johnson, a ditch rider named Richards, and a third man went to Pratt's farm to serve it. They found Pratt and another man, John Fort, at the head gate. Within a matter of minutes, Deputy Johnson was dead of a shotgun blast to the chest and Richards was wounded with a buckshot wound to the shoulder. Pratt retreated to his home nearby.

There are two versions of the story.

Richards said that he, Deputy Johnson and the third man rode up to the head gate and dismounted. Deputy Johnson said, "Good morning Mr. Pratt. I have a warrant for your arrest." Richards said Pratt fired immediately causing death and injury.

Pratt's version was something of a departure. He said that he did not know Johnson to be a deputy and was properly fearful when three armed men rode up and dismounted.

"Give me that gun!" Pratt reported Johnson as saying.

Backing off a few feet, Pratt responded, "I am on my own premises and will not be disarmed."

"Draw your arms men," Johnson said.

Pratt said he wasn't the first to fire but he acknowledged that he shot Johnson and Richards before he and Fort fled the scene.

Both the Pratt and Fort families were in Pratt's house as was Fort's nephew, Willie Niel; seven children in all. Joe Taylor soon showed up and began shooting at Pratt's house from a range of about 300 yards. One of his bullets passed through a wall and hit young Willie Niel in the shoulder. Pratt (or someone in the house) returned fire and Taylor fled. Soon other citizens began arriving and pouring a steady barrage of gunfire into the house. Several hundred shots were fired. Someone sent a telegram to Sheriff Miles Cicero Stewart at Eddy, the county seat, advising him of the situation in Hope and urging him to come as soon as possible. It was feared that the mob would lynch Pratt if he was not otherwise killed.

Late on Wednesday afternoon, Pratt surrendered to two local men, Dave Runyan and C. Wilburn.* Sheriff Stewart arrived on the scene and took Pratt into custody and removed him to Miller (now Artesia). From there he took him to jail at Eddy (now Carlsbad) by train.

A flurry of charges and countercharges were soon filed. On June 9, nearly the entire population of Hope was present in a courtroom in Eddy when a judge named Roberts heard charges that John Fort was guilty of assault for shooting at Joe Taylor from Pratt's house. That charge was dismissed and Joe Taylor was charged with assault for shooting Willie Niel. Then Fort was arrested again and charged with accessory to murder for the shooting of Bud Johnson. The disposition of those charges is not known.

On October 22, 1898, L. E. Pratt was indicted for murder and a change of venue to Chaves County was granted. On November 5, 1898, a jury convicted Pratt of 3rd degree murder and on November 12 he was sentenced to two years in prison. Judge Leland freed him on a $3,000 appeal bond. A month or so later, the judge realized that he didn't have the authority to free a convicted murderer on bond and ordered the arrest of Pratt. That seemed to mark the end of the affair.

Virtually nothing of a personal nature is known of Deputy Sheriff Bud Johnson.

* No source says so, but this may be Eddy County Deputy Sheriff Stone Wilburn who was wounded in a 1922 gunfight in Hope when Sheriff G. W. Batton was killed. (See page 15)

Albuquerque *Citizen*, May 31, 1898

Eddy *Argus*, May 28 & June 11, 1898

John F. Lewis, Eddy County Chief Deputy Sheriff, correspondence, September 14, 1995

(Thanks to former Eddy County Sheriff Jack Childress and Ron Grimes of Carlsbad.)

WILLIAM D. "KEECHI" JOHNSON

Chief Deputy Sheriff
Grant County, New Mexico

In late August of 1900, Grant County Deputy Sheriff Keechi Johnson set out from Silver City, New Mexico, in pursuit of cattle rustlers. He managed to capture one of them in the Upper Gila country of Socorro County, about 75 miles northwest of Silver City. On August 27, along White Creek,* as he began his return trip to the county seat with his prisoner, he was ambushed by a second rustler, shot and killed.

The offender was believed to have been a thief named Ralph Jenks who was subsequently arrested by deputies. On the ride to Silver City, Jenks unwisely made a grab for Deputy Ed Scarborough's shotgun. Scarborough shot him three times: twice in the chest and once in the head. Zealous law and order advocates demanded that the deputy be charged for murder in the killing of Jenks, but a judge directed the jury to return a verdict of not guilty, and they did.

Keechi Johnson was an unlikely lawman. He was born in Alabama in 1855. As a young man, he married and moved west, making stops in Taylor County, Texas and Eddy County, New Mexico before he arrived in Silver City. His trade over many years was that of house painter and wallpaper hanger. When James K. Blair was elected Grant County Sheriff in 1899, he appointed Johnson a deputy. Johnson appears to have created a formidable reputation in a short period of time. After his death, a local newspaper opined thus: "Johnson was one of the best and most fearless officers that Grant County has had in years and his loss will be keenly felt by Sheriff Blair and the law abiding citizens of that district."

* One source reports that the killing occurred along Raw Meat Creek which is in what is now Catron County.

Albuquerque *Journal Democrat*, August 31; September 6 & 13, 1900
Bob Alexander, *Lawmen, Outlaws, and S. O. Bs.*, High-Lonesome Books
Bob Alexander, *Six-Guns and Single-Jacks*, Gila Books

Robert K. DeArment, *George Scarborough, The Life and Death of a Lawman on the Closing Frontier*, University of Oklahoma Press

JAMES B. "JIMMY" JONES

Inspector
New Mexico Livestock Board

Inspector Jimmy Jones, 64, was killed on October 29, 1981 when the state-owned pickup truck he was driving rolled over three times on State Road 117 about 18 miles southeast of Grants in Cibola County. A passenger in the truck, livestock inspector Harold Valerio, 30, of Gamerco was severely injured but survived. Because neither man was wearing a seatbelt, both were thrown out as the vehicle rolled over.

Jimmy Jones had been a state cattle inspector for 25 years at the time of his death. He was selected inspector of the year for 1976. His mother, Maud, and a son, James III, survived him. His father, James Jones, Sr., served as Lieutenant Governor of New Mexico from 1943 to 1946. His brother, Preston, was a well-known Texas playwright. Jones was a survivor of the Baatan Death March during World War II. He was buried in the Grants Memorial Park.

Albuquerque *Journal*, October 30, 1981
Grants *Beacon*, October 30, 1981
Robert VanderHee, Captain, Special Investigations Division, New Mexico Department of Public Safety
Deanna Vanderlaan, New Mexico Crimestoppers (Formerly with the New Mexico Livestock Board)

TOM JONES

Chief Deputy Sheriff
Lincoln County, New Mexico

Lincoln County Sheriff A. S. McCamant got word on Friday, July 14, 1933, that two wanted Texas bank robbers and killers, Ed "Pearchmouth" Stanton, 45, and Glenn Hunsucker, 21, were hiding out on a dry-land homestead near Corona in the northern part of the county. The sheriff, along with deputies Tom Jones, Jack Davidson and Hubert Reynolds, set out at once in search of the outlaws. On Saturday they visited the farm in question and found that the suspects were not present. They returned the following day and found tire tracks, a sign that the outlaws had visited the place during the night.

The posse, augmented by Sgt. Barney Leonard (page 186) and Sam McCue of Chaves County followed a trail left Stanton and Hunsucker. They kept up the pursuit for most of Sunday across rugged country. After Leonard and McCue left the group, the posse came upon their quarry late Sunday afternoon east of Corona on the Nalda Ranch. The two outlaws concealed themselves in a wooded area that surrounded a broad dell. They opened fire on the officers without warning, killing Tom Jones almost instantly with a bullet to the head. Hunsucker advanced on the remaining lawmen, firing as he went, only to be shot down. He died about an hour later of eight bullet wounds. Stanton got away on foot.

Word of Deputy Jones' killing spread rapidly around Lincoln County and southeastern New Mexico and by Monday morning the sheriff had help from Capitan and Hondo, as well as from neighboring jurisdictions. His posse grew to more than twenty men. They resumed the search for Stanton. At about 3:00 Monday afternoon, the killer was spotted, still in the Ramon area. When Stanton realized he was cornered, he surrendered. Officers took him to jail in Carrizozo.

Officers from Tulia and Silverton in the Texas Panhandle arrived in Lincoln County on Tuesday morning. They positively identified Glenn Hunsucker and Pearchmouth Stanton as the two bandits who robbed a gasoline filling station at Tulia, Texas, and killed Swisher County Sheriff John C. Mosely on January 23, 1933. Hunsucker was also believed to have participated in a bank robbery at Olton, Texas and to have taken part in a gun battle with law officers at Bluitt, 50 miles south of Portales in 1932. Hale County, Texas, Deputy Sheriff Harve Bolin was shot and killed in that fight and Roosevelt County Deputy Sheriff R. L. Hollis was badly wounded.

Because officers feared that Stanton's friends would attempt to rescue him, the Lincoln County Jail was carefully guarded until Wednesday when Stanton appeared before a local magistrate and waived extradition back to Texas. Deputy Hubert Reynolds accompanied the four Texas officers in taking Stanton first to Roswell, where two other officers joined them for the trip to Clovis and then to Amarillo. No one attempted to interfere with the officers.

On September 28, 1934, Ed "Pearchmouth" Stanton was executed by electrocution at the Texas State Prison at Huntsville. All New Mexico charges against him were dropped on March 7, 1935.

As a sidelight to this story, after the killing of Deputy Jones, local citizens determined that the sheriff needed more firepower so they purchased a Colt model 1921 Thompson submachine gun for the department. The department still owns it (see photo below).

Deputy Jones' widow, Ola, served as superintendent of the Lincoln County Schools.

Alamogordo *News,* July 20, 1933
Albuquerque *Journal,* July 17 & 18, 1933
Artesia *Advocate,* July 20, 1933
Jack Davidson (Sheriff McCamant's nephew), September 24, 1990
Lincoln County *News,* July 21, 1933
Charlie Brown, Texas Department of Corrections, conversation, 1990
James McSwane, Sheriff, Lincoln County
Vernon Petty, Carrizozo, New Mexico, correspondence, June 1 & 28, 1990
Michael Shyne, Alamogordo, New Mexico, correspondence, May 14 1990

KENT KEARNEY

Deputy Sheriff
Doña Ana County, New Mexico

In early July, 1898, Doña Ana County Sheriff Pat Garrett (page 106) led a posse in pursuit of Oliver Lee and Jim Gilliland, both wanted in connection with the mysterious disappearance of Col. Albert J. Fountain (page 96) and his son, Henry, in late January of 1896. Members of the posse included José Espalín, Clint Llewellyn, Ben Williams and Kent Kearney. All were regular deputies and experienced gun hands except for Kearney, a former schoolteacher.

Garrett received a tip that Lee and Gilliland had been seen at the W. W. Cox ranch east of the Organ Mountains. The posse picked up the fugitive's trail and followed it for about 40 miles across the Tularosa Valley to Lee's Wildey Well* ranch, a few miles east of Oro Grande. They reached the remote ranch before dawn and moved in. Garrett found the house occupied by James Madison—who worked for Oliver Lee—and his wife Mary, their three children, and a stranger named McVey. Lee and Gilliland were not in the house and no one would say where they were. A search of the area soon revealed a ladder leading to the roof and Garrett surmised his quarry was up there. Sleeping on the flat roofs of adobe houses was common summer practice in the Old Southwest.

Garrett positioned his posse and himself to try and get a look at the roof. Kearney leaned a ladder from a shed roof to the house roof and started slowly up. He spotted a rifle barrel above him and fired. Garrett too began firing and Lee and Gilliland returned the shots. Kearney was hit immediately, first in the shoulder and then the groin. He fell off the ladder and down to the shed roof, and then to the ground. Espalín was pinned down beside the house and not in firing position. Williams returned fire from below a water-tank which, pierced by answering bullets, showered him with cold water. Open ground with no cover prevented him from moving out of the downpour. Llewellyn remained inside the house guarding the Madisons and McVey.

Lee and Gilliland had near-perfect cover and a 360-degree field of fire. The gun battle at Wildey Well became a standoff.

"Are you ready to surrender?" Garrett called to Lee.

"I don't think I will. I've heard you intend to kill me."

"You have no need to fear. You will be perfectly safe in my hands. Now will you surrender?"

"Who do you think has the best of it?" Lee asked. "You have got yourself into a hell of a close place."

"I know it," Garrett said. "How are we going to get out of here?"

"If you pull off, we won't shoot," Lee responded.

A humiliated Pat Garrett and his deputies withdrew and Lee and Gilliland let them go. The posse left Kearney behind. Mary Madison tended his wounds and removed the bullet from his groin. Later that afternoon he was taken first to Alamogordo and then to La Luz, where he died the following day.

Warrants were issued for Lee and Gilliland charging them with the murder of Deputy Kent Kearney but the two were never arrested or tried for that crime. They ultimately surrendered to authorities (not Pat Garrett) and were tried at Hillsboro, New Mexico, in May and June, 1899, for the murder of young Henry Fountain. They were acquitted and never tried again.

Oliver Lee went on to serve as a member of the New Mexico House of Representatives from 1918 to 1926, and the State senate from 1926 to 1932. Legend holds that even then he was armed at all times, but some historians say that was not so. As to Lee's character, former New Mexico Territorial Governor George Curry said: "He had a well-earned reputation as a good citizen, expert rancher, and efficient public servant." Not everyone in southern New Mexico agreed.

* Also spelled as Wildy Well and Wildey's Well.

A. M. Gibson, *The Life and Death of Colonel Albert Jennings Fountain*, University of Oklahoma Press

William A. Keleher, *The Fabulous Frontier*, University of New Mexico Press

Lt. West Gilbreath, Doña Ana County Sheriff's Department

Leon C. Metz, *Pat Garrett, The Story of a Western Lawman*, University of Oklahoma Press

New Mexico Legislative Council Service

Dan L. Thrapp, *Encyclopedia of Frontier Biography*, University of Nebraska Press

JAMES I. KENT

Deputy

Union County, New Mexico Sheriff's Department

A band of horse thieves busily plied their trade in northwestern Union County in the spring of 1909. In one case alone, they stole 28 head from the ranch of John King near Folsom. In early June, Sheriff D. W. Snyder learned that some of the horses had been sold to farmers around Richland in southwestern Kansas, and he immediately sent his deputy, Jim Kent, to Kansas to see what he could find. Kent recovered many of the horses and learned that some of the others had been traded for a team of mules and yet another team of horses. He picked up a trail in Richland that took him to Trinidad, Colorado. Kent learned there that a man named Clarence Hamilton sold both teams to a Colorado farmer. When Hamilton went to a local bank to collect for the mules and horses, Deputy Kent was waiting and arrested him. It didn't take long for Hamilton to tell Kent that the Jamison brothers, who maintained a "camp" in eastern Colfax County, only about five miles from the King ranch, actually stole the animals.

Deputies Kent, H. M. Williams* and Gay Melon were dispatched to arrest the Jamison brothers. They reached the King ranch on the evening of July 1 and spent the night there. It was still dark the next morning when the posse took the trail to the Jamison place, and the officers took positions of concealment outside the small adobe before full daylight. Shortly, one of the Jamisons exited the house to gather kindling and firewood for use in preparing breakfast. Deputy Kent followed him back inside and at gunpoint ordered, "Throw up your hands!" Kent's demand was immediately answered by a gunshot from an adjoining room. Kent, shot in the neck, fell to the floor, mortally wounded. Deputy Williams then approached the door and he too was shot and severely wounded. Deputy Melon hurried away from the scene and back to the King ranch for help. Williams, in great agony from a stomach wound, was able to reach his horse and mount, and he too started for the King ranch. His strength failed him, however, and he collapsed along the road where he was found later by a relief party from Folsom, unconscious from loss of blood.

News accounts of the time reported that the Jamisons stepped over and around Kent's body as they finished preparing and eating breakfast. Then they mounted up and rode west, toward Raton, but apparently not in great haste.

Meantime, Melon reached the King Ranch, and John King rode to Folsom where he sent a telegram to Sheriff Snyder:

July 2, 9:00 a.m.
Sheriff:
J. I. Kent killed at Jamison ranch. Take along posse from there
overland at once.

Sheriff Snyder and a three man posse set out from Clayton immediately and by riding hard overtook the killers about midnight at the George ranch, only 20 miles from the scene of the killing. One story is that the Jamisons surrendered themselves to Mr. George, who was a Justice of the Peace. The officers and their prisoners began the trip to Clayton at once, and arrived there at noon the next day. The Sheriff and his posse had covered a distance of more than 200 miles in about 29 hours.

Williams survived a long wagon ride in the hot sun to Folsom where a local doctor dressed his wound. The morning train then took him to Trinidad where the bullet could be removed.

James I. Kent was born in Bartols County, Texas** in 1875. He arrived in Folsom in 1904 and married Gladys Hittson in February 1905. Other survivors included his father, one brother and two sisters. An infant son preceded him in death. His obituary said this:

> He was a highly esteemed citizen, doing right by his fellow man for the sake of doing right, a friend to those for whom he professed friendship. His untimely death we greatly deplore and realize that one has been called from our midst whose place in our community will be hard to fill.

Complete details regarding the prosecutions of the Jamison brothers are not known. It is known that George Jamison was convicted of manslaughter for killing Deputy Kent, and sentenced to five years in the penitentiary.

* The *Clayton Citizen*, in one place identifies the deputy as I. F. or I. P. Williams. In another he is identified as H. M. Williams.

** The same source seems to have difficulty with place names, too. It is reported that the stolen horses were sold to farmers around a town called "Konantz" in Kansas. Maps dating back to 1917 do not show such a community. There is likewise no county in Texas named "Bartols."

Larry D. Ball, *Desert Lawmen: The High Sheriffs of New Mexico and Arizona, 1846-1912*, University of New Mexico Press

Clayton *Citizen*, July 2 & 9, 1909

Click, Mrs. N. H. (Cora), *Us Nesters in The Land of Enchantment*, privately printed

Lee Johnson, Sheriff, Union County, New Mexico, October 22, 1999

WILLIAM HARVEY KILBURN

Town Marshal
Silver City, New Mexico

Five cowboys from the Victorio Land and Cattle Company ranch rode into Silver City on Saturday afternoon, August 27, 1904. Fall roundup was scheduled to begin the following week and there'd be no opportunity to get back to town until the work was done. Drinking in the Club House and Palace Saloons was the order of the day and two of the cowboys in particular, Howard Chenowth* and Mart Kennedy far over-did it. At one point during the evening, the two engaged in a loud quarrel along a city street and Victorio ranch foreman Pat Nunn intervened. And before August 27th became August 28th, Chenowth tried to ride his horse into the Palace Saloon, only to be stopped by Nunn and deputy sheriff Elmore Murray.

It was close to two o'clock on the morning of the 28th when Nunn and Murray encountered the two cowboys on the street. One version of the story goes that Chenowth and Kennedy were fighting and Nunn interceded. Another version holds that Nunn simply told the two men to return to the ranch. Chenowth agreed to go and mounted his horse. Kennedy, angered at being ordered to cease his revelry, refused to go; said he'd quit the Victorio and he took his saddle off the company horse. He called Nunn an "ugly" name. The ranch foreman resented the remark—whatever it was—dismounted his horse, removed his gunbelt and placed it on the curb before he engaged Kennedy in a fistfight.

The fight didn't last long. Nunn was a bigger man, physically, and he was sober, too. He knocked the cowboy to the ground and stood over him as Chenowth removed Nunn's gun from its holster and announced that he would not allow anyone to harm his friend. Chenowth opened fire. The first bullet hit Nunn in the chest, exactly where he carried his watch in a shirt pocket. The watch was ruined but Nunn was not otherwise injured. The second bullet grazed the foreman's forehead and removed both eyebrows.

Deputy Murray began struggling to get the gun away from Chenowth. An elderly man named H. A. McGowan tried to help the deputy as Precinct Constable Perfecto Rodriguez approached the scene. He'd been visiting a nearby saloon, heard the shots and ran into the street to learn the cause of the disturbance.

"Get the gun!" He yelled at Murray.

"That is just what I am trying to do," the deputy responded just as Chenowth shot the constable in the chest, knocking him down.

Chenowth and Kennedy fled north on Texas Street with Deputy Murray close at hand, trying at the same time to take the gun away from Chenowth and preventing Kennedy from drawing the gun he wore at his side. Sources at the time reported that Deputy Murray had been friendly with the two cowboys which may account for the fact that Chenowth didn't shoot him.

Town Marshal William Kilburn, who lived only two blocks away, hurried to the scene and came upon the three men. Murray told Kilburn to get Chenowth's gun, but before the marshal could take any action, Chenowth shot the lawman in the neck rendering him immediately unconscious. The two cowboys broke away from Murray and fled the scene on foot.

A sizable crowd gathered. Constable Rodriguez was found to be dead from his wound (page 249) and Marshal Kilburn, severely wounded, was removed to Ladies' Hospital. He was not expected to survive. Neither of the two lawmen had been armed. Officers and citizens soon developed a plan to search Silver City for the killers. About then, Mart Kennedy walked into the Palace Saloon and ordered a drink. He announced that he'd done nothing wrong and shouldn't be arrested. He was quickly taken into custody. A Justice of the Peace named Newcomb had already been summoned and he'd issued murder warrants for both of the offending cowboys.

A jailer named Gill and three deputies, Charles Williams, John Burnside and John Collier, escorted Kennedy to jail, keeping a careful lookout for Chenowth. As the party passed Samuel Lindaner's dry goods store, Collier spotted Chenowth hiding behind some boxes on the sidewalk. He said nothing for some distance and then told Burnside what he'd seen. The group shortly encountered a citizen who provided Collier with a shotgun. Unfortunately, it was not loaded and the deputy was obliged to return to the Club House Saloon for ammunition. Then he moved carefully along the street until he stood in front of Lindaner's store, in the middle of the street.

Collier ordered Chenowth to surrender, several times, and Chenowth refused every time. At Burnside's warning, Collier took cover behind a tree in front of the Silver City Mercantile. Collier again ordered Chenowth to give up. Chenowth refused and advanced toward Collier, gun in hand. The cowboy stopped behind a sign post and started to take aim at the deputy, and as he did, Collier fired. Half a load of number 6 birdshot splintered the post and the other half hit Chenowth in the side of the head. It didn't kill him but he went down immediately. (One version of the story which appeared in an Albuquerque newspaper, is that Deputy Murray shot Chenowth. The above retelling is based on detailed accounts reported in the Silver City newspapers of the day.)

Marshal Kilburn died of his wound a week later. He was born in Missouri in 1864 but spent most of his adult life in Colorado and New Mexico. Kilburn served as a Grant County deputy under Sheriff Harvey Whitehill** before becoming Silver City Town Marshal in 1888. He served until 1891 and was reelected to the post in 1895 and again in 1903. His wife, Emma, was Harvey Whitehill's daughter. The Kilburns had four children: Hattie, Harvey, Bob and Jack who ranged in age from five to 12 years.

The local paper said this about Marshal William Kilburn:

> As a peace officer he was especially gifted. He was absolutely fearless in the discharge of his duties and at the same time exercised such good sense and judgment that even those whom he was compelled to exert his authority upon were his friends.

Howard Chenowth was convicted of killing both lawmen and sentenced to 50 years in prison. His lawyer, however, appealed the conviction and Chenowth remained in the Grant County Jail in Silver City awaiting the appeals court decision. On Christmas day in 1905, he escaped from the lock-up, apparently with the help of his family. Never recaptured, he spent many years living in South America where he married and raised a family. In 1927, New Mexico Governor Richard C. Dillon pardoned Chenowth and the killer returned to the United States a free man. One historian noted, "Except for that one voyage on a whiskey river many years ago, Chenowth's life had been honorable and productive."

Of course, peace officers Kilburn and Rodriguez had no opportunity to continue honorable and productive lives, thanks to the drunkenness and bad judgment of Howard Chenowth.

* The name is spelled variously, Chinowth, Chenowith, Chenoweth and Chinoworth. Historian Bob Alexander declares that Chenowth is the correct version.

** Whitehill was the first lawman to arrest William Bonney—Billy the Kid—for stealing butter, in 1875.

Albuquerque *Morning Journal*, August 29, 1904
Bob Alexander, *Lawmen, Outlaws, and S. O. Bs.*, High-Lonesome Books

Don Bullis, *Duels, Gunfights & Shootouts*, Rio Grande Books

Silver City *Independent*, August 30, September 6 & 9, 1904

Chief Thomas J. Ryan (Ret.), Silver City Police Department, correspondence, October 2 & 23, 1991

MICHAEL R. KING

Officer
Albuquerque, New Mexico, Police Department

One of Albuquerque's bloodiest days began at about 6:30 a.m. on August 18, 2005, when employees at the New Mexico Department of Transportation facility on Volcano NW, near the west end of Central Avenue, found the body of fellow worker, Ben Lopez, 54, dead from a gunshot wound. Investigating police officers found very little evidence to work with.

Then, at just before 5:00 p.m., Albuquerque police were called to Rider Valley Motorcycles near the far eastern end of Central Avenue in response to a reported robbery. They found the bodies of David Fisher, 17, and Garrett Iverson, 22, dead from gunshot wounds. Again, police found little evidence to work with, except that a witness provided a basic description of a suspect and the motorcycle he rode.

During the day, there had been considerable activity at Presbyterian Kaseman Hospital where a some-time patient named John Hyde, 48, had made threats against employees. Because of a series of communications disconnects and delays, Officers Richard Smith, 46, and Michael King, 50, didn't receive a pick-up order for Hyde until about 9:15 p.m., and did not arrive at his residence on Gold Street until about a half hour later. They arrived in separate police units, and evidence indicates that Hyde began shooting almost immediately. Officer King was hit before he could fire a shot, and Officer Smith left what cover he had to assist his partner, and was himself shot. Both officers died soon after they were transported to the University of New Mexico Hospital. Both officers had been wearing body armor.

A back-up officer arrived at the scene of the shootings as the suspect departed, and was able to broadcast a description of the motorcycle he rode. John Hyde was taken into custody at a little after midnight after officers spotted him near the intersection of Kathryn and Louisiana SE in Albuquerque. He attempted to evade the police, but wrecked his motorcycle before he was arrested. According to a news report, Hyde admitted that he'd shot the two officers.

The motorcycle Hyde rode matched the description of the bike seen at the

170

motorcycle shop killings. Also, the gun Hyde used in the police shootings—a British Webley revolver which had been modified to fire .45 caliber ammunition—matched the gun used to kill Ben Lopez, David Fisher and Garrett Iverson, he was charged with all five killings. Notably, at his arraignment, Hyde complained of his treatment: "My hair looks ridiculous. I was not allowed to groom myself." He also demanded his constitutional right to bond, but Judge Daniel Ramczyk considered him a flight risk and ordered him held without bail. Court action in the years that followed the commission of these crimes revolved around the contention that Hyde suffered from paranoid schizophrenia and bipolar disorder. It was alleged that he was off his medications and had a psychotic episode which led to these crimes. Four years after Officers Smith and King were killed Hyde remains confined to the State Hospital in Las Vegas, New Mexico. A news report dated October 10, 2009 noted that "Hyde is still sick. And he's not likely to get better."

Both officers had retired from the Albuquerque Police Department, and both discovered that they preferred police work to not working at all. Both returned to the ranks, only to meet tragic death.

Michael King joined the Albuquerque Police Department in 1982 and initially retired in 2002. He returned to active duty in 2004. He held a variety of assignments during his career and received a number of commendations. Chief of Police Ray Schultz said, "Michael loved being a street cop and that is what he always wanted to do." Bernalillo County Sheriff Darren White described Officer King a "gentle giant."

Albuquerque *Journal*, August 19 to 28; November 30, 2005; August 14 & 15, 2009
Albuquerque Police Department
Albuquerque *Tribune*, August 19 & 20, 2005
Santa Fe *New Mexican*, August 20, 2005

LEWIS ALEXANDER "ALEX" KNAPP

Officer

Albuquerque, New Mexico, Police Department

On the day New Mexico became the 47th state of the Union, January 6, 1912, Police Officer Alex Knapp and Police Chief Tom McMillan stood talking on First Street in downtown Albuquerque. At about 3:00 o'clock on that Saturday afternoon, a passing citizen told Officer Knapp that a drunk had passed out near the First National Bank at Central Avenue and Fourth Street. By the time Knapp arrived, the man in question was up and walking away. The officer approached and first asked the man where he lived; saying he would escort him home. The man apparently refused to say where he lived and Knapp told him he was taking him to jail. The man didn't resist as they walked along, but when the two of them were in front of Goff's Blacksmith shop on Copper Avenue, between Second and Third Streets, the stranger fired a .25 caliber pistol from his overcoat pocket. The bullet struck Officer Knapp in the chest, above the heart, punctured his lung and lodged in the back muscle.

Though severely wounded, Knapp wrestled the man to the ground and choked him into unconsciousness. Help arrived. Bystanders took Knapp to his home on Central Avenue before doctors ordered him removed to St. Joseph's Hospital. Other officers and citizens took Knapp's assailant, initially identified as Fred J. Watson, and still unconscious, to jail. Doctors were obliged to take "heroic" measures to save the man's life. Chief McMillan was anxious to take Watson to the hospital so that Knapp could identify him as the attacker. Officers carried an unconscious Watson to Knapp's hospital room on a litter and held him in a sitting position while Knapp made a positive identification.

For more than a week the Albuquerque newspaper provided medical updates daily. First reports called Knapp's wound "fatal." A day later, after a restful night, hope returned that he might survive. Then recovery seemed likely, barring any setback. But on January 15, Knapp succumbed to pneumonia, brought on by his wound.

A few days after the shooting, Chief McMillan learned that Fred J. Watson was in fact Theodore Goulet, 25, an ex-convict from Minnesota who was wanted there for parole violation. He was charged with first degree murder for the killing of Officer Knapp. Goulet attempted to break jail even before Knapp died, and on Sunday evening, April 28, 1912, he succeeded and managed to free himself.* He was captured two days later as he walked along the railroad tracks south of McIntosh in Torrance County. He did not resist arrest. Goulet was taken to the state penitentiary for safekeeping until his trial.

On September 26, 1912, Goulet went on trial for murder. The defense claimed that Theodore Goulet, at the time he shot Officer Knapp, suffered from "mental aberration" brought on by over indulgence in liquor; that Goulet had no memory of firing the shot that took the officer's life. It took the jury only one hour and twenty-five minutes on the evening of September 27 to find Goulet guilty of second degree murder. His sentence was set at 10 years to life in prison.

Alex Knapp's obituary read:

> Patrolman Knapp had been a member of the Albuquerque police force ten years. His record was a splendid one. He was known for his attentiveness to duty, fearlessness and kindness. He seldom carried a gun and on the day he was shot was unarmed.

> The dead officer was about 50 years old. He was born on a farm in Indiana. Early in life, after he had grown to manhood, he was a riverman on the Ohio. Later he was engaged in the grocery business in Jeffersonville, Ind. He came to Albuquerque eleven years ago and a year later became a member of the police force. Mr. Knapp was twice married. His first wife died about a year ago after having been an invalid for almost ten years. The widow who survives is a bride of but a few months.

* A second killer being held in the Bernalillo County jail, Sam Lyle, had hacksaw blades smuggled into the lockup. Lyle cut the bars in an effort to effect his own escape, but he failed to make the hole large enough to accommodate his bulk. Goulet, however, smaller in stature, was able to flee, leaving Lyle behind.

Albuquerque *Morning Journal*, January 7, 8, 9, 10, 12, 16 & 23; April 29; May 1 & 3; October
14, 26 & 27; and December 30, 1912
Albuquerque Police Department

ISHKOTEN KOTEEN

Officer
Jicarilla Apache Tribal Police Department

Officer Ishkoten Koteen, made a routine patrol in the southwestern part of the Jicarilla Reservation of northern New Mexico on Sunday evening, May 8, 1961. Along the way, he encountered Climaco Lucero, 27, stealing drip gas from a natural gas well. The two men exchanged shots almost immediately, with no effect. Lucero got to his pickup truck and drove away. Koteen got back into his police vehicle and took up pursuit. The officer managed to stop Lucero some distance away, and as he walked up to the pickup, Lucero leveled a rifle as Officer Koteen pulled his revolver. Both men fired at the same time and both were hit. Officer Koteen took a few steps and collapsed. Lucero sped away from the scene.

When the officer failed to return home Sunday evening, his wife began searching for him. She found his body about 5:00 o'clock Monday morning near his departmental truck. Officer Koteen was dead of two bullet wounds to the chest. The officer had two quirks regarding his sidearm that may have contributed to his death. One was that while he was left-handed, he carried his pistol on the right side. His practice was to draw with his right hand, then shift the gun to his left hand, which would certainly contribute to slowing access to the weapon. The other was that he regularly carried practice ammunition—wad cutters—in his .357 revolver rather that the magnum loads the gun was designed to fire, which would certainly reduce the weapon's range and effectiveness.

Lucero, a sawmill worker, managed to drive himself to his home in Gallina and his wife drove him from there to the hospital in Española. He reported that he'd been shot in the chest by accident while cleaning his gun, but hospital personnel reported the gunshot wound to authorities. FBI agents and New Mexico State Police questioned Lucero at the hospital and he admitted that he shot officer Koteen. He claimed the officer fired first, and he only defended himself.

Lucero was charged with first-degree murder and indicted in September 1961. On November 7, 1961, however, he entered into a plea agreement in which he pleaded guilty to second degree murder and was sentenced to 12 years in prison. Lucero benefitted from the services of attorney A. T. Montoya, a member of an important political family. Federal Judge Waldo H. Rogers' strong, and public, opposition to the death penalty also worked to the killer's advantage. "I am unequivocally against it [capital punishment]," the judge said.

Officer Koteen, 61, was a veteran of 33 years service as a tribal policeman. He lived at Otero Ranch, a tribal police substation located in Rio Arriba County near the Sandoval County line, not far from the village of Counselor.

Albuquerque *Journal*, May 9, 10, 11, 16, & 19; September 19; November 7 1961
Jicarilla Department of Public Safety
Santa Fe *New Mexican*, May 10, 1961

OWEN LANDDECK

Lieutenant
Farmington, New Mexico, Police Department

The Farmington Police Academy conducted a training exercise in August 1979, which dealt with officer handling of domestic violence calls. Lt. Owen Landdeck's role in the mock situation was that of deranged husband. The scenario called for Lt. Landdeck to become engaged in a scuffle with one of the responding officers, then to produce a gun and fire blanks at the other officer. At that point a cadet would return fire. The exercise went according to plan except that inadvertently the cadet's gun was loaded with live ammunition and he accidentally shot Landdeck. The bullet passed through the lieutenant's body and wounded Cadet Greg Willis who stood behind him. Landdeck died a short while later at the San Juan Regional Medical Center. An investigation conducted by District Attorney Paul Onuska concluded that the incident was a "tragic accident" with no evidence of criminal intent by anyone involved. No charges were filed.

Lt. Landdeck, 40, served ten years on the Albuquerque Police Department before he joined the Farmington Police Department in 1969. He founded the "Officer Bill" program in Farmington and he had previously served as President of the San Juan Mental Health Services, Inc. He also served on the Board of Directors of Childhaven.

"He was a part of almost every program for kids," said Farmington Detective Sergeant Gerald Steele.

"[Landdeck's death] is a great loss to the police department. He was a fine officer. Top notch," said Police Chief Robert Schmerheim.

His wife, Iris, a daughter, Brenda, and a son, Owen Jr., both teenagers, survived Lt. Landdeck. He is buried at Memory Gardens in Farmington.

Cadet Willis survived his wound and served 20 years with the Farmington Police Department.

Farmington *Daily Times*, October 10, 1972, May 2, 1975, December 20 & 27, 1977, August 19, 21 & 27, 1979

DAVID A. LANE

District Attorney
Sixth Judicial District Of New Mexico
(Grant, Hidalgo & Luna Counties)

David Lane, 39, was killed when the private airplane in which he was a passenger crashed in the Diablo Mountains near San Jose, California, on May 3, 1986. The plane was en route to New Mexico from San Francisco. James M. "Tuck" Grimes, 72, operator of the Silver City/Grant County Airport and attorney Thomas P. Foy Jr., 35, son of State Representative Thomas P. Foy Sr., both citizens of Silver City, also died in the crash which was attributed to fog and freezing rain.

His wife, Roberta, and daughter Kristie survived Mr. Lane. He served as Public Defender before he was elected District Attorney in 1984.

Albuquerque *Journal*, May 5 & 6, 1986

ROBERT P. LARSON

Agent in Charge
Metro Narcotics Agency, Doña Ana County, New Mexico

Near Tortugas, south of Las Cruces, on August 13, 1982, Metro Narcotics Agent Bob Larson purchased seven grams of cocaine from Richard Jimmy Montoya for $675. The officer made arrangements to purchase additional amounts of the controlled substance on Monday, August 23 from the same dope dealer. He arranged for backup and made other preparations, but Montoya postponed the meeting until Tuesday in the early afternoon. Larson rescheduled his backup officers and agreed to meet Montoya in a parking lot on Valley Drive in Las Cruces.

The meeting took place on schedule, but the deal didn't go down as planned. Larson got into Montoya's car and they drove away from the parking lot before backup officers realized what was happening. The move was unexpected and the officers last saw Larson in a green and white Chevrolet headed north on Valley Drive. As soon as the agents lost contact with Larson, they began an all points search, checking places Montoya was known to frequent. The search extended from El Paso on the south to Hatch on the north.

No luck.

Bob Larson's body was found in a room of the Coachlight Inn motel on the west side of Las Cruces. He'd been shot three times.

Montoya, 27, had no intention of selling cocaine during his second meeting with Larson. He only intended to rob him of the money he brought to make the buy. Montoya purchased a .22 magnum revolver and enlisted the assistance of his friend David "Yogie" Munoz of Las Cruces.

There was no chance they'd get away with the crime. In addition to the fact that Larson's back up officers knew who the dope dealer in question was, Montoya and Munoz were so inept that they locked their car keys in the motel room where they'd killed Larson, and they were obliged to break a window to get back in and retrieve them so they could leave the scene. Glass fragments and blood were later found on Munoz's trousers. The Chevrolet Montoya used to drive Larson away from the parking lot on Valley Drive was traced to Montoya's family. The motel clerk identified Munoz as the man who rented the room where Larson was killed. Montoya surrendered to police the day following the killing and Munoz gave himself up not long after that. Montoya and Munoz were both convicted of first-degree murder.

A native of Wisconsin, Agent Larson began his law enforcement career in the U. S. Army's Military Police. During the early 1970s he worked for the Brillion and Little Chute, Wisconsin, police departments where he got his first experience as a narcotics officer. He moved to New Mexico and first joined the Las Cruces Police department in April, 1978. In October 1978, he moved over to the Doña Ana County Sheriff's Department so he could work in the County Metro Narcotics Agency. Larson was named agent-in-charge of Metro Narcotics on July 1, 1982, less than two months before his death.

In earlier successes, Larson was responsible for the seizure of 1,200 pounds of marijuana in one case and 6,000 pounds in another. He was the only Metro officer to ever make a heroin buy. Larson received a letter of commendation from the City of Las Cruces in August 1980. Agent Larson was described by a fellow officer as "... a very dedicated person [who] loved his job."

Agent Bob Larson, 35, was survived by his daughter, Kim, and his father, Robert C. Larson. His body was transported to Peshtigo, Wisconsin for burial.

El Paso *Times*, May 16, 1984
Las Cruces *Sun News*, August 25, 26, 27 & 30, 1982
Doña Ana County Sheriff Cooney Sarracino, correspondence, October 24, 1989
West Gilbreath, Doña Ana County Sheriff Department, October 1994

RODOLFO "RUDY" LEDEZMA

Officer
Clovis, New Mexico, Police Department

Officer Ledezma patrolled the streets of Clovis on Sunday afternoon, May 28, 1995. He radioed the dispatcher that he had spotted a man who matched the description of a subject who had assaulted another police officer the previous week. At 1:36 he called the dispatcher again and gave his location as Manana Street. A minute or so later he drove across a curb at a very low rate of speed, hit a cinder block wall and then a parked car. Other officers were on the scene within seconds. Officer Ledezma was transported, unconscious, to Plains Regional Medical Center where he died about an hour later of a heart attack.

Rudy Ledezma joined the Clovis Police Department in 1992 after a 20-year stint in the U. S. Air Force during which he served in Operation Desert Storm. His wife, Dolores, served as a Curry County Sheriff's deputy and as a special agent in the Alcohol and Gaming Section of the New Mexico Department of Public Safety. The two of them attended the New Mexico Law Enforcement Academy together. Rudy received numerous commendations. Both he and Dolores were praised for their professionalism in the work they did, while off duty, assisting with a major auto accident on Interstate 40 near Santa Rosa in February 1995.

Officer Ledezma was born in Raymondville, Texas, on July 14, 1952. He graduated from high school in San Perlita, Texas. He and Dolores Garza were married on November 1, 1970. They were the parents of three daughters: Melissa, Teresa and Rebecca; and one son, Rodolfo II. Rudy Ledezma was buried at Lawn Haven Memorial Gardens in Clovis.

Amarillo (Texas) *Globe-News*, May 30, 1995
Clovis *News Journal*, May 30 & 31, June 2, 1995
Clovis Police Department Report
New Mexico Medical Examiner's Report
Raymond Mondragon, Deputy Chief, Clovis Police Department, June 2, 1995

ROBERT EARL LEE

Patrolman
New Mexico State Police

It was well after midnight when Officer Bob Lee received a telephone call from the Doña Ana County Sheriff's Department. A motorist on U. S. Route 70 east of Las Cruces was trying to flag down passing cars. The dispatcher didn't know whether or not an accident was involved. By about 2:00 a.m. on Tuesday, August 16, 1960, the officer was driving his patrol car east out of Las Cruces, toward the town of Organ. Suddenly, about six miles east of town, a 1953 Mercury pulled from the side of the road directly into Officer Lee's path.

The police car slid 273 feet, veering from the left to the right lane and going into a side-ways skid before the rear of the police car collided with the front fender of the vehicle in its path. The police car went airborne and landed on its top 78 feet from the point of impact then rolled over twice before coming to rest on its wheels. Officer Lee was ejected during the second roll and died at the accident scene of multiple injuries, including a fractured skull. The officer's wristwatch stopped at 2:11.

Officer Lee was not wearing a seat belt even though department policy at the time required their use any time an officer left city limits in a department vehicle.

Neither the driver nor passenger in the Mercury were injured.

State Police Chief A. P. Winston flew to Las Cruces and personally investigated the accident. He said he wanted to determine whether or not the Mercury's driver, Royce Longwood, 19, of San Angelo, Texas, could be charged with manslaughter. Evidence did not exist to warrant such a charge and Longwood was charged with failure to yield the right-of-way and fined $105.00.

Deputy State Police Chief Joe Black called Lee one of the finest young officers in the department and a good driver. Lee was driving a new patrol car, one he had picked up in Santa Fe the day before the accident.

Officer Lee's commander, Captain Archie White, said, "He will be missed by the entire force for he was a good officer and well liked by his brother officers, but

I believe I will miss him the most because I could place so much responsibility on him."

A native of Las Cruces, Lee, 29, joined the State Police in 1955 after a four-year stint in the U. S. Navy and two years in college. His survivors include his wife, Naomi, two daughters, Debra Kay and Kristen, and one son, Robert Eric. Robert Earl Lee was buried at Hillcrest Cemetery in Las Cruces.

Albuquerque *Journal*, August 17, 1960
El Paso *Times*, May 16, 1984
The Roadrunner (New Mexico State Police Association, Vol. 3, No. 2, Summer, 1992)
New Mexico State Police records

STEPHEN LOUIS LEE

Sheriff
Taos County, New Mexico

On May 13, 1846, the United States declared war on Mexico after Mexican troops crossed the Rio Grande and killed 11 Americans in west Texas (at least that is one version of events leading up to the Mexican War. There are others, including one that holds that the United States fired the first shots). On August 18, 1846, The Army of the West under the command of General Stephen Watts Kearny captured Santa Fe—without firing a shot—and thereby occupied New Mexico for the United States. Committed to a smooth transition from Mexican to American rule, Kearny appointed civil officials to run the new government. Charles Bent of Taos, a trader and the brother-in-law of famed scout Kit Carson, was named Governor and Donaciano Vigil of Santa Fe was named Secretary. General Kearny and the main body of his army left Santa Fe for California in late September. Colonel Sterling Price stayed behind with a garrison-sized contingent of troops.

By the late fall of 1846, Col. Price heard rumors of a conspiracy to kill and/or expel all the Americans in four northern New Mexico counties: Santa Fe, Rio Arriba, Taos and San Miguel. He was able to forestall a cabal in Santa Fe on December 21, but major uprisings against Americans occurred at Taos, Rio Colorado and Mora in January 1847. On the 19th, a mob made up of Mexican nationalists and Taos Pueblo Indians attacked the Taos jail and demanded the release of three Taos Indian prisoners held there for theft. Faced with an armed and hostile mob, Sheriff Stephen Lee complied and then fled to his house. The mob chased him there and shot him to death.

Before the day was over, others were killed: Governor Bent, Circuit Attorney James Leal, Prefect Cornelio Vigil, along with Narciso Beaubien and Pablo Jaramillo who were Taos residents. Seven Americans were slain at Rio Colorado and two at Arroyo Hondo.

Col. Price, advised of the massacre on January 20, started north on the 23rd with about 350 troops including a detachment of 79 mountain men recruited by Cerán St. Vrain, Charles Bent's partner. In spite of deep snow and bad weather, the Americans quickly defeated a rebel force of about 1,000 men at La Cañada on January 24 and a force of 700 to 800 at Embudo on January 27. The American troops reached, and surrounded, Taos Pueblo on February 4. The rebels awaited them inside the fortified mission of San Gerónimo. Price ordered the church bombarded with cannon and it was nearly destroyed. When the battle at Taos was over, about 200 rebels were dead, either killed in battle or quickly tried for murder or treason and executed afterwards. About 35 Americans were killed. On February 12, Donaciano Vigil, who became acting civil governor of New Mexico upon the death of Charles Bent, announced a "triumph" over the rebels.

Sheriff Lee, a native of Kentucky, reached New Mexico in 1824 and tried his hand at trapping before he became a trader and merchant based in Taos with interests in both Chihuahua, Mexico, and cities in the United States. Gov. Bent appointed Stephen L. Lee to the office of Taos County sheriff in spite of the fact they were business rivals. The exact date of Lee's appointment is not known, but history records that he was busy collecting taxes by October 1846.

Michael Antonucci, "Siege Warfare in the Southwest," *Wild West*, April, 1994

Larry D. Ball, *Desert Lawmen, The High Sheriffs of New Mexico and Arizona 1846-1912* University of New Mexico Press

James A. Crutchfield, *Tragedy at Taos, The Revolt of 1847*, The Republic of Texas Press

Shannon Garst, *William Bent and His Adobe Empire*, Julian Messner, Inc.

Myra Ellen Jenkins & Albert H. Schroeder, *A Brief History of New* Mexico, University of New Mexico Press

William A. Keleher, *Turmoil in New Mexico, 1846-1868*, University of New Mexico Press

Marc Simmons, *New Mexico, An Interpretive History*, University of New Mexico Press

Dan L. Thrapp, *Encyclopedia of Frontier Biography*, University of Nebraska Press

BARNEY F. LEONARD

Deputy Sheriff
Chaves County, New Mexico

Barney Leonard, known as "Sarge" and "Hawkshaw," cannot be easily categorized as a lawman. What made him unique was the fact that his left arm was missing below the elbow, the result of military action in Cuba during the Spanish American War in the late 1890s. He arrived in Roswell—employed by the New Mexico Military Institute as a firearms instructor—in 1909 and stayed for the remainder of his life. At various times he served as Roswell police officer—he was the city's first traffic cop, patrolling the streets on a Harley-Davidson motorcycle with a specially rigged handlebar to accommodate his missing left hand—game warden, constable and sheriff's deputy. Acting in the latter capacity cost him his life.

July 1933 was a costly time for New Mexico sheriffs. A Lincoln County gunfight on July 16 between lawmen and Texas bank robbers took the life of Deputy Sheriff Tom Jones (page 159). Outlaw Glenn Hunsucker was also killed. Hunsucker's partner, Ed "Pearchmouth" Stanton escaped and Sarge Leonard rode to the neighboring county to assist in the manhunt (he had been in on the hunt for the outlaws earlier that day, but was obliged to leave before the gunfight). Stanton surrendered to officers near Ramon on Monday the 17th. Deputy Sheriff William Meador of Torrance County was also killed in July 1933 (page 209).

Leonard got back to Roswell in time to go to an address on McGaffey Street in the southeast part of town where Sheriff John Peck and Police Chief Frank Young and an eight-man posse had cornered Frank Wallace, an Oklahoma fugitive.

In addition to robbery charges in Oklahoma and Colorado, the Albuquerque Police wanted Wallace for the kidnapping of Officer Jack Craig on the previous Friday, July 14. Wallace left Craig in a hotel room, bought a used car for $35.00 and headed out of town. The Torrance County sheriff reported seeing the car, a Ford Coupe, in Estancia, heading south. On Sunday, the same car was spotted in Roswell, at the residence of one of Wallace's relatives. Officers watched the house, hoping to nab Wallace when he came out. By late Monday afternoon, they had not seen the fugitive, and officers decided to move in.

With the house surrounded, Sheriff Peck ordered all inside to come out, and three women and two children emerged from the back door. The sheriff then ordered Wallace to come out with his hands up. Instead, Wallace opened fire with two .38 caliber revolvers. Barney Leonard was hit as he rushed toward the door. The bullet broke his spine. All other officers opened fire and continued shooting until it was quiet inside the house. Sheriff Peck ordered one of the women, Catherine Faris, back into the house. He told her to bring out the killer, or his guns. She came out with the guns. She said Wallace was dying. Bystanders counted 43 bullet holes in the house and doctors found seven bullet wounds in Wallace, but he was not dead.

"I should have given up," he said to Sheriff Peck.

"I gave you every chance," the sheriff replied.

"It will be over with soon enough." Wallace, 30, didn't utter another word before he died later that evening at St. Mary's Hospital.

Leonard also died later that evening.

Local newspaper headlines declared that, "Sarge Leonard has joined his final posse."

Alamogordo *News,* July 20, 1933

Albuquerque *Journal,* July 15 & 17, 1933

Artesia *Advocate,* July 20 & 27; August 3, 1933

Elvis E. Fleming, *Treasures of History IV, Historical Events of Chaves County, New Mexico,* iUniverse, 2003

Peñasco Valley *News and Hope Press,* July 21, 1933

Roswell *Daily Record,* July 22, 1990

TRANQUILINO CAMPOS LOPEZ

Assistant Jailer
Dona Ana County, New Mexico

The local paper reported the story.

> The killing of Tranquilino Lopez Saturday night [February 18, 1911] by mounted policeman Fred Higgins was one of the most deplorable occurrences in the history of Las Cruces.
>
> Higgins had arrested Lambert Reinhart and Manuel Candelaria in a downtown saloon and had taken them to jail. They threatened resistance and Higgins pulled his guns. Arriving at the jail he summoned the jailer. Reinhart called to the jailer to look out, as the man had a gun. When Lopez opened the door he immediately grabbed Higgins about the waist, apparently mistaking him for the prisoner and in the struggle which ensued Higgins gun was discharged, the ball passing through Lopez's body. Lopez was rendered unconscious and never recovered from the shock, passing away 6:25 Sunday morning.
>
> Higgins was taken into custody and given a preliminary hearing Tuesday. Judge Parker placed his bond at $10,000, which was furnished, and Higgins left for home in Roswell. He was sheriff of Chaves County and was town marshal. He has always borne a good reputation, and the killing of Lopez was evidently ruled accidental.
>
> Tranquilino Lopez was 54 years of age and left a family of wife, three sons and a daughter. He was formerly a farmer in this county, and came to Las Cruces from Garfield two years ago to take a position as guard at the jail. His funeral occurred Monday at Mesilla and was attended by a large number of friends and relatives. *

Fred Higgins served as sheriff of Chaves County from 1899 to 1904. Records also indicate that he was hired as a private in the New Mexico Mounted Police in 1907 and again 1909. He also served as Town Marshal in Roswell. Higgins was present when Roswell Marshal Roy Woofter was killed by Jim Lynch in May of 1911 (page 330).

* The news story as it appears here has been modified to clarify grammar, spelling, and syntax.

Certificado de Muerte, Territorio de Nuevo Mexico, February 19, 1911
Elvis E. Fleming, Archivist, Historical Center for Southeast New Mexico, correspondence, February 18 & December 9, 1999
Joseph E. Lopez (nephew), correspondence, February 24, 1999
Rio Grande *Republican*, February 24, 1911

HENRY M. LOVE

Posseman
Colfax County, New Mexico

Henry Love rode with the posse that engaged train robbers Sam Ketchum, Elza Lay and Harvey Logan in a gunfight at Turkey Canyon, near Cimarron, New Mexico, on July 16, 1899. During the fight, a rifle bullet struck Love in the leg and drove the blade of his pocketknife into his flesh. He had used his knife to treat cattle sick with blackleg—a form of anthrax—and the contaminated knife blade infected the cowboy with the disease and caused his death four days later at Springer. Colorado Sheriff Edward Farr (page 90) was also killed in the gun battle.*

Little is known about Henry Love. One source reports that he was employed as a cowboy for the Charles Springer Ranch at the time of his death.

* See page 90 for a complete account of the gunfight at Turkey Canyon.

Howard Bryan, *Robbers, Rogues and Ruffians, True Tales of the Wild West*, Clear Light Publishers

Charles Kelly, *The Outlaw Trail, A History of Butch Cassidy and His Wild Bunch*, Bonanza Books

Miguel A. Otero, *My Nine Years As Governor of the Territory of New Mexico, 1897-1906*, University of New Mexico Press

Dan L. Thrapp, *Encyclopedia of Frontier Biography*, University of Nebraska Press

GERALD PETER MAGEE

Officer

New Mexico Department Of Corrections

On August 30, 1981, corrections officers working in the penitentiary at Santa Fe—a maximum-security facility—discovered bars cut in a day room and an escape attempt underway. Officers Arthur LeSueur, Jóse E. Gutierrez and Gerald Magee entered Cellblock 6 to secure it and were taken hostage at gunpoint by prisoners. LeSueur and Gutierrez were locked in a cell but Magee was taken to another day room where inmates beat him with mop wringers and stabbed him 38 times. He died there.

Beginning at about 2:00 a.m., Warden Harvey Winans met with inmate Donald Stout who acted as spokesman for a group of prisoners attempting escape. Stout demanded that the inmates be released and that transportation away from the prison be provided. The Warden told Stout that the prisoners would not be released and transportation would not be provided under any circumstances. At about 4:30 a.m. Winans learned that Magee may have been hurt. He ordered the inmates to surrender immediately or an assault would be ordered on the area they occupied. More than 100 peace officers surrounded the prison by then.

Just before 5:00 a.m., LeSueur and Gutierrez were freed and five inmates were disarmed and taken to the administration building: Donald Stout serving 10 to 50 years for armed robbery; Thomas Wayne Crump serving life for first degree murder; Harmon Lee Ellis serving 10 to 50 years for escape; Alan Duning serving 6 to 55 years for armed robbery; and Wilfred L. LeBlanc serving 7½ to 30 years for burglary, auto theft and habitual offender. All five were subsequently, and temporarily, housed in the Sandoval County Jail at Bernalillo, from which facility they also made an unsuccessful escape attempt.

Three other inmates were charged with the murder of Magee. Juan Baca and Angel Munoz were tried and found not guilty. Charges against Antonio Aguilar were dismissed. Inmate Thomas Wayne Crump confessed to killing Magee at one point, but later recanted.

Magee, 33, a native of Ohio, had been a corrections officer for about 14 months at the time of his death. He had previously served as a police officer in Newton Township and Newton Falls, Ohio. He was not married. His salary at the time of his death was $1,189 per month.

Albuquerque *Journal*, August 31, 1981

Department of Corrections, Incident Report, Sept. 4, 1981 & Personnel Record
Résumé, Gerald P. Magee
Santa Fe *New Mexican*, September 14, 1981 & June 23, 1983

ELFEGO MARTÍNEZ

Deputy Sheriff
Taos County, New Mexico

The Albuquerque *Evening Review*, March 6, 1882, carried the following item:

> "Yesterday news was received at Santa Fe that the Pueblo Indians of Taos Pueblo and the peace officers of Taos County had a fight in which Eduyigen Miera was killed and Deputy Sheriff Elfego Martinez was mortally wounded.
>
> "It seems that some of the Pueblos had become drunk and were threatening to kill some Mexicans. They were arrested and put in jail, but by the help of the Pueblos managed to escape. Upon attempting to recapture them the sheriff and his deputies were shot [at] by about fifty armed Pueblos and a fight took place with the above mentioned result."

No other information about this incident has been found.

Frank Richard Prassel, *The Western Peace Officer, A Legacy of Law and Order*, University of Oklahoma Press

ISAAC BENJAMIN MARTINEZ

Acting Chief
San Ildefonso Pueblo Police Department

Residents of the Pojoaque Indian Pueblo reservation, north of Santa Fe, complained to tribal officials that Gerald James Viarrial, 31, was shooting a gun in the area. On Friday, April 8, 1994, the Pojoaque tribal court issued a warrant for Viarrial's arrest after he threatened two tribal members. At about 12:45 on Sunday morning, one of Viarrial's neighbors called the Pojoaque tribal police and reported that Viarrial was outside his house shooting a rifle. The police officer who took the report said he could hear shots being fired in the background. Less than an hour later, Pojoaque officers decided to call the Eight Northern Pueblos SWAT team to take Viarrial into custody on the warrant.

At about 3:30 on that Sunday morning, SWAT team members arrived and scouted the area. Dogs began barking and the scouts backed off. At 3:45 a.m., hoping to take advantage of the element of surprise, they rushed the house. Officers covered the back door and side windows as six officers, led by Chief Isaac Martinez of San Ildefonso Pueblo and Officer Tom Tapia of Tesuque Pueblo, entered the front door. Viarrial opened fire immediately. Martinez was hit with seven 7.62 millimeter bullets. He died at the scene. Officer Tapia was also hit, but saved by his body armor. The officers retreated and regrouped before a tear gas canister was lobbed into the house, forcing the occupants outside. Even then, Viarrial struggled with officers.

"I should have killed all you ... (expletives)," Viarrial said, according to an FBI report. "I know who you are," he said to Officer Tapia. "I'm going to kill you."

At a hearing on April 13, Viarrial's attorney attempted to have the suspect released to family members—his uncle, Jacob Viarrial, served as Pojoaque tribal governor—on his own recognizance. U. S. Magistrate William Deaton declined. The judge said he was persuaded to keep Gerald Viarrial in jail because marijuana, cocaine and alcohol had been found in his bloodstream following the shootings. At the same hearing, FBI Special Agent Greg Parrish testified that found inside Viarrial's house after the shootings were a 7.62 millimeter SKS semiautomatic rifle with 12 rounds left in the clip and 14 spent casings; a .357 caliber Ruger pistol with two spent rounds; and a bulletproof vest. Parrish also testified that Viarrial had numerous previous contacts with tribal police regarding harassment charges, domestic disturbances and threatening his wife.

Viarrial's trial for Martinez's murder took place in September, 1994. It took 12 days. The prosecution maintained that Viarrial waited armed and fully dressed for the officers before the shooting. The defense argued that Viarrial simply reacted to the invasion of his house in the early morning hours. It took the jury a day and a half to agree with the defense. Viarrial was acquitted.

Chief Issac Martinez started his law enforcement career as a patrolman with the Española Police Department. He also served as a Santa Fe County deputy sheriff and as an officer with the Bureau of Indian Affairs police. He was named acting chief of the San Ildefonso Police Department about three weeks before his death. His wife Shirley and a son, Issac Daniel Martinez, 14, survived him as did his parents, Elizabeth and Ben O. Martinez of Chimayó, two brothers, Ron and Robert, and a sister, Vivian (Martinez) Frietz of Las Cruces. He is buried at Nuestra Señora de Dolores Cemetery in Chimayó.

Albuquerque *Journal*, April 11, 13, & 14; September 14 & 30, 1994
Santa Fe *New Mexican*, April 11, 1994

JERRY MARTINEZ

Deputy Sheriff
Rio Arriba County, New Mexico

On Saturday, January 26, 1991, Rio Arriba County Deputy Sheriff Jerry Martinez went to Ricky Abeyta's residence near Chimayó to serve a restraining order. Abeyta had fired three shots at Ignacita Sandoval and Celina Gonzales on the previous Wednesday. The deputy didn't find Abeyta at home and departed before 4:00 p.m. Abeyta returned home soon after Martinez left. According to witnesses, he said, "*¡Con esto pagan!*" (With this I pay you back!) Then he began shooting the people there with a rifle. He killed five people immediately: three women, a man and a five-month-old baby.

Deputy Martinez returned to the scene, apparently as the initial shooting ended. Abeyta confronted the officer at gunpoint, and, according to witnesses, he shot the deputy twice in the head at close range. Martinez's body was found later beside his patrol car.

Abeyta also subsequently killed State Police Officer Glen Huber (page 145).

Other officers arrived as Abeyta managed to escape. Roadblocks were established and scores of officers took up the search for the fugitive. A helicopter rigged with night vision equipment was brought in. The fugitive evaded capture throughout the night and well into the next day. Then, at about 9:30 p.m. on Sunday evening, State Police officers received word that Abeyta, along with some of his family members, were at the District V State Police office in Albuquerque. The killer wished to surrender. Captain James O. Jennings, Sgt. Gary Smith and Officer Danny Lichtenberger took Abeyta into custody. Abeyta expressed concern that if he continued to run and hide, he would not be taken alive by police officers when they found him. He asked arresting officers not to hurt him, and said he did not want to be handcuffed. Captain Jennings told him that he would not be hurt, but that he *would* be cuffed. He was taken to Santa Fe without incident.

Tried for his crimes in November 1991, Ricky Abeyta was convicted on four counts of first-degree murder, two counts of second-degree murder and one count of involuntary manslaughter. Combined, and to be served consecutively, Abeyta's sentences totaled 146 years.

Jerry Martinez was born in Chimayó and graduated from Española High School. He studied criminology at San Francisco Community College and the College of Santa Fe. He served as a paratrooper with the U. S. Army. He planned to run for Rio Arriba County Sheriff in 1992. Deputy Martinez was survived by his wife, Lisa, and two children, Nick, 5, and Destiny, a two-week old baby; his parents, Roman and Molly Martinez; and a brother, Rocky.

Albuquerque *Journal*, January 27 & 28, 1991

Deputy Chief James O. Jennings, New Mexico State Police, conversations, summer 1995

New Mexico Department of Corrections Records

The Roadrunner (New Mexico State Police Association, Vol. 3, No. 2, Summer, 1992)

JUAN MARTÍNEZ*

Constable
Lincoln County, New Mexico

Sam, Mart, Merritt, Tom, John and Ben were the Horrell brothers of near Lampasas in central Texas.** Some of their neighbors called them "fun-loving cowboys" who regularly shot up the town but they were also the leading members of a group "...whose occupation was the branding, killing and skinning of other people's cattle." On March 14, 1873, in the Matador Saloon in Lampasas, Tom, Mart and Merritt, along with their brother-in-law, Bill Bowen and several other outlaws were confronted by Captain Thomas Williams of the Texas State Police who sought to arrest Bowen. In the gunfight that followed, four State Policemen, including Williams, were killed. Mart Horrell and three other men were later arrested and housed in the jail at Georgetown, Texas, between Austin and Waco. On the night of May 2, 1873 the remaining Horrell brothers, and about 30 other riders, stormed the jail and freed Mart and his friends. After that, the brothers rounded up their cattle, sold them and headed northwest to New Mexico.

The Horrell bunch arrived in Lincoln County in the fall of 1873. They bought a homestead/ranch and settled on the Rio Ruidoso not far from the present day village of Hondo. Other relatives and hangers-on also settled in the area. The county seat at Lincoln was the local hub of activity.

On December 1, Ben Horrell, along with Dave Warner and former Lincoln County Sheriff Jack Gylam rode into the town of Lincoln. Some said they "undertook to run the town." Others said they simply wanted to carouse in the saloons and brothels. Whatever the reason, they were armed and soon enough they were drunk and shooting their guns. Constable Juan Martínez demanded that they surrender their weapons, and they did. It wasn't long, though, before Horrell, Warner and Gylam were again armed and shooting up a brothel. Constable Martínez and four members of the police guard, accompanied by an interpreter, again confronted the miscreants. As the interpreter began to explain the situation to Horrell and his friends, Dave Warner—who had a long-standing grudge against Juan Martínez—suddenly pulled his pistol and shot the constable, killing him instantly. Warner was killed on the spot by return fire and Horrell and Gylam fled, only to be chased down and also killed by the police guard.

The Horrells considered the death of brother Ben as murder, and retaliation was swift. A few days after the gunfight in Lincoln, two prominent Hispanic citizens were found murdered on the Horrell ranch. Efforts by Sheriff Alexander Hamilton "Ham" Mills and a posse to arrest the Horrells failed when they discovered that the Texans had "forted up" in their house on the Rio Ruidoso. On December 20, the Horrells returned to Lincoln and shot-up a wedding *baile*, killing four Hispanic men and wounding one woman. Again, efforts to capture the Horrells were unsuccessful, and other clashes between the Texans and Hispanic citizens occurred. Toward the end of January, 1874, a Horrell outlaw associate, Edward "Little" Hart, murdered Deputy Sheriff Joseph Haskins for no reason other than that Haskins was married to an Hispanic woman.

The Horrells, no longer welcome in southeastern New Mexico, began a retreat in early 1874, heading back to Texas. About 15 miles west of Roswell, they encountered five Hispanic freighters and killed all of them. Estimates are that a total of more than a dozen Hispanic citizens were killed by the gang during the course of the so-called Horrell War of 1873-74.

But Texans were no longer hospitable to the clan, either. Citizens of Lampasas took pot shots at them when they returned to town, but none of the Horrells were killed. By 1876, the Horrell brothers were engaged in a feud with cattleman/gunman John Pinkney Calhoun "Pink" Higgins.*** Higgins shot Merritt Horrell to death in the Matador Saloon that year. In 1878, Mart and Tom Horrell were arrested for robbing and killing merchant J. F. Vaughn at a place called Rock School House on Hog Creek in Bosque County. A mob of masked citizens, estimated at 100 strong, stormed the jail at Meridian and killed both outlaws in their cell on December 15, 1878. Only Sam, the oldest of the brothers, managed to avoid a violent death.

History records nothing of a personal nature about Constable Juan Martínez. One writer refers to his "hardihood" in taking the initiative to disarm the drunken gunmen. Given the character of the times, there is no question that he showed considerable devotion to duty.

* One source indicates that the Constable's name was Martín.

** John Horrell was killed in a gunfight in Las Cruces, New Mexico, before the events described here. The family name is also spelled *Harrell* or *Harrold*, depending on the source.

*** A really bad idea on the part of the Horrells. Pink Higgins became one of the most feared gunmen in Texas.

Yolanda Cline, Fort Sumner, New Mexico, correspondence, August 21, 1990
Maurice Fulton, *History of the Lincoln County War*, University of Arizona Press

Lily Klasner, *My Girlhood Among Outlaws*, The University of Arizona Press

Cindy Martinez, Lincoln County Heritage Trust, correspondence, September 11, 1995

Frederick Nolan, *Bad Blood, The Life and Times of the Horrell Brothers*, Barbed Wire Press

P. J. Rasch, "The Horrell War," *New Mexico Historical Review*, July, 1956

C. L. Sonnichsen, "Hot Heads and Hair Triggers, The Horrell-Higgins Feud," *I'll Die Before I'll Run, the Story of the Great Feuds of Texas*, University of Nebraska Press

Dan L. Thrapp, *Encyclopedia of Frontier Biography*, University of Nebraska Press

Robert M. Utley, *High Noon in Lincoln, Violence on the Western Frontier*, University of New Mexico Press

Walter Prescott Webb, *The Texas Rangers, A Century of Frontier Defense*, University of Texas Press

John P. Wilson, *Merchants Guns & Money, The Story of Lincoln County and Its Wars*, Museum of New Mexico Press

(Special thanks to Coleen Salazar of the Lincoln County Heritage Trust.)

LOUIS McCAMANT

Special Officer
Atchison, Topeka & Santa Fe Railroad Police

On April 25, 1924, Railroad Special Police Officer Louis McCamant boarded an eastbound freight train for the ride from Gallup to Belen. At the coal stop near Wall, New Mexico, in Valencia County, three men asked a conductor if they could ride. He told them they could not; that a Special Officer was aboard who would not allow it. As the train began moving, the three illegally boarded a coal car and Officer McCamant saw them do it. As he approached them along the tops of the cars, one of the men threw a large iron bolt with great force. It struck the officer in the face causing him to fall off the moving train, and under it. The entire train ran over him, mangling his body and cutting it into two pieces.

An initial coroner's inquest returned a verdict of accidental death, but further investigation by J. R. Froman, chief of special officers, located the bolt at a point near where McCamant was killed. The shape of the bolt was consistent with injuries to McCamant's face; injuries not likely caused by his fall or contact with the train's wheels or undercarriage.

J. L. Berry of Sweetwater, Texas, James C. Carlton of Brookline, Arkansas, and John C. Edwards of Knoxville, Mississippi were arrested at Los Lunas and charged with murder. Berry claimed that he'd been working at McCarty and didn't know the other two men; that he only met them when he boarded the train. Charges against him were subsequently dropped. Carlton and Edwards were indicted for murder.

Louis McCamant, 24, was the son of former McKinley County Sheriff J. H. McCamant and he'd lived in Gallup for some years. Only a few weeks before his son's death, the elder McCamant's ranch house near Thoreau had burned to the ground.

Gallup *Independent*, April 30 & May 7 & September 12, 1924
Cpl. Sam Gomez, Gallup Police Department, Correspondence, January 31, 1990

J. A. McCLURE

Special Agent
Atchison, Topeka & Santa Fe Railroad Police

A railroad line known as the Belen Cut-off opened in the early 1900s. One unforeseen result of the new line was that it offered thieves an opportunity to rob freight cars as slow-moving trains crawled up the steep grade in the Abo Pass between Belen and Mountainair, New Mexico. On Wednesday, January 25, 1911, two railroad officers were sent to investigate the thefts. They boarded an eastbound train at Belen. One agent got off at a flag stop to send a telegram before they reached the Abo Pass and Agent J. A. McClure continued on alone. He was never seen alive again.

When McClure failed to return, the chief of the railroad police, Ben Williams, took charge of the investigation. Immediately suspected in the disappearance was a homesteader named F. B. Howe and his two sons, Robert and Guy, who lived near the railroad at Abo. They were leading members of a loosely organized group known as the Abo Pass Gang.

On Friday, January 27, a posse of officers headed by Billy Olds, a railroad special agent, and Lt. John Collier of the New Mexico Mounted Police, reached Abo to conduct a thorough search for McClure. The search was futile the first day, but on the afternoon of the second day, Agent McClure's body was found, head down, in a deep well on property belonging to F. B. Howe. Also found close by were several large caches of goods stolen from railroad cars.

Investigation revealed that McClure had been shot from ambush. He had apparently discovered that thieves were stealing corn from a boxcar, and by following a trail of kernels left by a leaking grain bag, he located the outlaw camp. As he neared it, the thieves opened fire, hitting the officer in the wrist, arm and stomach. After he had fallen, McClure was shot a fourth time, in the top of the head, the bullet exiting at his chin.

By Sunday, several posses were in pursuit of Howe and his sons, and the Santa Fe Railroad offered a $500 reward for arrest and conviction. Ben Williams believed that the outlaws would head for Mexico, and he was right.

The Howes boarded a southbound freight train and rode all the way to Fort Hancock, Texas, about 50 miles south of El Paso. When they attempted to cross into Mexico, they were stopped by Thomas L. O'Connor, a United States Customs Guard, and M. R. Hemley, a Justice of the Peace. The outlaws opened fire at once and O'Connor fell, mortally wounded, and Hemly received a bullet wound to the arm. The Howes stole O'Connor's gun and ammunition before they fled east, toward Sierra Blanca, Texas. (Why they did not continue into Mexico is not known.)

At that point, Texas Rangers joined with New Mexico lawmen in pursuit of the killers. At about 9:00 p.m. on Tuesday, January 31, the posse overtook the Howes. A gunfight erupted immediately and Robert Howe, the younger of the brothers, was wounded in the leg. His older brother and father abandoned him and fled into a thicket, firing as they ran. Officers surrounded the thicket and prepared to stand siege until the next morning.

In only an hour, though, the remaining Howes, father and son, emerged from the brush, guns in hand, and firing as they ran toward the law officers. Officers returned fire and both outlaws fell, shot dead. They were buried at Fort Hancock, Texas.

J. A. McClure was about 40 at the time of his death. He'd been employed by the railroad for many years serving previously as a conductor, brakeman. He was survived by a wife and child who resided in Texas.

Albuquerque *Morning Journal*, January 28, 29, 30, 31, 1911
Don Bullis, *Duels, Gunfights & Shootouts: Wild Tales from the Land of Enchantment*, Rio Grande Books
"The Abo Pass Gang," by Randy Dunson
Dallas *Morning News*, January 31, 1911
Robert Howe, Letter to his sister, January 31, 1911 (Thanks to Frank C. Wimberly)

JAMES McGRANE JR.

Deputy
Bernalillo County, New Mexico, Sheriff's Department

Just after midnight, in the early morning hours of Wednesday, March 22, 2006, Bernalillo County Deputy Sheriff Jim McGrane stopped a 1991 Dodge pickup truck near the intersection of New Mexico Routes 333 and 337 in the village of Tijeras, east of Albuquerque. Deputy McGrane did not know who was driving the truck in what had all appearances of a routine traffic stop. Within seconds, literally, he was dead of a gunshot wound to the head.

A nearby resident heard two shots and reported seeing the officer lying in the road. It was also reported that the truck sped south into the canyon. Officers responded to the scene very quickly, but there was no help for the fatally wounded officer. Ownership of the pickup was soon traced to a suspect named Michael Paul Astorga, 31, an ex-convict who had spent time in prison for possession of heroin, weapons violations, vandalism and traffic violations. He was also the subject of an outstanding warrant for first degree murder. Astorga's truck was located at a residence near the village of Escobosa in the Manzano Mountains, but no one was present. Literally hundreds of officers fanned out across Albuquerque, Bernalillo County, and surrounding communities. It appeared that Astorga had disappeared. By March 23, a reward of $50,000 was being offered for the information leading to Astorga's arrest.

Early efforts to locate the suspect were unsuccessful, but by Sunday, April 2, investigators had developed solid information that Astorga was hiding out in Juarez, Chihuahua, Mexico. Information was passed along to Mexican authorities and they arrested Astorga about four hours later. They escorted him to the Mexico/United States border where American authorities took custody of him, and returned him to New Mexico.

As this book goes to press in late 2009, Astorga remains confined in the Maximum Security wing of the New Mexico State Penitentiary in Santa Fe. A trial date had not been set.

James McGrane Jr., 38, was raised in Albuquerque and graduated from Hope Christian School. He joined the New Mexico State Police in 1996, but left the department after six months to work for the U. S. Postal Service, where his father was employed. He joined the Bernalillo County Sheriff's Department in December 2002 and requested assignment to the East Mountain Substation. He is said to have enjoyed the rural atmosphere. He was survived by his wife Connie, parents James and Rita McGrane, and sister Ida.

Albuquerque *Journal*, April 4, 2006
Albuquerque *Tribune*, March 23, 2006; September 10, 2007
News accounts abundant

MICHAEL ROBERT "BOB" McGUIRE

City Marshal
Albuquerque, New Mexico

On Saturday night, November 20th, 1886, Marshal Bob McGuire and his deputy, E. D. Henry, went to Martíneztown, northeast of Albuquerque's new town, to arrest outlaws, John "Kid" Johnson and Charlie Ross. The two were members of a gang of robbers and rustlers and the officers held arrest warrants for both.

After searching around for a while, McGuire and Henry found the outlaws holed up with two young women in a one-room adobe house, eating supper. One of the women opened the door and stepped out for a pitcher of water as McGuire and Henry tried to step in and all three fell down in a confused heap. The outlaws quickly realized what had happen, grabbed their guns and opened fire. The lights went out as the officers returned fire and the women took cover under the bed. McGuire was hit in the chest, abdomen and right arm. Deputy Henry was hit twice in the chest and once in the right leg. When a lamp was lit and the smoke cleared, Henry lay dead on the floor. Marshal McGuire was down, but alive. The outlaws were gone.

Charlie Ross was hit, too. One bullet struck his shoulder and lodged against his shoulder blade and another one grazed his head. A Santa Fe Railroad detective (and former Albuquerque city police officer) Carl Holton and Police Officer Pete Isherwood tracked Ross to an area called Hell's half-acre, where they arrested the killer.

As a result of the Martíneztown gunfight, the Albuquerque Morning *Journal* for November 23, 1886 reported thus:

> The city council are going to give the policemen latitude hereafter in the use of firearms in making arrests. They have had orders never to use their arms except in case of being fired on. Hereafter any criminal may be shot by the police if he makes a show of his arms or attempts to use them.

Marshal McGuire died of his wounds on November 26.

Charlie Ross recovered from his wounds. On January 3, 1887, he escaped from the Bernalillo County jail. One source says Ross' girlfriend slipped him a key; another that Ross and jail inmate Peter Trinkaus of Gallup, a convicted murderer, bribed a guard. Ross left a note addressed to the editor of the Albuquerque *Daily Democrat*:

County Hotel, January 3, 1887, to Mr. Roberts of the Democrat: Please say in your paper that hearing there is a reward offered for my partner, Johnson, that I have gone to find him. Tell the boys not to feel uneasy about my absence, and as the weather is such that they might take cold, it may be better for their health to stay at home. We'll turn up in time, and don't you forget it.

/S/ C. Henry Ross, with his hair parted in the middle.

Ross was recaptured on January 27 after an attempted train robbery west of Grants and returned to jail in Albuquerque. He escaped again in July 1887, and was never recaptured.

Kid Johnson, described as "...full of cowboy swagger, wears a Chihuahua hat and wears his pants in his boots," received wounds to the neck and foot in the gunfight. He got to his horse and left town, crossing the Rio Grande near Isleta. At the Rio Puerco he joined up with an ox train and train's captain doctored his foot until he was able to put a boot on and continue his flight. Johnson was later arrested in El Paso on charges of killing the two Albuquerque officers. It was decided that not enough evidence against him existed to justify trial on those charges, and they were dropped. Never tried for the murder of the two officers, Ross and Johnson both lived to old age.

Robert McGuire was the second Albuquerque City Marshal. Local sources at the time said his death was "...a loss to the town of an honest, effective, and fearless officer and respected citizen." Albuquerque's flags were flown at half-staff to honor Marshal McGuire and Deputy Henry. The Marshal's brother took his body back to his native Oswego, New York, for burial.

Henry, a native of Henry County, Ohio, was buried in Albuquerque.

Albuquerque *Morning Journal*, Nov. 23 & 27, 1886
Howard Bryan, "Off the Beaten Path," Albuquerque *Tribune*, Nov. 20, 1961
Howard Bryan, *Albuquerque Remembered*, University of New Mexico Press
Marc Simmons, *Albuquerque, A Narrative History*, University of New Mexico Press

KENNETH SHAWN McWETHY

Officer
Albuquerque, New Mexico, Police Department

Officer Shawn McWethy, 23, took note of a suspicious looking man near the intersection of South Broadway and Pacific Avenue in Albuquerque. The date was Saturday, February 1, 1986. The time was about 4:15 in the afternoon. Officer McWethy lost sight of the man and stopped his police car near a trash-littered alley. He called the dispatcher and gave his location. He had no way of knowing that an auto parts store nearby had been robbed only moments before. The crime had not yet been reported.

A white over blue Ford or Mercury rolled to a stop behind the police car. A man walked quickly to the driver's side of the police unit. He produced a .22 automatic pistol and opened fire. Five bullets hit the officer's body armor but in a reflex action McWethy raised his arm as if to ward off the shots and four other bullets hit his body between his armpit and the top of the bulletproof vest. One of them severed his aorta. McWethy was able to grab his police radio microphone and utter just two words: "I'm shot!"

An hour later the young officer lay dead at the University of New Mexico Hospital.

Dozens of officers responded to the scene and a massive search was undertaken for the white over blue car. Roadblocks were established on main roads in and out of Albuquerque. Rewards totaling $5,000 were offered for information leading to the arrest and indictment of the killer. On Wednesday night, February 5, Albuquerque Police Department officers arrested Vincent Paul Candelaria, 33, at the home of his ex-wife in Albuquerque's South Valley. He was booked on suspicion of murder.

Candelaria had an arrest record going back 19 years to the time he was arrested for burglary at the age of 14. By 1980 he was serving a 70 to 225 year sentence in the New Mexico Penitentiary for armed robbery. In one of his series of robberies, he had exchanged gunshots with police officers after holding up a supermarket. During the 1980 prison riot he served as a negotiator between inmates and prison officials, and because of that, after Toney Anaya became governor in 1983, Anaya reduced Candelaria's minimum sentence. Candelaria was paroled in 1985.

Candelaria was tried in 1988 and again 1989 for killing Shawn McWethy, but both trials resulted in hung juries. Finally, in November 1989, he pleaded no-contest to charges of armed robbery, conspiracy to commit armed robbery, and being an habitual offender. Judge H. Richard Blackhurst sentenced Candelaria to 21 years for the armed robbery which he allowed to run concurrently with the 65 to 215 year sentence he was already serving; he imposed three years for conspiracy, which he suspended; then he added eight years under the habitual offender statute. The net result of the sentences was an additional four and one half years in prison. Candelaria could be eligible for parole as early as the year 2000. None of these sentences had anything to do with the death of Officer Shawn McWethy.

Candelaria died of cancer in Salinas Valley State Correctional Facility in California in July 2002. He was serving 70 to 220 years for a series of armed robberies.

Officer McWethy's parents, Kenneth and Helen McWethy, and brothers Matthew, Joseph, and Patrick survived him. His father, a former Albuquerque Police officer, served as head of the U. S. Secret Service office in Albuquerque at the time of his son's death. The elder McWethy later served as Bernalillo County undersheriff. Shawn's brother, Matthew, completed the Albuquerque Police Academy in February 1987. The Albuquerque Police Valley Substation is named for Kenneth Shawn McWethy.

Albuquerque *Journal*, February 2, 3, 4, 5, 6 & 7, 1986; February 28, 1987; November 7, 1989; July 23, 2002
Albuquerque Police Department

WILLIAM MEADOR

Deputy Sheriff
Torrance County, New Mexico

Jack Layman's arrest record began in California where he was arrested for armed robbery three times in the late 1920s. He returned to New Mexico and was soon arrested and convicted of robbing the mayor of Estancia in Torrance County. Freed from prison in the spring of 1933, he took up residence with his mother in Albuquerque. On the evening of Thursday, July 27, 1933, he and two other men went to Old Albuquerque where they found a bootlegger and got drunk. Deputy sheriff Frank Mann received a disturbing the peace report and when he tried to arrest Layman and his friends, Layman slashed at the officer with a knife but only managed to cut Mann's shirt. Mann cracked his assailant on the skull with his gun butt, but Layman managed to escape while the deputy arrested the other two men.

Officers soon found out who Layman was, and they learned that his mother lived on south Edith Street. They also learned that his brother-in-law, Charles Spencer, owned two residences in Mountainair, Torrance County. When Layman was not found in Albuquerque, Bernalillo County Sheriff Felipe Zamora and Deputy Mann, joined by Torrance County Sheriff Rex Meador, and his son Billy, who also served as a deputy sheriff, and other deputies, drove to Mountainair.

On Friday evening, after dark, Sheriff Meador, Billy Meador and Torrance County deputy Tom Kane went to the residence occupied by Spencer and his family while the other officers went to the second residence owned by Spencer. Sheriff Meador described what happened next.

"As we approached the house, Charlie Spencer came out and asked what we were after. I told him we wanted to search his house for a man we had reason to believe was there. Spencer refused on the ground we needed a search warrant, and after 20 minutes argument, Tom Kane was sent back to get such a warrant."

After Kane left, Spencer invited the Meadors inside. As they approached the house, they met Johnny Layman, Jack's 21 year old younger brother. After a short delay, the front door was opened and they began to enter the house, Johnny Layman going in first, followed by Spencer, then the sheriff, and finally Billy Meador. Just as the sheriff got inside, the lights went out. Rex Meador flicked on his flashlight and spotted Jack Layman coming toward him with a gun in his hand.

"Dad! We've been trapped!" Billy Meador shouted.

Johnny Layman and Charlie Spencer got between Jack Layman and the sheriff and Jack headed for the back door. Billy Meador saw what was happening and ran from the front door and around the house in time to meet Jack Layman as he exited the back door.

"Layman fired first, and immediately afterwards my boy returned the fire. As he fell to the ground he emptied his gun at the fleeing fugitive," Sheriff Meador said.

Charlie Spencer placed himself between the sheriff and the back door which prevented Rex Meador from firing at Jack Layman as he fled. One of the deputies who had gone to Spencer's other house, however, observed the gunfight between Billy Meador and Jack Layman, and he fired at the fleeing fugitive. One of the deputy's bullets hit Layman in the leg but he none the less made good his escape.*

Officers rushed Billy Meador to an Albuquerque hospital while Sheriffs Rex Meador and Felipe Zamora, and Deputy Frank Mann, coordinated a search for Jack Layman. In short order more than 100 officers began combing the scrub pine country south of Mountainair, and by Saturday afternoon more than 200 officers were involved, along with bloodhounds from the state prison.**

Billy Meador died at 9:16 p.m. on Saturday. Sheriff Meador stepped from his son's hospital room and called his deputy, Wallace Crawford, in Mountainair. "The boy is dead," he said. "Get that __!"

But that wasn't to be. The search intensified on Sunday and Monday, but Jack Layman couldn't be found. Officers believed at one point that the fugitive had stolen a horse hobbled nearby and made good his escape on horseback. Others suspected that he had help and fled the area in an automobile. Layman's mother thought her son would be found dead in the brush. Sheriff Meador called off the manhunt in the Mountainair area on Tuesday evening, August first. Surveillance was maintained at Layman's mother's house in Albuquerque.

On Friday evening, August fourth, exactly one week after he shot Billy Meador, Jack Layman's flight ended. Bernalillo County Sheriff Felipe Zamora, Deputy Frank Mann and two other deputies stopped a car operated by A. N. "Dad" Gragg, an Old Albuquerque bootlegger, on Fourth Street, north of Albuquerque. As officers lifted the cover on the luggage compartment, Layman fired a shot from a .32-20 revolver, which struck no one. Sheriff Zamora immediately tossed a tear gas bomb into the compartment. He also fired a single shot which struck Layman in the finger. Layman surrendered without further ado.

Jack and Johnny Layman, and Charles Spencer were all charged with first degree murder in the death of Billy Meador. At a trial held in Las Cruces in November 1933, Jack Layman was convicted of second degree murder and sentenced to 75 years in prison. Johnny Layman and Charles Spencer were acquitted. Jack's conviction was overturned by the New Mexico Supreme Court, however, and he was retried in August 1935. His second trial resulted in a conviction for manslaughter. Jack was sentenced to ten years in prison.

Billy Meador, 21, was survived his mother and a sister, Geraldine, 17, in addition to his father. His funeral at Estancia was described as one of the largest in Torrance County history.***

* Jack Layman's mother later claimed that young Meador was shot inside the house, by accident, by one of the officers at the scene, and not by her son, who, she said, was not armed. That theory was largely disproved by the fact that Billy Meador was shot outside the house and Sheriff Meador never fired a shot. The second deputy who did fire at Jack Layman aimed his shots away from the house.

** A request for bloodhounds was initially refused because state officials claimed they had no money to pay to transport the dogs, and their handlers, to the Mountainair area. Friends of the Meador family pledged the necessary funds and the dogs arrived on Saturday evening, too late to do any good.

*** Billy Meador was the third New Mexico sheriff's deputy to be killed in the line of duty during July 1933. Lincoln County Deputy Tom Jones (page 159) and Chaves County Deputy Barney Leonard (page 185) were the other two.

Albuquerque *Journal*, July 28, 30, 31; August 2, 3, 5, 6, 7, 8; November 30, 1933
Amarillo *Globe*, July 31, 1933
Clovis *Evening News-Journal*, August 30, 1935

EMILIO MESTAS

Sergeant
Clayton, New Mexico, Police Department

At about 7:30 on Wednesday evening, July 18, 1973, an altercation erupted at the A-1 Texaco gas station on south First Street in Clayton, New Mexico. Local youths and station owner Leland Jacobs, a city councilman, engaged in a fistfight after the youths directed abusive language toward Mrs. Jacobs. Punches were thrown and Councilman Jacobs, somewhat "roughed up," filed assault and battery charges against six young men in a red and white Chevrolet.

Later that evening, Clayton police officers attempted to serve the warrants at an address on Polk Street on the west side of town, only to be met with a barrage of rocks and bottles from the 35 to 40 youths hanging around the house. The officers retreated without making any arrests. At about 10:00 p.m., Clayton Mayor Ed Heringa went to the house and tried to talk to the youths and received nothing but insults and threats. The Mayor then decided to call in all off duty city police officers—including Sgt. Emilio Mestas—and to request assistance from the New Mexico State Police and the Union County Sheriff's Office.

Officials assigned eleven State Policemen under the supervision of Sgt. Bill Holder of Springer. The officers began arriving before midnight. Sgt. Holder reported everything quiet at that time, but his officers, along with city police and deputy sheriffs continued to patrol the streets. Several carloads of local youths were also observed cruising the streets of Clayton.

Sometime after midnight, Holder and State Police Officer Frank Rice stopped a red and white Chevrolet matching the description of the vehicle involved in the disturbance at the A-1 Texaco. As the officers stepped out of the police car, the Chevrolet sped away at a high rate of speed. Holder, Rice and other officers took up pursuit as the car fled to the house on Polk Street. Again officers were bombarded with rocks and bottles when they attempted to arrest the occupants of the fugitive vehicle. All police officers in town then assembled at the Polk Street location. As officers began exiting their vehicles to move in on the suspects, shots were fired. One hit Sgt. Mestas in the right side of the head, near the temple; one broke the spotlight on a police vehicle and another hit the door of a cattle inspector's car.

Police officers did not return gunfire. Holder and Rice immediately loaded Officer Mestas into a State Police car and took him to the hospital in Clayton. He was later transferred to Northwest Texas Hospital in Amarillo where he died on the operating table just before 6:00 a.m. on Thursday, July 19, 1973.

More State Police officers were ordered to Clayton. Police Roadblocks surrounded the town. Officers at the house on Polk Street arrested the six subjects wanted on the original warrant. They found a handgun, marijuana and pills under the seat of the red and white Chevrolet. Later on Thursday morning they arrested the primary suspect in the shooting, Lawrence Eugene "Larry" Vigil, son of the Clayton city clerk. He was charged with first-degree murder.

Vigil was indicted by the grand jury on August 6, 1973 and his trial date was set for early December. A series of motions and a question about the constitutionality of the New Mexico murder statute resulted in delays, and the venue was changed from Clayton and Union County to Ratón and Colfax County. Finally, on June 12, 1974, a Ratón jury found Vigil guilty of voluntary manslaughter. At the killer's sentencing, Judge Santiago Campos said this: "I remember the testimony very vividly in this case. I remember that the jury itself chose to extend all the leniency and all the consideration which I think is justifiable." Vigil was sentenced to two to ten years in prison. Since he'd spent 142 days in jail awaiting trial, he was eligible for parole after serving only eight months.

Officer Emilio Mestas, 55, was a 13 year veteran of the Clayton Police Department. A local resident remembered him this way:

> His purpose in dealing with teenagers was not necessarily to enforce the law by the book, or to create a police record, but rather to teach teenagers some small degree of responsibility for their actions. As a teenager, my encounters with Emilio were numerous, and I considered him to be fair yet firm. He would see that kids in our town got home safely. He cared about the local kids, and most of their families. A word from Emilio to a youngster's father brought quick results."

So many folks attended the officer's funeral that loudspeakers had to be installed outside because St. Francis Xavier Catholic Church was filled to overflowing. The caravan of cars to the cemetery was the longest in Clayton history.

A wife, Maxine, and nine children: Charles, 19, Loretta, 16, Tammy, 14, Eileen, 12, David, 10, Michelle, 8, of Clayton, and Angela, Arthur and Louis of Roswell, survived Emilio Mestas.

Albuquerque *Journal*, July 20, 1973

Union County *Leader*, July 25, August 1, 8 & 15, October 24, December 5, 1973;
   May 29, June 5, 12 & 19, July 10, 1974

James E. Atkins, Chief, Clayton Police Dept., correspondence, January 4, 1989

Nick Payton, Editor and Publisher, Union County *Leader*, correspondence, January
   4, 1996

LEWIS H. MICKEY

Special Officer
Atchinson, Topeka & Santa Fe Railroad Police

Santa Fe Railroad authorities at Clovis had been notified to be on the lookout for Leslie Starr, 16, suspected of robbing a store at Mountainair. At about 2:00 a.m. on Saturday morning, March 21, 1925, Special Officer Lewis Mickey found Starr hiding in the ice compartment of a refrigerated car which had just arrived at the Clovis rail yard from Mountainair. Mickey arrested the boy and began searching him. He missed a .32 caliber automatic pistol Starr had strapped around his neck. As the officer stooped to search the youth's lower body, Starr pulled the gun and fired six times, several bullets passing through Mickey's body. Mickey pulled his own gun after he fell. His third shot hit Starr with telling effect. The two were found on top of the car, lying about ten feet apart, Starr dead and Mickey dying.

The officer died about three hours later.

Leslie Starr was from Curry County. His parents lived about twenty miles south of Clovis.

Lewis H. Mickey and his family had lived in Clovis for some years at the time of his death. A wife and two small children survived him. The Clovis Masonic Lodge conducted his funeral.

Albuquerque *Morning Journal*, March 22, 1925
Clovis *News-Journal*, February 22, 1981
Unidentified Clovis newspaper clipping, March 25, 1925

CHRISTOPHER MIRABAL

Patrolman
New Mexico State Police

Officer Christopher Mirabal, 35, was en route to his Alamogordo home on the evening of June 13, 2007, just before seven o'clock. Very soon after he called the dispatcher to say that he was going off duty, his State Police motorcycle hit the right curb of North Scenic Avenue, and then skidded and crashed into a parked semi trailer. He was only a few blocks from his home. He was pronounced dead less than an hour later at a local hospital.

State Police Chief Faron Segotta said, "We believe he saw something that was obvious or flagrant that he chose to take some type of enforcement action against. The distance that he probably observed the violation to the point where he lost control is probably a quarter of a mile. He may not have had time to radio in."

Officer Mirabal, a native of Alamogordo and a nine year veteran of the State Police, was assigned to the motorcycle unit in 2004. He was survived by his wife, Nichole, a daughter Kennedie, 9, and a son Nathan, 4. Governor Bill Richardson ordered the state's flags lowered to half staff in honor of Officer Mirabal.

Albuquerque *Journal*, June 15 & 16, 2007
Arthur Ortiz, Director, New Mexico Law Enforcement Academy, September 4, 2009

LARRY BRYAN MITCHELL

Officer
Gallup, New Mexico, Police Department

A 911 operator in Gallup, New Mexico, received a hang-up call at about 10:40 on the evening of May 29, 2001. A follow-up phone call was answered by the daughter of Robert Kiro. She told the dispatcher that her father and his girlfriend, her mother, were fighting. When responding officers arrived at Kiro's mobile home, they learned that the girlfriend and the couple's three children had fled the scene. Kiro remained inside, firing random shots from a 9-millimeter pistol.

Kiro, 34, continued firing sporadically throughout the night. His girlfriend reported that he had been drinking and taking crack cocaine. Family and friends made several efforts to talk Kiro into surrendering, but he consistently refused.

"He demanded that we come in and get him," one officer at the scene said.

At about 6:00 a.m. on May 30, as Kiro continued to fire his gun, the decision was made to end the standoff by removing him from the mobile home. Officers first lobbed teargas canisters into the home and then six SWAT officers entered the structure. Two officers, Larry Mitchell and Michael Mitchell (who were not related), turned to the left inside the door while other officers turned to the right. Kiro was hiding in a bedroom to the left, and he opened fire. One of his bullets struck Larry Mitchell under his left armpit, less than one inch from the body armor that might have saved his life.

Larry Mitchell fell to the floor and Michael Mitchell began dragging him away from the line of fire when Kiro fired again, striking Michael in the shoulder. Michael Mitchell avoided serious injury when his body armor stopped the bullet. He succeeded in pulling Larry Mitchell out of the mobile home. Larry Mitchell was pronounced dead at a Gallup hospital a short time later. Michael Mitchell was treated for a bruise on his shoulder and released.

Kiro remained inside the mobile home until later in the morning when he voluntarily surrendered. He was charged with an open count of murder, plus three counts of attempted murder, seven counts of aggravated assault on a police officer, aggravated assault on a household member and child abuse. In early June, Robert Kiro was indicted on those charges, plus shooting at an occupied building. After more than three years of procedural delays—during which Kiro escaped from jail and was recaptured—he entered an Alford plea in which he acknowledged that he would accept the consequences of a guilty plea without actually admitting that he killed Officer Mitchell. In August 2004, Kiro was sentenced to 34 years in prison.

Larry Bryan Mitchell was 23 years old at the time of his death. His wife, Erica, and son, Dillon, 2, survived him. District Attorney Karl Gillson said, "He was a young, bright, diligent law enforcement officer. He had a professionalism and a vigor for his work. He will be missed in so many ways."

Albuquerque *Journal*, May 31; June 1, 3, 10; November 18, 2001; December 6, 2002; July 5, 2003; August 16 & 17, 2004
Albuquerque *Tribune*, May 31; June 4, 2001

BARNEY D. MONTOYA

Sergeant
Gallup, New Mexico, Police Department

Barney Montoya was a native of Gallup, New Mexico, and joined the city police department in 1959. He began as a jailer before he moved to patrol. While serving as a field officer, he and another officer responded to a "man with a gun" call. The suspect began firing at the police car as the officers arrived, and Officer Montoya was severely wounded in the leg, but managed to return fire, as did the other officer. The offender was killed at the scene. Officer Montoya suffered considerable pain and was obliged to take a leave of absence afterwards.

Dedicated to police service, he returned to work as uniformed desk sergeant.

On Saturday evening, September 4, 1977, Sgt. Montoya remained on duty after his normal shift ended so that he might assist Officer Alfredo Martinez in booking an unruly drunk. That task completed, Sgt. Montoya left the police station en route to his home. Moments later the vehicle he was driving was struck broadside by a drunk driver who ran a clearly posted stop sign. He died of multiple injuries the following morning at McKinley General Hospital.

The driver of the other car, Jerome Francis Reed, was convicted of vehicular homicide in September of 1978.

Sgt. Scott Montoya, Sgt. Barney Montoya's son, wrote the following:

> Every night I watched for the headlamps of my dad's vehicle to reflect off the wall outside. With this I knew he was home safe again. This night was like no other. I saw the lights, and a sense of relief came over me. Then I heard the scream from my grandmother. I knew it was dad. I knew he was gone.

In addition to his son Scott, Sgt. Montoya was survived by his mother and another son, Danny. He was interred at Sunset Memorial Park in Gallup. Sgt. Montoya's wife had died only seven months earlier.

Robert Cron, Chief, Gallup Police Department, Correspondence, February 11, 2008
Gallup *Independent*, July 28, 1972; September 6, 1977

Gallup Police Department, Accident Report, September 4, 1977
Frank Gonzales, Chief, Gallup Police Department, Correspondence, September &
       November 1977
McKinley County District Court, miscellaneous papers

GILBERT MONTOYA

Officer

Moriarty, New Mexico, Police Department

At a little after 1:00 o'clock on the morning of February 16, 1967, Moriarty policeman Gilbert Montoya received a phone call at home from a local merchant's son. Wallace Wilson reported that a burglar alarm had gone off at the Moriarty Trading Company, a combination hardware, dry goods and feed store. The alarm was the type that sounded at the merchant's house, 250 yards away, and not at the store itself. Officer Montoya got out of bed, dressed, put on his police jacket and a pair of slippers, took his gun and badge and headed out the door. He told his wife he'd be back in fifteen minutes.

A few minutes later, Wilson called the Montoya residence again. He said he'd seen two men and some activity at the store. He wondered if the officer had left yet. Mrs. Montoya said that he had. A short time later, Wilson called Moriarty Police Chief John Davis. Wilson said he'd seen two men running from the store, and one vehicle hurriedly departed the area while another car remained near the store. The chief said he'd be there immediately.

Chief Davis found Officer Montoya lying on his back at the rear of his car, unconscious but alive. The officer's service revolver was missing. Davis noted a bump on the back of the officer's head and thought he'd been slugged. Montoya's breathing seemed to stop and Davis did mouth-to-mouth resuscitation and got it started again. Help arrived and Officer Montoya was taken by ambulance to Baatan Memorial Hospital in Albuquerque. He was dead on arrival. An autopsy revealed that the officer had been shot in the back of the head with a small caliber, probably a .22, firearm. The bullet had not exited the officer's head.

A few years before, a State Police officer had a close call with a burglar when he investigated a break-in at the same trading post. After that, it was agreed between Moriarty officers and State Police officers that they would call each other for backup before responding to burglary calls late at night. Officer Montoya did not make a call to the State Police dispatcher because the radio in his police car had been disconnected in preparation of it being installed in a new police car recently purchased by the city. His emergency red lights had also been deactivated.

The State Police, the Torrance and Bernalillo County sheriff's departments, and Chief Davis undertook a massive investigation. The method of operation used by the Moriarty thieves was similar to the one used by a group of burglars recently arrested in

Albuquerque on suspicion of about 50 residential and commercial burglaries all over New Mexico. Three suspects were soon identified: Carl Bell, 19, Ray Raney, 23, and Noah Oldfield, also 23. Raney and Oldfield were cousins. After further investigation, the three were arrested, and on February 24, 1967, Carl Bell confessed.

Bell said the three men broke into the store and when Montoya arrived Raney and Oldfield were outside. Montoya caught Oldfield and ordered him to place his hands on the side of the police car so he could be searched. Bell saw what was happening from inside the store and shot the officer with a single action revolver loaded with .22 caliber short ammunition. The three then fled the scene. They took Officer Montoya's gun because they feared he'd regain consciousness and begin shooting.

Bell showed officers where the murder weapon had been thrown from the car in Tijeras Canyon. They found it hanging on a tree branch. Bell also helped officers locate other items that had been stolen from the Moriarty Trading Company. In a plea bargain arrangement, Bell pled guilty to voluntary manslaughter and burglary. More than 30 years later, in July 1999, Bell was back in trouble with the law. The Bernalillo County Sheriff's Department, in a case involving a methamphetamine deal that went bad, charged him with two counts of first-degree murder.

Officer Montoya, 31, is the only Moriarty Police officer to be killed in the line of duty. He began his law enforcement career and a Military Policeman in the U. S. Army. He served as police officer in both Mountainair and Belen before he joined Moriarty Department about a year before his death. He was survived by his wife, Jean, and a son, Cary, 9. He was buried at the Moriarty Catholic Cemetery.

Albuquerque *Journal,* July 17 & 20, 1999
Albuquerque *Tribune*, February 16, 1967
Richard Alexander, Former Chief, Moriarty Police Department
Bill G. Cox, "Just Get Them," *Official Detective Stories*, issue and date unknown

EDWARD L. MORENO

Liquor Inspector
New Mexico Alcohol Beverage Control Department

Liquor agents Eddie Moreno, normally stationed at Santa Rita, and Lalo Sanchez, normally stationed at Deming, were temporarily assigned to Gallup. At about 11:30 on the evening of March 3, 1970, they went to the American Bar to talk with the owner. Before entering, they ordered several men to move from a parking area in front of the saloon. Several minutes later, from inside the bar, Agent Moreno saw four men around the state car and he went outside to investigate. When Agent Sanchez went outside a short time later, he found Moreno lying on the sidewalk, badly beaten and bleeding from a single gunshot wound to the head. He'd been shot with his own gun which was found nearby.

Two men, Julian Martinez of Window Rock, Arizona, and Nelson Loretto of Gallup, were charged with the crime.

Agent Moreno, 38 years old in 1970, initially survived the attack, and responded to treatment. After several years in nursing facilities in Albuquerque and El Paso, he died on July 13, 1975, at Fort Bayard Medical Center as result of complications from the assault and gunshot wound. He was buried at Fort Bayard National Cemetery with full military honors. His wife, Norberta, survived him as did his six children: son Edward and daughters Norberta Anderson, Teresa Moreno, Diana Mahan, Margaret Coplen and Mary Camile Moreno.

Agent Moreno's son, Edward, is a sergeant with the New Mexico Department of Corrections in Santa Fe. He previously served as Chief of Police in Santa Clara, New Mexico.

In commemoration of what would have been Agent Moreno's sixtieth birthday, his family presented Grant County Deputy Sheriff Louis Tavison with Kevlar body armor in the hope that Deputy Tavison's family can have a measure of peace of mind when the officer is on duty.

Albuquerque *Journal*, March 9, 1970
Norberta Mareno (widow) undated correspondence
PERA Report of Disability, July 17, 1970

JULIAN NARVAEZ

Deputy Sheriff/Sergeant
Bernalillo County, New Mexico

Bernalillo County Sheriff's Sgt. Julian Narvaez was on his way to meet his friend Oswald Vigil to have coffee. The date was Wednesday, March 26, 1969. At 10:10 a.m., in front of a Conoco gas station in the 1900 block of Isleta Boulevard in Albuquerque's South Valley, Narvaez conducted a felony traffic stop on a blue 1960 Chevrolet with Texas plates. Four men occupied the car.

The driver, Flavio Javier Fraire, 22, got out and after talking with Narvaez, the officer ordered the car's other occupants out. The man riding in the front passenger seat, Pete Garcia, reached inside his coat as if for a gun. Narvaez and Garcia struggled and Garcia dropped a .22 caliber pistol and made a grab for Sgt. Narvaez's service revolver. Shots were fired. Garcia was hit in the lower back and Narvaez took a bullet in the stomach and fell to the ground. Garcia then shot Narvaez three more times in the back with his own gun. One of the bullets hit Sgt. Narvaez in the heart. He died at the scene. The other three men put Garcia in the car and fled the scene, leaving the officer lying in the street.

Albuquerque police officers Ray Rivera, Lamar Register and Arthur Acosta stopped the blue Chevrolet at the corner of Trumbull and Second SE a short time later. Arrested in addition to Farire were Pete Baca, 27, and a 16 year old juvenile. They had already dropped Garcia off at the hospital and fled.

Pete "Cabezas" Garcia, an admitted heron junkie and narcotics dealer, survived his wound. He was arrested and charged with murder. In late August and early September 1969, Garcia was tried for the crime and the state sought the death penalty. Garcia admitted shooting the officer but claimed Sgt. Narvaez attacked him without provocation and shot him first, for no reason. Defense attorneys attacked Sgt. Narvaez's character as a police officer. They claimed he had a particular dislike of junkies and on previous occasions had assaulted them.

Prosecutors refuted the allegations with witnesses who attested to Narvaez's popularity among residents of the South Valley, where he patrolled. Several law enforcement officers, from the State Police and the Albuquerque

Police Department, testified they had never seen Narvaez behave in an improper manner.

On September 6, 1969, after 14 hours of deliberations, the jury reported to Judge Robert W. Reidy that they were unable to reach a unanimous verdict. The Judge declared a mistrial. Garcia was never convicted of killing Sgt. Narvaez and eventually disappeared into Old Mexico. Rumors filtered back to Albuquerque that Garcia was killed in Mexico some years later.

Sgt. Narvaez, 31, was an eight-year veteran of the sheriff's department at the time of his death. His wife, Sally, and a son Gerald survived him. His daughter, Julie, was born after her father's death. As an adult, she married a Bernalillo County deputy sheriff. Julian's parents, Mr. and Mrs. Julio Narvaez of Albuquerque, four sisters and three brothers also survived him. Julian Narvaez was buried in Mt. Calvary Cemetery.

Bernalillo County Sheriff's Department Chief Deputy Ben Herrera said this: "He was a very efficient man, one of my best—an A-1 policeman in my book."

District Attorney Alexander Sceresse echoed that sentiment: "Julian Narvaez was an excellent officer, and a very personable fellow. You never passed him up without getting a big smile and hello."

Albuquerque *Journal*, March 27 & 28; August 26, 27, 28, 29 & 30; September 3, 4, 5 & 6

Albuquerque *Tribune*, March 26, 28 & 29; August 25

Joe Bowdich, Sheriff, Bernalillo County

Julie Naranjo, Daughter

Ray Rivera, Sheriff, Sandoval County (former APD officer) conversation, January 4, 1996

(Thanks to Roni Sparks, Public Information Officer, Bernalillo County Sheriff's Department.)

MAX RAY OLDHAM

Motorcycle Officer
Albuquerque, New Mexico, Police Department

Motorcycle Officer Oldham, 22, was on routine street patrol on Friday night, February 21, 1959, near the intersection of Lomas Boulevard and Las Lomas Road NE, in Albuquerque. He was struck head-on by a car being driven the wrong way on Lomas by a 59 year old drunk driver. The impact was so severe that Officer Oldham's helmet was torn from his head and offered him virtually no protection during the crash. He died of head injuries 17 hours later at Presbyterian Hospital without regaining consciousness.

The motorcycle Officer Oldham rode the day of his fatal accident was the same motorcycle Officer Richard Armijo rode when he was killed in an accident five months earlier (page 8).

Officer Oldham's wife, Arvella, and a daughter, Kelly Sue, survived him. He was buried at Sunset Gardens in Albuquerque.

Albuquerque *Journal*, February 22 & 24, 1959
Albuquerque Police Department

ROBERT AMERIDTH OLINGER

Deputy Sheriff
Doña Ana County, New Mexico

On April 13, 1881, a court at Mesilla, New Mexico, sentenced William H. Bonney (Billy the Kid) to die on May 13 of the same year at the town of Lincoln. Sheriff Pat Garrett assigned Doña Ana County Deputy Bob Olinger and Lincoln County Deputy J. W. Bell to guard Bonney until his date with the hangman. Bonney escaped from custody on April 28, 1881, by killing both officers (page 19).

Olinger, variously referred to as "Pecos Bob" and "The Big Indian" was a native of Ohio. Not a well-liked man, he was generally considered a loud-mouth and a bully. He is known to have killed several men. After his death, his mother said of him, "Bob was a murderer from the cradle and if there is a hell, I know he is in it."

In the interest of impartiality, it should be noted that Lily Klasner, in her autobiography, wrote that Olinger was much maligned and treated unfairly by historians of the Lincoln County War. She described him as a quiet young man who worked as a ranch foreman before he became a lawman. It should also be noted that Lily Klasner was engaged to marry Bob Olinger.

Olinger also served as a deputy U. S. Marshal.

George Curry, 1861-1947, An Autobiography, University of New Mexico Press (Curry incorrectly identifies the deputy as Bill Ollinger.)

William A. Keleher, *Violence in Lincoln County,* University of New Mexico Press

Lily Klasner, *My Girlhood Among Outlaws,* University of Arizona Press

Marc Simmons, *When Six-Guns Ruled, Outlaw Tales of the Southwest,* Ancient City Press

Dan L. Thrapp, *Encyclopedia of Frontier Biography,* University of Nebraska Press, 1988

Paul Trachtman, "The Gunfighters," *The Old West,* Time Life Books

John P. Wilson, *Merchants, Guns & Money, The Story of Lincoln County and Its Wars,* Museum of New Mexico Press

MANUEL "MANNY" OLIVAS

Patrolman
New Mexico State Police

Officer Manny Olivas was busy at the scene of a two car accident on Interstate 25 near Ribera in San Miguel County on Friday, February 1, 1985. Occupants of the two wrecked vehicles had already left the scene. Another State Police Officer, Tom Meserve, on his way home to Las Vegas from Santa Fe, stopped to assist Olivas by putting out flares. Meserve had departed and Officer Olivas was taking measurements along the edge of the road near the Pecos River Bridge when he was struck by a pickup truck. Knocked 70 feet off the roadway, Manny Olivas was dead at the scene. A wrecker driver responding to the first accident found the officer a few minutes later.

Officer Meserve was called out to participate in the search for a pickup truck with damage to the front end. He began by checking motel parking lots in Las Vegas and in the third one he located a 1979 GMC pickup with damage to the right front. Its owner, Mickey Dean Copeland, 40, of Albuquerque, was subsequently arrested and charged with Driving While Intoxicated (DWI) and vehicular homicide; his blood alcohol level was .20, twice the legal presumptive level for intoxication.* Copeland claimed he was so drunk that he didn't remember hitting anyone, but he thought he remembered hitting a deer. Convicted of vehicular homicide, Copeland was sentenced to three years in jail, but served one year.

Manuel Olivas, 32, was born in Chihuahua, Mexico. His family immigrated to the U. S. in 1962 and settled at Floyd in Roosevelt County. He graduated from Floyd High School in 1973 and enrolled in Eastern New Mexico University. He began his law enforcement career working as campus police officer while he went to school. Officer Olivas graduated from ENMU in 1978 with a Bachelor of Arts Degree in Spanish Education. He later served with the Portales and Roswell Police Departments.

His wife of ten years, Socorro, and daughter Veronica, 6 survived the officer. His son, Manuel Jr. was born four months after his father died. Manuel Olivas was buried in Portales.

* The presumptive level for DWI was .10 at the time. It has since been changed to .08.

Albuquerque *Journal*, February 4, 1985
Agent Tom Meserve, New Mexico State Police, conversation, December 12, 1995
Las Vegas *Daily Optic*, April 30, 1985
Mrs. Socorro Olivas, correspondence, April 1990
Portales *News-Tribune*, February 4, 1985
Rio Grande *Sun*, February 7, 1985
The Roadrunner (New Mexico State Police Association, Vol. 3, No. 2, Summer, 1992)

PHILIP OLIVAS

Deputy Marshal
Mesilla, New Mexico

At about 11:20 on the evening of Tuesday, September 1, 1992, Mesilla Deputy Marshal Philip Olivas stopped a pickup truck driven by John R. Sadecki, 23, of Hatch, for a traffic violation on Doña Ana County Road 34, near its intersection with Union Avenue. Sadecki immediately jumped out of his vehicle and fled on foot. Officer Olivas, a martial arts expert, chased the subject, also on foot, along the county road and then east on an unlighted Union Avenue where he tackled Sadecki. As Olivas struggled with the suspect he asked a by-stander to go to his car and call for assistance. The citizen made the radio call at 11:44 p.m.

A Doña Ana County Deputy en route to the station at the end of his shift responded to the call. He turned down Union Avenue from which point he could not see Deputy Olivas' police unit. When he realized that the two men were fighting in the street, it was too late to avoid hitting them. Sadecki was dead at the scene and Officer Olivas died about 30 minutes later. Sadecki had fled from Olivas because he was driving with a revoked license.

Third Judicial District Attorney Doug Driggers later cleared the deputy of any wrongdoing and no charges were filed in the matter. An investigating officer said this: "The accident was especially tragic because we had a Mesilla marshal who was doing his job killed by a Doña Ana County sheriff's deputy who was doing his job."

Deputy Olivas, 25, was a lifelong resident of Las Cruces. His parents, Jesús and Rosa Olivas, with whom he resided, and brothers James Jacob and John Paul survived him. He was buried at the Masonic Cemetery in Las Cruces.

Albuquerque *Journal*, September 3 & 9, 1992
Las Cruces *Sun-News*, September 2, 3 & 4, 1992
Lt. West Gilbreath, Doña Ana County Sheriff's Department

FILIMON J. ORTIZ

Corrections Officer
New Mexico Department Of Corrections

It was about 6:00 on the morning of June 11, 1952 when Captain Juan Griego of the Department of Corrections found the body of Corrections officer Filimon Ortiz lying face-up on the floor in Cellblock 1. The captain felt no pulse and found the body to be cold. Officer Ortiz had been stabbed with a small knife and bludgeoned with a lead pipe. The murder of Filimon Ortiz proved to be one of the most baffling cases in the annals of crime in New Mexico.

No blood was found around the body of the victim, indicating that he was killed elsewhere and his body placed in Cellblock 1.

All prisoners in Cellblock 1 were accounted for, and each was securely locked in his respective cell.

Officer Ortiz carried no keys and therefore could not have opened any of the cells, even if he wanted to, or been forced to.

The doctor who conducted the autopsy placed the time of death at about 1:00 a.m., and yet a corrections officer reported seeing Ortiz alive at 4:00 a.m.

A small pen knife was found wrapped in a handkerchief on a table in Cellblock 1 and a length of lead pipe was found near the body. No one could explain how they got there.

The crime was never solved and circumstances surrounding Officer Ortiz's death were never discovered.

Filimon Ortiz, 54, was survived by his mother, Eloisa Q. Ortiz, three brothers and three sisters. He had previously been employed at Los Alamos and at the Japanese Internment Camp in Santa Fe.

Warden Robert J. Tansy, Penitentiary of NM, Correspondence, May 13, 1988
Santa Fe *New Mexican*, June 11, 1952

JUAN LEO ORTIZ

Deputy Sheriff
San Miguel County, New Mexico

On August 12, 1978, Deputy Juan Ortiz patrolled in the Santa Fe National Forest west of Las Vegas, New Mexico. He was looking for four horsemen who'd been reported harassing campers and vandalizing campgrounds. He encountered a subject named Frank Trujillo who pointed a .22 caliber rifle at the officer. Ortiz drew his gun and fired, killing Trujillo.

The District Attorney initially filed a murder charge against Ortiz but on September 1, 1978, District Court Judge Joe Angel dismissed the charge on the ground that the deputy acted in self-defense.

On Sunday afternoon, September 18, at about 5:00 o'clock, Juan Ortiz and his family worked in a field across the road from their home at Rociada, about 27 miles northwest of Las Vegas. They were busy stacking hay. Two shots were fired and Juan Ortiz fell to the ground, shot in the chest and mortally wounded.

A search soon began for the assassin or assassins. Three sets of horse tracks and two spent .300 Savage rifle cartridges were found about 200 yards away. The tracks led north, into the National Forest and toward the village of Tres Ritos. But even with the use of a State Police helicopter, the riders were not captured. No one was ever prosecuted for killing Deputy Juan Ortiz.

Deputy Ortiz, who had been a deputy for only five months, had announced his intention to leave the sheriff's department. His resignation would have been effective on Monday, September 18, the day after he died.

Albuquerque *Journal*, September 18, 19, 21, & 22, 1978
National Law Enforcement Memorial Fund, Washington, D. C.
Santa Fe *New Mexican*, September 19, 1978 & September 6, 1979

LEE VICENTE PEÑA

Town Marshal
Taos, New Mexico

On Wednesday evening, December 20, 1944, Marshal Lee Peña was called upon to quell a disturbance at a local tavern. A man, a stranger, apparently drunk, had displayed a gun in the bar and threatened other patrons. The marshal entered the bar and escorted the young man into the street without any difficulty. They had taken but a few steps when the stranger pulled a .32 caliber revolver and shot the marshal in the left side of the chest at point-blank range. A crowd quickly gathered and Marshal Peña was rushed to the hospital, but was dead upon arrival.

Meanwhile, the gunman was subdued and temporarily locked up in the Taos County Jail. He was soon transferred to the Colfax County Jail in Raton because the authorities in Taos feared he would be lynched.

The gunman claimed to be Albert Edwin Ellis, 27, of Monte Vista, Colorado, but he carried a social security card in another name. His true identity was yet a third name: Henry Gonzales, a deserter from the U. S. Army. On June 3, 1945, Gonzales pleaded guilty and Judge Henry Kiker sentenced him to three life terms in prison without parole. He actually served 14 years.

Lee Peña, 49, a native of Nacogdoches, Texas, and a veteran of World War I, had served as marshal under three Taos city administrations. He was also the truant officer for the Taos County School System. He was very well regarded in the community. His funeral—conducted with full military honors—was one of the largest ever seen in Taos. All schools and businesses were closed upon that sad occasion.

He was survived by his wife, Emelia Lujan Peña and seven children: Gloria, 18; John, 14; Marcia, 13; Theresa, 9; Rosella, 5; Charles, 3; and Michael, 1. A daughter, Margaret, 22, from a previous marriage also survived Marshal Peña.

On December 29, 1944, the Taos Village Council voted to pay the marshal's funeral expenses. Since no fund existed for that purpose, money had to be transferred from the Light and Power and Driver's License funds. It was also agreed that the village should look into purchasing insurance for police officers and firemen.

Jose G. Lucero, Chief, Taos Police Department, correspondence, 1989
Santa Fe *New Mexican*, December 21, 1944
Minutes, Special Meeting, Taos Village Council, December 29, 1944
John O. Peña & Marcia Peña, correspondence, November 5, 1999

LYON PHILLIPOWSKY(I)

Deputy Sheriff
Lincoln County, New Mexico

The following item appeared on the front page of the Santa Fe *New Mexican*:

Affray in Lincoln County

"A friend gives us the following account of a difficulty at Lincoln resulting in the death of one of the parties. He says a shooting affray took place at Lincoln city, Lincoln county [*sic*], on the 21st inst. [October 21, 1874], between William Burns and Lyon Phillipowsky, deputy sheriff, which resulted in the death of the latter. Mr. Burns was a clerk in the employ of L. G. Murphy & Co. Phillipowski [*sic*] entered the store late in the evening very much intoxicated and grow [*sic*] quite insulting to Burns, who attempted to evade any difficulty with him; but the latter drew his pistol threatening Burns' life, and went on the outside and challenged Burns, who procured a pistol and went out. Phillipowski [*sic*] commenced firing at him; the latter returned the fire and it was kept up until Phillipowsky fell, mortally [wounded] and died early next morning. The Coroner held an inquest over the body who returned a verdict that Burns was justifiable [*sic*]."

William A. Keleher in *Violence in Lincoln County* mentions this event. Frederick Nolan in *Bad Blood* mentions Phillipowski [*sic*] but doesn't mention the events surrounding his death, or William Burns. Lily Klasner in *My Girlhood Among Outlaws* refers to a Jewish settler in Lincoln County named Philip Bowski who, she says, became county clerk. She makes no mention of this shooting.

In spite of Phillipowski's general obscurity, it is known that he was born in Poland and came to New Mexico as private in the Fifth California (Volunteer) Infantry—the California Column—in 1862. He settled in Lincoln County after being mustered out and served for a time as an interpreter with the Mescalero Apache for the Indian Bureau, though no mention is made as to how he became conversant in Athabaskan. While he is reported to have been a Republican—he served as secretary to the Lincoln County Republican convention in 1871—he was closely associated with such notable Democrats as Lawrence Murphy and Emil Fritz; in fact served as clerk when Murphy was Lincoln County probate judge. He also owned a ranch on the Rio Ruidoso. The drunken and aggressive behavior which led to his death is described as a departure from his normally "mild-mannered" demeanor. He served as a deputy under Sheriff Alexander Hamilton Mills at the time of his death.

Phillipowsky's name is embossed on the Law Enforcement Memorial Monument at the New Mexico Law Enforcement Academy in Santa Fe, whether it deserves to be there, or not.

William A. Keleher, *Violence in Lincoln County, 1869-1881*, University of New Mexico Press

Lily Klasner, *My Girlhood Among Outlaws*, University of Arizona Press

Darlis A. Miller, *The California Column in New Mexico*, University of New Mexico Press

Santa Fe *New Mexican*, November 6, 1874

John P. Wilson, *Merchants, Guns & Money, The Story of Lincoln County and Its Wars*, Museum of New Mexico Press

ROBERT FRANCIS PURCELL

Security Police Officer
United States Atomic Energy Commission

On February 11, 1950, Officer Purcell, 30, along with Officer Warren Fleshman returned to New Mexico from the East Coast carrying "national security assets." The airplane in which they traveled crashed west of Albuquerque, killing both officers and the pilot, Hugh Williams, 31, of Albuquerque. (page 94.)

Robert Purcell, a World War II veteran, was survived by his wife, Francene, and a two year old daughter, of Los Alamos, and his mother and brother of Denver, Colorado. An honor guard escorted his remains there for interment.

Albuquerque *Journal*, February 11 & 12, 1950
Albuquerque *Tribune*, June 13, 1957
Certificates of Death, State of New Mexico, February 12, 1950
Allen M. Osborn, Albuquerque, correspondence

JOSÉ FRANCISCO QUINTANA

Patrolman
New Mexico State Police

Officer Joe Quintana left the New Mexico State Police during World War II, early in 1943, to join the U. S. Army Air Corps as a flying instructor. He held the army rank of lieutenant. He was stationed in England when he was killed in an airplane crash on March 24, 1944. He had previously served with the New Mexico National Guard's 111th Cavalry Regiment and the 200th Coast Artillery Anti-aircraft Regiments.

Officer Quintana, 29, a native of Santa Fe, joined the State Police in 1937. He was assigned to Chama, Socorro and Albuquerque before joined the Army Air Corps. His son, Alex, retired from the State Police with the rank of Captain.

The Roadrunner (New Mexico State Police Association, Vol. 3, No. 2, Summer, 1992)

Assistant Chief A. B. Martinez, New Mexico State Police, memo dated February 28, 1943

Assistant Chief A. B. Martinez, memo to the attention of the Chief's Office, March 28, 1944

WILLIAM RAINBOLT

Deputy
Chaves County, New Mexico, Sheriff's Department

Chaves County sheriff Fred Higgins was out of town at mid February in 1901, and his chief deputy, and brother-in-law, twenty-five year old Will Rainbolt was in charge. The young deputy received information that Oliver Hendricks, a young cowboy, was packing a gun at a dance being held in the southwestern part of Roswell. Accompanied by his brother, Mody, Rainbolt drove his buggy to the dance and soon located Hendricks who was engaged in a dance. The officer waited patiently until the music stopped before he approached Hendricks. Rainbolt asked the young man to give up his gun, which Hendricks did. Rainbolt then told Hendricks to get into his buggy so that he could take him to jail.

At about that time, Oliver Hendricks' brother, Nathan, appeared and attempted to talk Rainbolt out of arresting his younger brother. Rainbolt was not persuaded, whereupon Nathan drew his own gun and shot the deputy before the officer had any chance to draw his own gun. The bullet hit Rainbolt in the right arm, passed through or near his heart, and lodged under the skin on the left side.

"They have killed me," Rainbolt said to Mody just before he died.

The Hendricks brothers mounted a single horse and rode out of town, toward a cow camp at Eight Mile, west of Roswell. There they secured two fresh mounts and continued their flight, to the west. A posse soon took up pursuit of the killer, but was unsuccessful. The local newspaper said the posse's failure was due to ineffectual leadership since the sheriff was away and the chief deputy was dead.

A young wife and child, as well as his parents, survived Deputy Rainbolt. His funeral was held on Sunday, February 10, and the officer was interred at the South Side Cemetery in Roswell. The tragic affair was "largely attended."

Rumors later circulated that there was more to the affair than met the eye. Some said there was bad blood between Rainbolt and the Hendricks brothers which resulted from a confrontation two years previous in which Rainbolt shot the McElroy brothers. It was said that the McElroys and the Hendricks' were friends and the Hendricks brothers had gone about armed for the purpose of settling the score with Rainbolt at the best opportunity. Another rumor suggested that Deputy Rainbolt had been seen drinking whiskey shortly before he was killed.

Sheriff Higgins returned to Roswell in time for his deputy's funeral, and began a pursuit of the killer, but it was too late. Higgins was able to trace Nathan

Hendricks several years later, and returned him to Roswell for trial. Hendricks claimed self-defense and was found not guilty of murder. He was released and returned to his new home in South Dakota.

The local newspaper editorialized thus:

> The tragic death of Deputy Sheriff Will Rainbolt is another proof that heavy fines for carrying concealed weapons are not entirely successful in preventing the practice. In the absence of something better it would be a good thing to make the fine an even $100 and see how that would work. The time has long passed in this country when it is necessary for anybody to go armed, and as long as they do, murder is at our elbow all the time. The pernicious habit of carrying a gun is responsible for more murders than either whiskey or women, the two great prompters of crime.

Roswell *Record*, February 15, 1901

Roswell *Daily Record*, June 2 & August 4, 2000

Bonney, Cecil. *Looking Over My Shoulder: Seventy-five years in the Pecos Valley*

Fleming, Elvis, Historian, City of Roswell, correspondence, December 9, 1999 & January 7, 2000

JOHN T. "JAKE" RAMSEY

Sergeant
New Mexico State Police

State Police Sergeant John "Jake" Ramsey and State Police Officer Joe Aven were severely injured on August 6, 1953 in a head-on collision with a vehicle occupied by five members of a Chicago family on highway U. S. 180 about 14 miles east of Hobbs, New Mexico. Ramsey died at the scene and Aven died the following day. Three people riding in the other car were also killed. E. W. "Bill" Long, acting chief of the Hobbs Police Department, a passenger in the State Police car, was injured but survived.

The officers had been en route to Sweetwater, Texas, to complete an investigation and to attend the funeral of Sheriff Robert L. McReynolds of Gaines County who was killed in an automobile accident earlier that week.

Sgt. Jake Ramsey, 39, was survived by his wife, Bernadine, two sons, Carl, 18, and Darwin, 17, and a daughter, Bonnie, 5. He joined the State Police in 1949 and was promoted to sergeant in 1951. He had previously served as a Quay County deputy sheriff and a Gallup city police officer. Described as "fearless," Ramsey once took an armed fugitive into custody without drawing his own gun. He was buried in Tucumcari.

Hobbs *Daily News-Sun*, August 6, 1953
Roadrunner (New Mexico State Police Association, Vol. 3, No. 2, Summer, 1992)

DONALD W. REDFERN

Officer
Albuquerque, New Mexico, Police Department

Patrolman Donald W. Redfern had completed his shift and was on his way home when a flash flood occurred in Albuquerque's north valley late on the evening of Wednesday, August 15, 1951. The officer was near his residence when he was assigned to direct traffic in the 6700 block of North Second Street. His wife watched him work from a nearby ditch bank. Suddenly a southbound car hit a vehicle parked close to where the officer stood, caromed off of it and slid sideways toward the officer. Redfern saw the car coming toward him and tried to get out of the way. He didn't make it. His body was thrown about 47 feet; his gun and holster were ripped from his body and found, along with his flashlight, about 35 feet away. The car skidded nearly 150 feet before it hit the officer and went on to hit two more parked cars. Donald Redfern was dead on arrival at St. Joseph's Hospital.

The driver of the car that hit Officer Redfern was a 21 year old Airman from Kirtland Air Force Base named Earl M. Maier. He admitted that he'd been drinking just prior to the accident. He claimed he was traveling at about 50 miles per hour when he saw the officer. Police officers had to protect Maier from assault by local residents who witnessed the accident and wanted at him. Maier was charged with manslaughter.

Officer Redfern, 27, was a two and one half year veteran of the Albuquerque Police Department. In addition to his wife, a young son, Walter, survived him. Assistant Police Chief Frank Doyle said that Officer Redfern had an excellent record and was one of the department's most popular officers.

Donald Redfern was buried at Sunset Memorial Cemetery in Albuquerque.

Albuquerque Police Department
Albuquerque *Tribune*, August 16 & 18, 1951

SAMUEL REDHOUSE

Officer
Navajo Tribal Police Department

The McKinley County Sheriff's Department received a 911 call at about 8:00 a.m. on Monday, February 17, 1997, from a man who said he had a rifle and a pistol. FBI agents later described the caller as troubled, despondent and angry. Officers traced the call to the Navajo community of Iyanbito, about 15 miles east of Gallup, to the residence of Richard Roy Smith. Six officers responded to the call: four McKinley County deputies and two Navajo tribal policemen. They interviewed Smith's 10-year-old son who said his father was out shooting at dogs.

Officers began tracking Smith. They located him when he opened fire on them from behind some rocks with a .22 caliber, lever action, rifle. A single bullet struck officer Redhouse under the right arm. As Smith raised up to continue firing, Navajo Police Sergeant Ed Marble and McKinley County Deputy Pat Martinez opened fire. Smith was shot in the head and died at the scene.

Officer Redhouse was declared dead upon arrival at the Gallup Indian Medical Center.

Under conviction in federal court for child sexual assault, Richard Roy Smith, 56, was scheduled to surrender himself to the U. S. Marshal's Service to begin serving a prison sentence on February 18, the day after he was killed. Albuquerque FBI Agent Doug Beldon described Smith's actions as suicide by cop. "He lured the officers into a situation where he knew they would have to shoot," Beldon said.

Samuel Redhouse, 34, was a six year veteran of the Navajo Police Department. He was stationed at Crownpoint. A resident of Lukachukai, Arizona, he was survived by a wife and two children.

Albuquerque *Journal*, February 18, 19, & 20, 1997

BRUCE A. RICHARD

Public Safety Officer
Alamogordo, New Mexico, Department Of Public Safety

DPS Officer Bruce Richard and ambulance technician Norma Sutherland responded to a two car collision on U. S. 70 west of Alamogordo at about 1:00 a.m. on Sunday, September 2, 1984. One car had pulled into the roadway from a lounge parking lot and collided with a second vehicle. Richard and Sutherland were at the rear of the ambulance when a semi truck jack-knifed as it approached the accident scene and struck them. Both were pinned between the truck's right rear tires and the ambulance, which was carried about a hundred feet after the impact. Officer Richard died shortly after the collision of massive internal injuries. Norma Sutherland was critically injured, but survived.

Officer Richard, a two-year veteran of the Alamogordo DPS, had previously received an Honorable Service Award and a Commendation from the VFW. His mother, Joanna Smith, survived him.

Alamogordo Department of Public Safety
Albuquerque *Journal*, September 3, 1984

THOMAS A. RICHMOND

Deputy Marshal/Sergeant
Mesilla, New Mexico

It was a *routine* traffic stop that became anything but *routine*.

The date was Wednesday, July 13, 1988, and the time was about 5:15 p.m. Sgt. Tom Richmond used radar to check for speeding motorists on Snow Road in Mesilla, just south of Las Cruces in Doña Ana County. Traffic enforcement was a big part of the officer's job. He observed a red Toyota pickup which seemed to be exceeding the 35 mile per hour speed limit; his radar unit confirmed that the truck was traveling at 49. Sgt. Richmond engaged his red lights and made a *routine* traffic stop. He got out of his police car and started to walk toward the Toyota. Suddenly, shots were fired and the officer was hit. He went down but managed to draw his own weapon and return fire as the pickup sped away. Sgt. Richmond died at the scene.

Tom Richmond had no way of knowing that the E-Z Pawnshop in Las Cruces had been robbed at gunpoint only 15 minutes before he stopped the pickup. It might not have mattered if he'd known about the robbery because the offender changed vehicles after he fled the pawnshop. Richmond had no way of knowing that the Toyota's two occupants were ex-convicts, both armed and suspected of robbing the pawnshop. He had no way of knowing that one of the occupants was wanted by Las Cruces authorities for the armed robbery of a liquor store a month before. And that day, of all days, Sgt. Richmond neglected to wear his bulletproof vest.

A private citizen named Billy Salopek also had no way of knowing about any of these events when he saw a stranger near a relative's house in a pecan grove about five miles from the scene of the shooting. Salopek thought the man had burglarized the house and he approached him. The man produced a pistol but Salopek disarmed and held him until officers arrived a few minutes later. Arrested was Raymond Clark, 27. The second suspect, Angel Carreon, 38, was captured near the residence of John Salopek, Billy's uncle. Carreon resisted arrest and officers were obliged to use force to restrain him.

Both offenders had served time with the New Mexico Department of Corrections: Clark for a robbery in 1978 and Carreon for a heroin trafficking conviction in 1981. Carreon also served time for aggravated battery. They were both charged with the murder of Tom Richmond. On March 20, 1989, Clark pleaded no contest to first degree murder and was sentenced to life in prison. On March 23, Carreon was allowed to plead guilty to possession of a firearm by a felon and to being an habitual offender. He was sentenced to eight years.

Tom Richmond and his wife of 35 years, Carol, migrated to southern New Mexico from Middletown, New York, in June of 1985. He'd previously worked as a private investigator and later as a deputy sheriff in Orange County, Goshen, New York. He joined the Mesilla Marshal's Department in October 1985, and was promoted to sergeant in 1986. In addition to his wife, daughters Dorothy, Donna and Diane, and son David survived him. Sgt. Richmond was buried in Mesilla.

Lt. Benjamin Archuleta, a Doña Ana County deputy sheriff and a resident of Mesilla paid Sgt. Richmond the highest compliment when he said, "He made a difference."

Albuquerque *Journal*, March 23, 1989
Lt. Benjamin R. Archuleta, "Death of a Deputy," Doña Ana County Sheriff's Department,
Employee Newsletter, July, 1988
El Paso *Times*, July 14, 15 & 19, 1988
Las Cruces *Sun-News*, July 17, 1988
Correspondence, Carol Richmond, May 6, 1990
Lt. West Gilbreath, Doña Ana County Sheriff's Department

DANIEL C. RIVERA, JR.

Inspector
New Mexico Motor Transportation Department

Inspector Danny Rivera was working at the Anthony Port of Entry on Interstate Highway 10, south of Las Cruces, on July 11, 1989. At about 10:00 a.m. he observed a semi-truck pass by without stopping. He took up pursuit at a high rate of speed and collided with the truck before he realized that it had pulled over and stopped. He died at the scene. Inspector Rivera was not using his seat belt and investigating officers reported that seat belt use might have prevented his death.

A resident of Anthony, Danny Rivera had been employed by the Department of Transportation for seven years at the time of his death. He attended the New Mexico Law Enforcement Academy in 1987 and was then assigned to patrol duties in District 4. He had previously served in the U. S. Navy and Naval Reserves.

Inspector Rivera, 30, was survived by his parents, Daniel and Ampro Rivera, brothers Oscar, Johnny, Ricky, Gilbert, and Rudy, and a sister Dolores. He and his fiancé, Leticia Flores, had planned to marry in January of 1990.

Deming *Headlight*, July 12, 1989
Lt. West Gilbreath, Doña Ana County Sheriff's Department
Cpl. Cesar Marmolejo, "D. O. T. Officer Killed in Traffic Stop," Doña Ana County
        Sheriff's Department, *Employee Newsletter*, August, 1989
New Mexico State Police, Fatal Report, July 11, 1989

AUSTIN A. ROBERTS

Officer/Pilot
New Mexico Game And Fish Department

The winter of 1959-60 was a hard one. The New Mexico Department of Game and Fish undertook an operation to airdrop hay to antelope starving in deep snow in San Miguel County. Officer Austin Roberts piloted a Game and Fish Department plane when it crashed on January 4, 1960, between Trujillo and Maes, near State Road 104, east of Las Vegas. Roberts and his passenger, O. C. Gray, also a Game and Fish Officer, were killed (page 115).

Officer Roberts joined the Department of Game and Fish on August 1, 1949, and was stationed at the Glenwood Hatchery in Catron County. He later transferred to a biological research project studying the eating habits of merganser ducks. In 1954 he became a district conservation officer and served in that capacity until January 1958 when he was promoted to department pilot.

A resident of Santa Fe, Officer Roberts was survived by a wife and three daughters. Lake Roberts, located in Grant County between Silver City and the Gila Cliff dwellings is named for Officer Austin A. Roberts.

Albuquerque *Journal*, January 5, 1960
Ms. Jerry Montgomery, Public Affairs staff, New Mexico Department of Game and Fish, correspondence, December 5, 1989

PERFECTO RODRIGUEZ

Precinct Constable
Silver City, New Mexico

Constable Perfecto Rodriguez was shot to death in the early morning hours of August 28, 1904 as he attempted to help a Grant County deputy sheriff disarm two drunken cowboys in Silver City. Town Marshal William Kilburn was also killed. (Page 166).

Constable Rodriguez, 45, was well known in Grant County and Southern New Mexico as he had been active in politics for many years. He'd previously served as deputy U. S. Marshal in addition to several terms as constable. A wife and six children survived him. The local newspaper said, "...[his] remains were followed to their last resting place by a large number of friends."

Albuquerque *Morning Journal*, August 29, 1904

Bob Alexander, *Lawmen, Outlaws, and S. O. Bs.*, High-Lonesome Books

Silver City *Independent*, August 30, September 6 & 9, 1904

Chief Thomas J. Ryan (Ret.), Silver City Police Department, correspondence, October 2 & 23, 1991

ROBERT SETH ROMERO

Agent
New Mexico State Police

Agent Romero had been in Española in late September 1967, working on a meeting between land grant leader Reyes López Tijerina, some of his followers, and Attorney General Boston Witt. Returning to Santa Fe in the early hours of September 30, about three miles south of Española, Agent Romero collided with a loaded logging truck that was crosswise and blocking U. S. Route 64. He was killed instantly.

Robert Romero, 39, served in the U. S. Army as a paratrooper in 1946-47. He served with the Santa Fe Police Department from 1953 to 1956 and joined the State Police in 1959. After duty assignments in Glorieta, Pecos and Cuba, he was transferred to the Narcotics Division. Romero was so successful there that he and his family began receiving threatening phone calls. In 1963 he was assigned as special investigator to the Attorney General's Office and beginning in October of 1966 he spent a lot of time investigating the Alianza Federál de Mercedes Reales take-over of Rio Arriba County's Echo Amphitheater. Attorney General Witt described Agent Romero as "A good officer who had a lot of good sources of information."

Agent Romero was also responsible for establishing a youth recreation program in the village of Pecos. He spent money out of his own pocket to get the program started. The New Mexico State Senate memorialized his efforts in 1962 and he was awarded the Veterans of Foreign Wars Bronze Medal for Citizenship for 1961-62. The State Senate also memorialized Agent Romero after his death.

A native of Santa Fe, Robert Romero was the youngest son of Mr. & Mrs. Facundo Romero. His wife, Clara, one son and three daughters survived him. He was buried at the Santa Fe National Cemetery. His daughter, Cindy, served as a Santa Fe County deputy sheriff, Santa Fe city police officer and investigator for the First Judicial District Attorney's Office.

Albuquerque *Journal*, October 1, 1967
New Mexico Law, Official Sheriff's & Police Magazine, June, 1962

The Roadrunner (New Mexico State Police Association, Vol. 3, No. 2, Summer, 1992)

Mrs. Clara G. Romero, correspondence, November, 1999

Santa Fe *New Mexican*, May 29, 1990

ROBERT ROSENBLOOM

Patrolman
New Mexico State Police

Assigned to the Albuquerque State Police District, Officer Bob Rosenbloom had applied for a position as agent in the Criminal Investigations Bureau in Santa Fe, and he'd been accepted. On November 8, 1971, he made arrangements to sell his house. All he needed were orders from Santa Fe to begin his new job.

Just after eating dinner with his wife that evening, Officer Rosenbloom received a telephone call from headquarters. He was instructed to relay a trial witness to Grants. While en route back to Albuquerque, sometime after 10:30 p.m., Rosenbloom stopped an east-bound 1972 Ford Galaxie four door sedan about eight miles west of Albuquerque. He may have stopped it for a traffic violation or because he suspected it was stolen. At 10:41, he radioed the dispatcher and requested a check on the vehicle's California license plate. When the dispatcher attempted to respond with the information at 10:55, there was no answer. At 11:11, a citizen called the dispatcher on Officer Rosenbloom's police radio and said the officer had been hurt. He requested an ambulance.

Sgt. C. A. Hawkins arrived on the scene a few minutes later. He found the officer lying face down, a single bullet wound to his throat. Officer Rosenbloom gripped his flashlight with one hand and his gun with the other. The weapon was just clear of the holster and had not been fired. His hat had rolled down the embankment. Officer Rosenbloom was dead.

About 30 minutes after the shooting, a Bernalillo County deputy sheriff spotted the car in Albuquerque's south valley. The deputy pursued the car for about three miles at speeds up to 120 miles per hour before he lost sight of it near the intersection of Coors Boulevard and Gun Club Road. Albuquerque Police officers found the car the next day on San Ygnacio SW. It had been rented from the Hertz agency in San Francisco, California, and then stolen.

Near the car officers found luggage, three military rifles and a 12 gauge shotgun. They also found an abundance of revolutionary literature, bomb-making materials and hundreds of rounds of ammunition. Evidence indicated that the occupants of the car were members of a militant group called the Republic of New Africa which advocated the establishment of a Black nation in the Southern United States. About 250 officers from federal, state and local law enforcement agencies participated in the search for the killers.

There was no sign of the wanted men for nearly three weeks. Then they made a move. They kidnapped a wrecker driver, and his wrecker, and used it to get them close to a TWA 727-jet liner at the Albuquerque International airport. They commandeered the plane and ordered it flown to Africa but flight personnel convinced them the plane didn't have the range to make such a long trip. They settled for Cuba and all passengers were allowed to leave the plane when it landed for refueling at Tampa, Florida. The plane returned from Havana to Miami on November 29.

The three killers were identified as Charles Hill, 21, of Albuquerque; Robert (or Ralph) Goodwin, 24, of Berkeley, California; and Michael Finney, 20, of Oakland, California. Finney, who adopted the African name Mancha, is believed to have fired the shot that killed Officer Rosenbloom. In interviews in Cuba since their escape, they said they were able to hideout with other members of the Republic of New Africa in Albuquerque. Then, for two days, they hid in the desert near the airport waiting for an opportunity to hijack an airplane. Word also reached the United States that Goodwin died in a drowning accident in 1973. The other two have remained free in Cuba for nearly a quarter century.

In 1995, Governor Gary Johnson of New Mexico made a request to the U. S. State Department that renewed efforts to extradite the two back to New Mexico be made. At this writing (2009), the killers remain in Cuba.

A native of Brooklyn, New York, Officer Rosenbloom previously served on the New Mexico State University Police Department and the Las Cruces Police Department. He joined the State Police in 1965. He was survived by his wife, Linda, and two children, Tammy and Robbie, aged two and one, respectively, at the time of their father's death. Many New Mexicans contributed to a $17,000 education fund for the Rosenbloom children.

Tomás Martínez, "A Routine Check Ended in Death," *Impact* Magazine, Albuquerque *Journal*, October 9, 1979
Albuquerque *Tribune*, November 9, 1991 and July 6, 1995
El Paso *Times,* May 16, 1984
New York *Times*, November 29, 1971
The Roadrunner (New Mexico State Police Association, Vol. 3, No. 2, Summer, 1992)

PETER "PETE" ROSS

Sergeant
New Mexico State Police

On Friday, August 29, 1986, a major cooperative marijuana eradication effort was underway in the mountains west of Artesia, New Mexico. It involved four helicopters, one of which transported seven peace officers: four State Policemen and three Customs Service agents. When it crashed at about 11:30 a.m., all aboard were severely injured, but Sergeant Pete Ross suffered most with broken neck, shoulder, arm and ankles, as well as from internal injuries. Ross remained a quadriplegic for the remainder of his life. He died on February 6, 2005 at the age of 52 years.

After he recovered enough to get around in a wheel chair, Ross attended Law School and became a prosecuting attorney of the Second Judicial District (Bernalillo County), and served there for 12 years. He worked in the felony Driving While Intoxicated, Repeat Offender, and Violent Crime Divisions, among others. He was considered a very professional prosecutor. Bernalillo County Metropolitan Court Chief Judge Judith Nakamura said, "[Pete Ross' death] is a tragic blow to many of us.... It is a sad day because of the way he touched so many of us here in this court and in many other jurisdictions in New Mexico."

In addition to his official duties, Ross was President of the Paralyzed Veterans of America, Chairman of the Governor's Committee on Concerns for the Handicapped, and a member of the Governor's Veterans Service Commission. He also worked hard toward a better understanding between prosecutors and law enforcement personnel and conducted orientation classes to that end.

Pete Ross was a native of Albuquerque and served four years in the U. S. Marine Corps before he joined the State Police in 1974. His wife, Ann, and five children survived him, as did 10 grandchildren. In addition to all the things he did in his life, Ross was also something of a legal historian. In 2001 he had published an item which detailed the investigation surrounding the murder of famed New Mexico Sheriff Pat Garrett (page 106) in 1908, and the shoddy way the prosecution of his alleged killer was handled.

An editorial in the Albuquerque *Journal* concluded with this: "Now is the time to honor the memory and sacrifice of Pete Ross, who honorably and indefatigably served New Mexico and his nation for 30 years."

Albuquerque *Journal*, February 12, 2005
Don Bullis, "Pete Ross: Historian," Rio Rancho *Observer*, October 17, 2001
Rio Rancho *Observer*, February 10, 2005
Santa Fe *New Mexican*, August 30, 1986 & August 23, 1989
Wild West, December 2001

TRUETT EUGENE ROWE

Special Agent
Federal Bureau Of Investigation

The warden of the Oklahoma State Prison at McAlester described George Guy "Bud" Osborne as "a punk, a louse, a habitual liar and absolutely unreliable." Osborne was released in October, 1936 and arrested again in the spring of 1937 at Eufala, Oklahoma, for auto theft. He soon escaped from jail and made his way to Pampa, Texas, where he stole a car and headed toward New Mexico. Because his criminal activities took him across state lines, Bud Osborne became of interest to the FBI.

Special Agent Truett E. Rowe, 33, worked out of the FBI's El Paso Field Office (which at the time took in all of New Mexico). In late May, 1937, Rowe learned that Bud Osborne had a brother, Wes Osborne, living near Gallup. The agent took a bus to Albuquerque and then another one to Gallup.

On June 1st, Rowe walked into the office of Gallup Police Chief Kelsey Pressley and asked for a ride out to the Osborne place. Pressley didn't know where Osborne lived and suggested the agent try the Sheriff's Department. Rowe learned that Sheriff Dee Roberts was away from the office, fishing near Ramah, and he returned to the police department. Pressley agreed to drive the federal officer.

After asking around, Pressley learned that Osborne's small ranch was near Stinking Spring, 17, or so, miles south of town. The chief found it with no trouble. Wes Osborne, his wife Ethel, and 13 year old son, J. W., greeted the officers in the door yard as Bud Osborne fled from the house to the barn. Young J. W. went into the barn and told his uncle that Chief Pressley was outside with a man in a gray suit. Bud and his nephew walked out of the barn. Agent Rowe identified himself and asked the suspect to go to Gallup for questioning. Bud agreed but asked to be allowed to change clothes and pack some things. Rowe agreed and followed the ex-con into a bedroom in the small clapboard house. Chief Pressley kept an eye on other members of the family, including Bud's 17 year old wife, Betsy Louise. Pressley heard a shot and Bud Osborne suddenly appeared in the doorway, a gun, a .32 caliber revolver, in his hand. The chief drew his own gun but it misfired and

Osborne fled out the back door and disappeared into some brush.

Agent Rowe made it to the yard in front of the house where he dropped to his hands and knees. He was losing a lot of blood. He asked the chief to get him to a hospital as soon as possible. Pressley and Wes Osborne got the agent into the car and Pressley headed for Gallup. Later Chief Pressley recalled hearing the agent plead: "Open the door and give me some air! For God's sake, chief, give me some air!"

Pressley said all the windows were rolled down in his car and he was driving 80 miles per hour. At St. Mary's Hospital, Sister Mary Carina, a nurse, declared the agent dead.

After he fled the house, Bud Osborne doubled back and took J. W.'s horse which was saddled and standing near the barn. He mounted up and headed for a bluff called The Hogback west of Stinking Spring.

Undersheriff Dwight Craig heard news of the shooting. He recruited three Navajo trackers and along with Deputy Sheriff Lawrence "Bobcat" Wilson headed for Stinking Spring in pursuit of the killer. They picked up Bud's trail and were following it when Chief Pressley and Assistant Police Chief Les Mahoney arrived at Wes Osborne's house. The chief saw a rider herding cows along an arroyo and coming toward the house. Pressley, himself a cattleman, noticed that the drover's stirrups seemed much too short. The officers quickly drove their cars into the small herd and Assistant Chief Mahoney pulled down on the rider with a shotgun.

"You aren't as smart as you thought you were," Pressley said.

"No, but I damn near got away with it," Osborne said.

Federal Agents from El Paso, St. Louis and Kansas City converged on Gallup. They transferred Osborne from the McKinley County Jail to Albuquerque. At his trial in September, Osborne claimed the shooting was an accident. He said he'd dropped the gun as he and Rowe struggled, and it accidentally discharged. The jury didn't buy it and on September 30, 1937, Bud Osborne was convicted of first-degree murder. He was sentenced to life in prison but was released in the late 1960s. Bud Osborne died in Dallas in 1975, thirty-eight years after he killed Truett Rowe.

Agent Rowe was born at Amity, Arkansas, and educated in Oklahoma City and Houston, Texas. He served in the army and with the Border Patrol before he applied to the FBI in 1934. Famed FBI agent Melvin Purvis (the man who led the hunt for John Dillinger and participated in the gunfight which resulted in the bank robber's death outside the Biograph Theater in Chicago on July 22, 1934) wrote on Rowe's application: "Applicant has a natural investigative ability. [He is] a sharpshooter who is familiar with dangerous situations. He is all right in that respect." The FBI accepted Rowe in 1935.

On the day he died, Truett Rowe carried in his pockets and on his person an eighty-cent round-trip train ticket between Albuquerque and Gallup, $8.49 cents in cash and a loaded .38 caliber Colt revolver.

Agent Rowe was survived by his wife, Victoria. She received two checks from FBI Director J. Edgar Hoover: one for about $1,000 and a second for about $5,000. The money came from a fund made up of voluntary contributions by the 634 agents which made up the FBI in 1937. She also got a job as a secretary with the FBI field office in Chicago. Hoover said Agent Rowe's death was an "... irreplaceable loss of a devoted public servant." The agent was buried at Oklahoma City.

The FBI was created in 1908. Truett Rowe was the ninth agent killed in the line of duty, and the only FBI agent killed in New Mexico.

Albuquerque *Journal*, June 2, 3 & 4; September 28, 29, & 30, 1937

Bart Ripp, "The day that Truett Rowe was shot." Albuquerque *Tribune*, May 25, 1987

James W. Nelson, Special Agent in Charge, FBI Albuquerque, correspondence, October 24 and November 17, 1989

Tom Kneir, Special Agent in Charge, FBI Albuquerque, correspondence, November 7, 1995

WARREN RUIZ

Deputy Sheriff
Sierra County Sheriff's Department

The item in the Albuquerque *Journal* for October 5, 1942, read, in part:

> Deputy Sheriff Warren Ruiz, 51, of Hot Springs, was killed late
> Saturday night while attempting to help a fellow officer during
> a brawl outside a roadside tavern south of here [Hot Springs,
> now called Truth or Consequences].

> A coroner's jury found that Ruiz was beaten with a blunt in-
> strument and shot, apparently with a .22 caliber pistol that had
> been wrested from Deputy Sheriff Ed Martinez of Dona Ana
> County during the brawl.

> [Martinez] attempted to break up an altercation and arrest the
> participants. ...A fight ensued in which Martinez lost his gun
> and badge. It was then that Ruiz appeared on the scene and
> went to Martinez' help.

Two men, Horatio Apodaca and Willie Luchini were arrested in the matter,
but available resources do not disclose the disposition of the case.

Albuquerque *Journal*, October 5, 1942
Las Cruces *Sun-News*, October 6, 1942
Las Vegas *Daily Optic*, October 5, 1942
Paula Moore, *Cricket in the Webb*, University of New Mexico Press, 2008

J. B. "JERRY" RUSK

Private
New Mexico Mounted Police

The news item read:

> "J. B. Rusk, the well-known and efficient mounted policeman, died at 5 o'clock yesterday afternoon in a hospital in Alamosa, Colo. of pneumonia. Death was unexpected although Mr. Rusk had been ill for almost a week. He contracted the illness on a trip to Denver where he presented requisition papers to the governor of Colorado for the person of J. W. King, city marshal of Antonito. The sheriff of Rio Arriba county, Silviano Roybal, met Mr. Rusk at Antonito and took the prisoner in charge and he is now being held pending action on a charge of larceny. Mr. Rusk was taken to the hospital at Alamosa where he died.

> "Mounted Policeman Rusk was about 40 years old, a native of Kansas and a member of the territorial Mounted police since April 1, 1907. He was considered by his superiors and by his associates to be one of the most efficient and fearless upholders of the law in the sparsely settled districts of northern New Mexico. There were few offenders in that section who one time or another had not felt the strong arm of the law through the agency of the indomitable officer. He made his headquarters at Chama, Rio Arriba County.

> "There is mourning among the boys in the mounted police office who valued him for his friendship as well as for his efficiency and as an officer of the law."*

The New Mexico Mounted Police existed from February, 1905, to February, 1921. The small group of lawmen was organized on a military structure: The chief was a captain, his assistant a lieutenant, with sergeants and privates at the lower ranks. Jerry Rusk is the only member of the Mounted Police known to have died while a member of the organization.

* The above news item appeared identically in both of the following papers:

Albuquerque *Morning Journal*, January 10, 1912
Santa Fe *New Mexican*, January 8, 1912
Chuck Hornung, *The Thin Gray Line - New Mexico Mounted Police*, Western Heritage
      Press

JEFFREY C. RUSSELL

Traffic Officer
Albuquerque, New Mexico, Police Department

Officer Jeff Russell normally rode his police motorcycle to work, but on the morning of Tuesday, January 8, 2002, he drove his police car. He was en route to the Gerald Cline substation to do follow-up work on a fatal accident he had previously investigated. As he traveled west-bound on Interstate Highway 40, near the Carnuel exit east of Albuquerque, he pulled into the left lane to pass a semi truck and slammed into a State Highway Department road sweeper which occupied a portion of the traffic lane. Witnesses said that Officer Russell had no opportunity to avoid the collision. He died as a result of the accident. The driver of the sweeper was not seriously injured, and was not charged with any offense.

Jeff Russell, 46, was a 16 year veteran of the Albuquerque Police Department. Other officers often called him "Josey," after the Outlaw Josey Wales. Russell was an avid fan of Clint Eastwood and his movies. Albuquerque Police Captain John Gonzales called Officer Russell "a gentle cowboy. I think that's how he would like to be remembered," he said.

The officer was survived by his wife, Doreene, and four children: Tamara, Emily, Laufen and Clint. He was interred at the Mountain Valley Cemetery in Edgewood, New Mexico.

Albuquerque *Journal*, January 9, 11, 12, 20 & 27, 2002

WILLIAM "BILL" L. RUTHERFORD

Sheriff

Otero County, New Mexico

In early February, 1923, two young thieves named William G. LaFavers (or LaFaver, LaFavors or LaFores),* 19, and Charles Hollis Smelcer (or Buck Smitzer), 21, stole a saddle and other tack from a rancher in northern Lincoln County. Soon arrested for the crime, they were taken before a magistrate in the village of Corona and sentenced to jail at the county seat in Carrizozo. Lincoln County deputies A. S. McCamant** and Graciano Yrait*** took custody of the two and started for Carrizozo.

McCamant rode in the back seat of the Ford touring car with LaFavers and Deputy Yrait drove. Some distance from town, on a rough road, LaFavers made a grab for McCamant's pistol that the officer carried in his pocket. The two men struggled until McCamant kicked open the car door and both fell out onto the roadway as the car came to a stop. The deputy's gun fell into the dirt and LaFavers was able to grab it before McCamant could retrieve it. Smelcer grappled with Yrait, too, but he was getting the worst of the fight until LaFavers took charge of the situation at gun point. The outlaws debated killing the deputies but finally forced the officers to walk away and they covered them with a rifle until they were out of sight. LaFavers and Smelcer took the car and fled. The officers had to walk 12 miles to the closest telephone.

LaFavers and Smelcer headed south. They stopped in Carrizozo and bought .30-30 caliber ammunition for the rifle they'd taken from the officers and then continued on to Tularosa. They had some trouble with the Ford and stopped there to have it repaired. Then they headed for Alamogordo.

Sheriff Bill Rutherford of Otero County returned to Alamogordo on the evening of February 13 from a trip to Santa Fe. At about 8:30 p.m. he received a phone call from Harry Straley, a deputy to Lincoln County Sheriff Ed Harris. Straley told Rutherford about LaFavers and Smelcer, described them, and warned that they were armed and "desperate characters." A short time later, Sheriff Rutherford stepped out of the Warren Drug Store at the corner of 10th Street and New York Avenue and saw a car matching the description of the Lincoln County car pull to the curb. Two men occupied the Ford; one behind the wheel and one in the rear seat. The sheriff walked up to the car.

"If you have no objection, I would like to search this car," a witness heard the sheriff say.

The car suddenly lurched backward, then shot ahead. Rutherford stepped up on the running board and reached inside. Witnesses believed that he tried to turn off the gas. A loud BANG filled the air and witnesses thought a tire had blown up but the sheriff fell away from the car and was left lying in the street as the Ford ran over a curb stone and sped away. A citizen named O. M. Smith soon knelt at the sheriff's side, but there was nothing he could do. The bullet hit Rutherford in the neck, killing him almost instantly. Witnesses and bystanders were puzzled about what became of the sheriff's hat. It was nowhere to be found and yet he'd been wearing one when he approached the Ford.

Word of the sheriff's murder spread around Alamogordo quickly. A "fast car" occupied by former sheriff Howard Beacham and car dealer Shorty Miller headed south out of town on the Orogrande Road. A second car, occupied by Deputy Sheriff H. M. Denny and a citizen named Louis Wolfinger, headed southwest along the Las Cruces Road. District Attorney J. Benson Newell directed much of the search and sent out word to authorities in all directions. Thirty minutes after the shooting, a tourist car arrived in Alamogordo from the south and the driver reporting passing a south-bound Ford touring car driving at a high rate of speed. All concerned believed it to be the fugitive car.

Shorty Miller's Buick ran out of gas north of Orogrande and he and Beacham were obliged to walk into the little town for gas. By midnight officers learned that Lincoln County sheriff's Ford had been located abandoned near Orogrande. Bloodhounds were ordered and a large posse was on hand to follow the dogs, but they were unable to go beyond the railroad track, for some unknown reason. A detachment of troops from Fort Bliss arrived at early morning and an airplane took up a search of the area. A special train with a railroad carload of horse-mounted possemen also arrived from Alamogordo and a second train made up of an engine, boxcar and caboose stopped in Orogrande with deputies from Lincoln County.

As the day progressed, one of the posses searching south and east of Orogrande discovered a sheep-lined coat known to have been taken from one of the Lincoln County deputies when the outlaws escaped custody. The manhunt centered in that area and in the early afternoon posseman M. L. Bradford, riding horseback, spotted the fugitives as they saw him and opened fire with the rifle. Bradford was hit in the leg and returned fire, emptying his pistol without hitting either of the wanted men. The killers retreated behind a small hill and soon saw two other mounted possemen riding in their direction, and then a posse of men on foot approached. They raised a white cloth of surrender and put down their guns.

In their flight, the two had covered about 15 miles from the point where they abandoned the car. They had circled and were returning to the El Paso road where they intended to steal a car when they were caught. By 6:45 p.m. on February 14, LaFavers and Smelzer were locked away in the Otero County jail.

Smelzer was wearing Sheriff Rutherford's hat.

A grand jury convened on February 26 and indicted the outlaws on charges of first degree murder. The two were tried at Alamogordo and on Thursday, March 1, 1923, just 23 days after they killed the sheriff. The jury took 35 minutes to convict them of the crime. On Saturday, March 3, LaFavers and Smelzer were sentenced to hang on April 6, the penalty to be executed in the Otero County jail yard.****

Defense attorneys appealed the convictions but before a higher court could hear the case, Governor James Hinkle commuted Smelcer's sentence to 40 to 50 years and LaFavers' to life imprisonment. Smelcer was paroled to Glendale, California on April 10, 1931 and Governor Arthur Seligman pardoned him on April 21, 1932. LaFavers was paroled to Amarillo, Texas, on December 23, 1936 and pardoned by Governor John E. Miles on April 13, 1939.

Bill Rutherford, 40, was a well-known and prominent stockman in southern New Mexico. His obituary read, in part;

"He was one of the most popular men of Otero County and had probably the widest acquaintance in the Southwest of any man in the county. He had been a resident of the county [Otero] for the past fifteen years, coming here from Marshall, Mo."

Rutherford served two terms in the New Mexico legislature before he was elected sheriff in 1922. He'd been a lawman for six weeks at the time of his death. He was survived by his mother and father who lived at Marshall, Missouri, where the lawman was buried.

*One source identified LaFavers as "Bill Morris."
** A. S. McCamant later became sheriff of Lincoln County (See Tom Jones, page 160).

*** A story which appeared in the Albuquerque *Journal* said a Lincoln County deputy named Pete Lucino alone escorted the prisoners.

**** New Mexico counties performed their own hangings until 1931 when the state took over that chore and changed the method from hanging to electrocution.

Alamogordo *News,* February 15 & 22, March 1 & 8, 1923

Albuquerque *Morning Journal,* February 14 & 15, and April 6, 1923

Howard and Blanch Brooks, Memories, Oral history tapes, Alamogordo Public Library, September, 1975. Howard Brooks was a member of one of the foot posses which pursued LaFevers and Smelzer. He incorrectly stated that the State Police brought in bloodhounds. The New Mexico State Police Department was not created until 1935.

Murray E. Morgan (1906-1988), Report on the Rutherford affair prepared in 1976 and presented to the Alamogordo Public Library in June, 1981. Morgan called the Rutherford murder "One of the major tragedies in the history of Alamogordo."

David Thomas, Alamogordo DPS, undated correspondence.

(Special thanks to Mrs. Josephine Anderson of Alamogordo for providing the Brooks and Morgan documents.)

CLEMENTE SALAZAR
Special Town Marshal
Bernalillo, New Mexico

The annual San Lorenzo fiesta is a major social event in the town of Bernalillo, the seat of Sandoval County. The celebration in 1950 was no exception but early on the morning of August 11, the celebration took a tragic turn.

The bars closed and the *bailes* ended at 2:00 o'clock on Friday morning. Different witnesses told different versions of the story. Some claimed that Bernalillo had been *invaded* by young men from Albuquerque who caused all the problems. One alleged observer said a bunch of men ran toward the altercation, all of them armed and that he heard many shots fired. One man told investigators he heard seven shots, another heard five and yet another heard only two. District Attorney Paul Tackett, after reviewing initial investigations done by Town Marshal Guadalupe Quintana and Sheriff Emiliano Montoya, believed that a fight broke out—perhaps over a woman—after a dance ended and Marshal Salazar was set upon when he attempted to break it up.

When other officers reached Marshal Salazar, they found him dead. He'd been shot twice; once in the neck, just above the sternum, and once in the left chest. Both his eyes were blackened indicating that he'd been severely beaten and he'd been stabbed with an ice pick-like weapon. His own gun was missing and never recovered. Witnesses reported seeing Frank Fernandez, 25, of Armijo (south of Albuquerque) with a gun in his hand. Marshal Quintana shot Fernandez in the foot and arrested him. Sam Baca, 18, of Bernalillo, received a bullet wound to the hip in the altercation.

Fernandez was treated at Veterans Hospital in Albuquerque, then charged with murder and placed in the Sandoval County jail. He was bound over for trial on August 28, 1950 and subsequently convicted of second degree murder and sentenced to 50 to 75 years in prison. He appealed the conviction and was released on a $20,000 bond. While free, he was arrested several times on a variety of charges including possession of marijuana, assault and battery, and accepting stolen property. On September 22, 1952, the New Mexico Supreme Court upheld his conviction and sentence and he was returned to prison.

Special Town Marshal Clemente Salazar, 36, was survived by his wife, Adelina, and four children: Casindo, 4, Rudy, 7, Francis, 9, and José, 11.

Albuquerque *Journal*, August 12, 13, 15, 16, & 29, 1950
Emily Aguilar, Bernalillo Police Department, March 13, 1996

ANDREW P. SANDERSON

Agent
Federal Bureau Of Narcotics And Dangerous Drugs

Andrew P. Sanderson, a Federal Narcotics Bureau Agent stationed at Denver, Colorado, was killed in an automobile accident which occurred after a tire blow-out resulted in the vehicle's rollover near Lordsburg, New Mexico, on September 23, 1944. His passenger, another agent, named White, was not seriously injured.

No other information regarding Agent Sanderson has been located. Sheriff Oscar Allen of Hidalgo County reported that the agent was en route to El Paso at the time of the accident.

Las Vegas *Daily Optic*, September 25, 1944
Santa Fe *New Mexican*, September 25, 1944
U. S. Department of Justice, Drug Enforcement Administration, *Briefing Book*, June 1991

STEPHEN SANDLIN

Officer
Mountainair, New Mexico, Police Department

Officer Stephen Sandlin, 21, was found dead on the floor of the Mountainair police station on the evening of May 7, 1988. He had been shot once in the head with his own .357 magnum service revolver which was found near his body. He was on duty at the time. The New Mexico State Police, the New Mexico Attorney General's Office and the Federal Bureau of Investigation have investigated the circumstances surrounding Officer Sandlin's death. The FBI reported in October 1989 that no final determination as to the nature of the incident had been made. In May of 1995, however, New Mexico Attorney General Tom Udall declared that the death was the result of a homicide, not a suicide. No one has ever been arrested and prosecuted for the crime.

A resident of Bosque Farms, Stephen Sandlin had been a Mountainair police officer for eight weeks—at a salary of $204 per week—when he died. His father, Tom, of Albuquerque and his mother Eileen Sandlin Martin of Springer, survived him. His father was a former Albuquerque police lieutenant. Officer Sandlin was also survived by a son, Robbie, 2.

Albuquerque *Journal*, May 14, 23; July 29, 1989; March 4, 1990; May 19 & 22, 1995
Federal Bureau of Investigation, correspondence, October 24, 1989
Thomas A. Sandlin, correspondence, November 10, 1999

GEORGE ADOLPHUS SCARBOROUGH
Range Detective/Deputy Sheriff
Grant County, New Mexico

On April 2, 1900, Deputy George Scarborough received a telegram in Deming from rancher Walt Birchfield requesting help in searching for some cattle thieves. Scarborough joined Birchfield at San Simon, Arizona Territory, and the two men took to the trail on April 3. Late in the day, they were ambushed and both were shot; Scarborough in the leg, just above the knee (the bullet also killed his horse), and Birchfield in the arm.

Birchfield erected a small fort out of rocks to protect the deputy, and then rode for help.

He returned in the early morning hours of the following day and found Scarborough alive but suffering greatly. The Deputy was taken to the railroad station at San Simon and then on to Deming. Doctors operated in an effort to save the officer's leg, but they couldn't save his life. He never came out of the anesthetic and died early on the morning of April 5, 1900.

No one was ever arrested and charged with Scarborough's murder. An El Paso news item reported that a posse encountered "fugitive murderers" Burt Alvard, Bravo Johnson and William Stiles, who, it alleged, had "ambushed and murdered" George Scarborough. Stiles, it was reported, died in the gunfight. The problem was that the news item was in error on just about every count. Alvard, Johnson, and Stiles were in jail in Arizona when the officer was killed, and Stiles is known to have lived on for some years. Two other men, George Stevenson and Jim Brooks, were subsequently arrested by Grant County, New Mexico, Deputy W. D. "Keechi" Johnson (page 156) and locked up in the jail at Silver City. They escaped in late May 1900, and were never recaptured.

Geroge Scarborough had served as a peace officer for most of his adult life; as a Texas sheriff and Ranger and Deputy U. S. Marshal, before he assumed his duties in New Mexico in 1897. As a deputy marshal, Scarborough killed John Selman (April 5, 1896) who was noted as the man who murdered Texas killer John Wesley Hardin by shooting him in the back (April 19, 1895). Note that in one of history's coincidences, Selman and Scarborough died four years apart, to the day.

Deputy Scarborough, a native of Louisiana, was 40 years old at the time of his death. He was survived by his wife, Mollie, and seven children. His son, 20 year old Ed, served for a time as a deputy sheriff, constable and Arizona Ranger, but was convicted of murder in 1915 and sentenced to prison, from which he escaped, never to be captured.

A newspaper of the day said this: "[George Scarborough's death] removes one of the best known characters in this section. He was brave as a lion. This is the universal testimony of all who knew him."

Albuquerque *Journal Democrat*, April 6, 11 & 15, 1900
Robert DeArment, *George Scarborough, The Life and Death of A Lawman on the Closing Frontier*, University of Oklahoma Press
Leon Metz, *The Encyclopedia of Lawmen, Outlaws, and Gunfighters*, Checkmark Books
Leon Metz, *John Selman, Gunfighter*, University of Oklahoma Press
Dan L. Thrapp, *Encyclopedia of Frontier Biography*, University of Nebraska Press.

JOHN "KEVIN" SCHULTZ

Officer
Pojoaque Pueblo Police Department

Officer Kevin Schultz and his family participated in a church-sponsored fishing trip on Saturday, August 17, 2002. The policeman observed a 12 year old boy lose his bait and go into the water after it, only to get into water well over his head. Schultz had to run for some distance before he could dive into the water and get to the boy. He was able to get the child, unconscious, to shallow water. The boy regained consciousness and saw that Schultz was face down in the water. Efforts to revive the officer were unsuccessful.

The boy's father said, "He saved my son's life. My son lost consciousness. I could never imagine someone giving me such an amazing gift as to save my son's life." Taos County Sheriff Charlie Martinez concurred. "The young boy was definitely drowning."

Officer Schultz, 44, moved to Santa Fe from Kansas City, Missouri, about two years before his death. He worked for the Santa Fe County Sheriff's Department for a time before he joined the Pojoaque Police Department. He moved to New Mexico to help with the start-up of Sangre de Cristo Bible Church, with which he served as youth pastor. He was the chaperone of the group on the fishing trip. He was survived by his widow, Cheryl and an eight year old son, Keagan.

He was well regarded by his law enforcement colleagues. Pojoaque Police Sergeant Andy Gutierrez said, "No matter what kind of day it was, Kevin would show up and put a smile on everyone's face. His main joy was Cheryl and Keagan. He would spend hours talking about them. He's a hero in our hearts."

Albuquerque *Journal*, August 20, 2002
Santa Fe *New Mexican*, August 20, 2002

C. B. SCHUTZ

Constable, Lordsburg Precinct*
Grant County, New Mexico

According to news reports from the mining town of Pyramid, south of Lordsburg, a man by the name of U. Sierra got drunk one day in early May of 1893 and went after Constable C. B. Schutz with a "heavily loaded quirt." He intended to kill the lawman, but instead got arrested for his trouble. A local judge named Medbury sentenced Sierra to sixty days in the Grant County jail at Silver City.

On Sunday evening, May 7, two men, Celso Analla and David Ramires, burglarized T. R. Brandt's store at Stein's Pass of $50.00 while the storekeeper was at home eating supper. Suspected of the crime, one of them confessed and a Judge McGrath bound them over to the grand jury at Silver City.

On Thursday, the 11th, C. B. Schutz and another constable named Ownby set out from Lordsburg to Silver City with the three prisoners in tow. Ramires and Sierra, shackled hand and foot, rode in the front seat of the wagon beside Schutz who drove the team. Analla, also handcuffed, rode in the rear seat with Constable Ownby who sat on his pistol, presumably so that he had quick access to it. As the wagon crossed Cactus Flat, about nine miles south of Silver City, Analla suddenly pushed Ownby off the wagon and grabbed the lawman's pistol. Hearing the scuffle, Schutz turned to see what the matter was just as Analla shot him in the head. Schutz fell from the wagon and Analla shot him twice more, once between the shoulder blades and once in the right shoulder.

Ownby attempted to get back on the wagon, to recover his gun, but was repulsed. Analla ordered him to run for his life and Ownby complied as the outlaw fired shots at him, none of which took effect. After the constable was gone, Analla realized that Ownby had the keys to the shackles they all wore. He ordered Ramires and Sierra to pursue Ownby but it was a useless effort. The two, chained together, soon gave up. Analla robbed Schutz's body of gun and watch before the three outlaws got back up on the wagon and set out for Silver City.

They encountered an old man south of town and paid him five dollars to get them a file and some whiskey. Later that evening, Ramires and Analla went on into town and purchased food and more whiskey, and then they disappeared. Sierra spent the night with the old man and next morning, still wearing one handcuff, surrendered himself to Grant County Sheriff Andrew Laird. Sierra reported the murder of Schutz and claimed that Analla and Ramiers put him off the wagon

274

about eight miles from town and forced him to walk. It took him the better part of the night, he said, to make the trek to town in a pouring rain, and he walked the streets until dawn. The flaw in his story lay in the fact that his boots and clothing were free of mud.

Telegrams were sent to all points asking authorities to be on the lookout for the killers. Sheriff Laird and another man rode south and encountered Ownby a mile or so from town. The constable was very ill, suffering from pneumonia induced by exposure to rain and cold the nightlong. They found Schutz's body and subsequently the abandoned wagon. Posses were sent out in every direction but to no avail. The rain had obliterated any tracks they might have left.

History records nothing of a personal nature regarding C. S. Schutz.

* Lordsburg was in Grant County until Hidalgo County was created in 1919.

Silver City *Enterprise*, May 19, 1893

EDWARD SEAMAN

Town Marshal
Loma Parda, New Mexico

In the late summer of 1872, a Texas cattleman named John Hittson decided that the time was right for him and 30 or so cowboys to mount a raid against New Mexico farmers and ranchers whom he believed had, over a period of years, stolen Texas cattle and horses; or in the alternative, had bought the stolen animals from the *Comancheros** who had stolen them in the first place. This Texas troop ranged up and down eastern New Mexico, plundering as they went, and by some estimates, confiscated 15,000, or so, head of livestock wherever they found them.

As a part of this effort, a small group of Texans arrived in the village of Loma Parda, near Fort Union,** and demanded virtually all of the stock in sight. A group of citizens led by Marshal Seaman (who was also the postmaster) held the Texans at bay, and they left town. When they returned, the contingent had grown to 25 or 30 cowboys. The first encounter was with a local resident, Julian Baca, who refused to surrender two of his horses. When he tried to get into his house, the Texans assaulted him and beat him with pistols "until his body was black." His neighbor, Toribo Garcia attempted to help, only to be shot in the back and killed. Marshal Seaman arrived in the meantime, and was promptly cursed by the Texans before he was slashed across the face with a rifle barrel (which put out his left eye). He tried to flee to safety into a corral only to discover that the enclosure was full of Texans who were busy appropriating livestock. He again tried to escape, only to be blocked by horsemen. Finally he was able to flee, but was soon shot down. "The ball entered the back part of the head and came out just above the forehead tearing away quite a large piece of the skull, and causing instant death." When the village *alcalde* protested, he, too, was shot, a bullet passing through both of his legs.

Hittson, for his part, claimed that he had no part in any killings, and that if any of his riders killed anyone, it was only because they were provoked into it, or acting in self-defense. In any case, no one was ever prosecuted for the murders of Toribio Garcia or Marshal Edward Seaman.

Nothing of a personal nature is known about Edward Seaman.

* *Comancheros*, according to some historians, were simply traders who dealt with the Comanche Indians and not criminals as they are often portrayed in popular literature and movies.

276

** Loma Parda was a small settlement, primarily of sheep raisers, until Fort Union opened in 1851. From then until the fort closed, the town operated as recreational area for soldiers on leave, with all that implies. It reverted to its former status after the fort closed in 1891. Very little of the town remains today. It is on private property and not accessible to the public.

Fabiola Cabeza de Baca, *We Fed Them Cactus*, University of New Mexico Press
Robert Julyan, *The Place Names of New Mexico*, University of New Mexico Press
Charles L. Kenner, "The Great New Mexico Cattle Raid—1872," *New Mexico Historical Review*, October 1962
Miguel Otero II, *My Life on the Frontier*, University of New Mexico Press
The Weekly New Mexican, September 24, 1872

E. C. "DAVE" SERNA

District Attorney
Sixth Judicial District Of New Mexico
(Grant, Hidalgo & Luna Counties)

District Attorney Dave Serna, 54, died in a single car accident on the evening of October 14, 1977. He had served the Sixth Judicial District as District Attorney for 21 years at the time of his death.

Born at Rincón in Doña Ana County, Dave Serna studied at both Western New Mexico University at Silver City and New Mexico State University at Las Cruces. He received his law degree from Tulane University in New Orleans, Louisiana, and established a law practice at Silver City in 1950. He was elected District Attorney in 1956.

A Western New Mexico University Regent, he was also a member of the United Latin American Citizens, state and national District Attorneys associations, the Commission on Criminal Justice Planning, the Knights of Columbus, and others.

Dave Serna was survived by his wife, Barbara; three sons, David, Richard and Jeffrey, of Albuquerque; his mother, Mrs. Margaret Serna of Silver City; one brother and two sisters.

The District Attorney was described as a "...pioneer Mexican-American lawyer in southwestern New Mexico."

Albuquerque *Journal*, October 17, 1977
National Law Enforcement Officers Memorial Fund

278

RONALD E. SHORES

Patrolman
Questa, New Mexico, Police Department

Officer Ron Shores established a roadblock by parking his police car across both lanes of a two-lane bridge on State Road 3 near Questa on November 3, 1977. The Taos County Sheriff's department had requested his assistance in stopping a car believed stolen in Santa Fe and being pursued by Taos County deputies. The car approached the roadblock at a high rate of speed, struck the police unit, and then slammed into Officer Shores who was on foot behind the car. The officer died at the scene of massive head and internal injuries.

It is noteworthy that Officer Shores was able to stop a car approaching from the north just before he was killed, and the vehicle was operated by Questa Mayor Max Ortega. "In giving his own life, he definitely saved the mayor's," Questa Police Chief Robert Taggart said.

The fleeing vehicle continued for a few hundred yards after the collision before it stopped and its driver fled on foot. Taos County officers quickly apprehended him. The driver of the car, Albert Romero, 20, of Taos, was charged with manslaughter, possession of stolen property, and aggravated battery on a police officer. He was later convicted.

Patrolman Shores, 27, had been with the Questa Police Department less than two months at the time of his death. His father, Leon Shores, and a four-year-old son survived him.

Albuquerque *Journal*, November 5, 1977
Questa Police Department, correspondence, November 21, 1989
Santa Fe *New Mexican*, November 4, 1977
Taos *News*, November 10, 1977

WILLIAM "BILL" SIBRAVA

Deputy Sheriff/Lieutenant
Bernalillo County, New Mexico

Albuquerque attorney Joe Mercer, 57, a former state senator and one time candidate for governor, was aware of his son's deteriorating mental condition. Police had been called to the home of Stephen Mercer, 33, in southeast Albuquerque on at least two occasions when the younger Mercer threatened violence to himself and/or others. One standoff lasted 45 minutes and the other seven hours. By Friday afternoon, May 27, 1994, the elder Mercer had taken the legal steps necessary to have his son temporarily, and involuntarily, committed to the Veterans Administration Medical Center in Albuquerque for evaluation.

Joe Mercer took the "Certificate of Evaluation" to the Bernalillo County Sheriff's Department and asked that it be served. Lt. Bill Sibrava, assistant commander of the Civil Division agreed to do so. Sibrava had long experience in the Civil Division and he was considered the department's expert in the use of Verbal Judo and used it often to avoid violent conflict in the course of his work. Aware of Stephen Mercer's mental condition, Sibrava decided that he would have a better chance of taking him into custody if he wore civilian clothing. He also elected to leave his bulletproof vest at the office. Sgt. Allan Rider and Deputies Shawn Benavidez and Phil Duran accompanied Lt. Sibrava and Joe Mercer to the younger Mercer's residence on Richmond southeast in Albuquerque.

The men stood in Stephen Mercer's living room as Joe Mercer tried to talk his son into submitting peacefully to the commitment order. The younger Mercer had a pistol in his hand which he held close to his stomach. Even so, the officers in the room did not draw their own weapons.

"Look," the elder Mercer said to his son, "you need to go to the hospital; you need to get an evaluation; we need to see what's bothering you."

Suddenly, Stephen Mercer began firing his gun. One bullet hit his father. It passed through one lung and shattered the elder Mercer's spine. Two bullets hit Lt. Bill Sibrava and though mortally wounded, Sibrava managed to pull his own gun and shoot Stephen Mercer at close range. Deputies Benevidez and Duran also drew and fired. Sgt. Rider did not shoot because the other officers were in his line of fire. When the shooting stopped, the younger Mercer had been hit 15 times. He was dead at the scene. Joe Mercer and Bill Sibrava both died at the hospital a short time later. On October 12, 1994, a Bernalillo County grand jury took five minutes to find the deputies justified in shooting the younger Mercer.

Bill Sibrava was a 19-year veteran of the Bernalillo County Sheriff's Department and a five-year veteran of the Civil Division at the time of his death. He'd planned to retire in July of 1995. Lt. Sibrava was survived by his wife of 19 years, Angelita, two daughters, Sabrina 18, and Sheree, 16.

Sheriff's Department Sgt. Bill Martinez said this:

"I've worked many years with him. He [was] the kind of man other deputies would like to emulate. He was the kind of professional other deputies could count on and follow into a dangerous situation. He was the type who would rather talk to an individual than have a confrontation."

Albuquerque *Journal*, May 28, 29, 30 & 31; June 1; and October 13, 1994
Bernalillo County Sheriff's Department
Angelita Sibrava, conversation, October 29, 1999

JOSEPH RALPH SILVA

Lieutenant
New Mexico Department Of Corrections

Lt. Ralph Silva, a corrections officer at the Southern New Mexico Correctional Facility west of Las Cruces, wrote a disciplinary report on inmate James Edward Pettes for possession of a shank; a prison-made knife. After the prison disciplinary committee found Pettes guilty of the infraction, Pettes asked to meet with Lt. Silva. They met in a captain's office at about 5:30 p.m. on Friday, April 3, 1987.

The prison control center became alerted that something was wrong when Lt. Silva activated the emergency switch on his portable radio. A captain and two corrections officers rushed to the office in time to see Pettes leaving and to find the lieutenant lying on the floor, bleeding profusely from the head. A bloody two by four board lay on the floor nearby. Ralph Silva died later that night of his injuries.

Pettes was serving life in prison for the murder and attempted rape of Carol Gordon, a 33-year-old mother of three in Las Cruces in 1983. He pleaded guilty but mentally ill. Pettes previously served time for the armed robbery of a laundry in Las Cruces. Shortly after he was paroled on the armed robbery charge, he was arrested and convicted of rape. After he was paroled on the rape charge, he killed Mrs. Gordon. He was convicted of voluntary manslaughter in the killing of Lieutenant Silva.

A four-year veteran of the Corrections Department, Ralph Silva previously served as a Doña Ana County Sheriff's Deputy, a Las Cruces Police officer and a New Mexico State University Police officer. The Corrections Department had commended him for exemplary performance of duties. Two sons, Fernando Rey, 1½, and Adam Joseph, two months, and his parents, Salvador and Josie Silva of Las Cruces survived Lieutenant Silva, as did a sister, Priscilla Rodriguez, and two brothers, Rudy and Alberto.

Albuquerque *Journal*, April 4 & 8, 1987
Lt. West Gilbreath, Doña Ana County Sheriff's Department

New Mexico Department of Corrections, correspondence, November, 1989
Albert Silva, correspondence, May 21, 1990 & November 15, 1999

LOUIS SILVA

Night Marshal
Gallup, New Mexico

There had not been a night for a dozen years when Officer Louis Silva did not try the door of every business in Gallup. He was out and about and doing that chore in the early morning hours of September 15, 1930. Near the Atlantic and Pacific Garage, he encountered a suspicious character whom he attempted to question about the burglary of the K & M drug store hours before. A gun was stolen in the burglary and apparently the suspicious man used the same weapon to shoot and kill Officer Silva.

R. S. Avery, a bus driver, claimed to be an eyewitness to the killing. He described the slayer as a "Negro of small size." The description was sent out statewide and suspects were soon rounded up in Santa Fe, Raton, Clovis and Tucumcari. All had alibis.

On October 4, a murder complaint filed by Manuel Silva, the officer's son, against the witness, R. S. Avery, was heard before Judge Reed Holloman. The hearing lasted all day and the courtroom was packed, but when it was over Judge Holloman ruled that insufficient evidence existed to hold Avery for the murder. He was freed and soon left town for Oconia, Montana, to attend to the estate of his parents who had been recently murdered. He said that he would return to Gallup at any time to assist in concluding the Silva murder investigation. The matter was not concluded. No arrest was ever made for the crime in spite of the fact that rewards totaling $1,250 were offered by the business community and the city government.

Louis Silva had lived in Gallup for about 30 years at the time of his death. He had been night marshal for 12 years. He was survived by a wife and six children, three boys and three girls. The local newspaper commended Officer Silva under a headline that read:

SILVA MURDER CASE STILL A DARK MYSTERY
"The bereaved family have [*sic*] the heartfelt sympathy of the

entire community in the death of the husband and father who died like a soldier 'in the line of duty'."

Gallup *Independent*, September 19 & October 10, 1930
Cpl. Sam Gomez, Gallup Police Department, correspondence, 1989

FRANK A. SJOLANDER

Patrolman
Albuquerque, New Mexico, Police Department

Albuquerque Police Officer Eugene Casey spotted the car at about an hour after midnight on Wednesday morning, December 1, 1954. It bore Texas plates and matched the description of a car used in several recent armed robberies. It was parked on Gold Avenue near the intersection of Arno Street. Casey radioed Officer Frank Sjolander and asked his help in checking a boarding house at 124 Arno to see if the car's owner could be identified.

Before the officers could knock, the door opened and gunfire erupted. The fight that followed was fast and furious. Both officers were hit but both returned fire. When the smoke cleared both officers were down and one of the outlaws, James Leroy Spahr, 22, was dead. Frank Sjolander died at the hospital about 45 minutes later. Gene Casey survived his wounds.

Investigation revealed that a second shooter along with Spahr was one James Church Isted, A. K. A. George Townsend, 21. He fled the scene of the gunfight by jumping out a window and made his way, afoot, to a residence on Lopez Street, southwest, where Lawrence Jay Snow, 20, joined him in flight. Snow was an accomplice in the armed robberies. Both men were California parolees.

The manhunt on December 1 and 2—some said it was the largest in the history of Albuquerque—soon centered a dozen or so miles south of town, around Isleta Pueblo and Bosque Farms. A railroad shack near Isleta station was found broken into and looted and the operator of a trading post at Isleta Pueblo positively identified a photograph of Lawrence Snow as the man who had been at the store seeking food. Officers from many different departments surrounded the Pueblo while Isleta police officers checked buildings on the reservation. No luck.

Things changed on Friday morning. The ground search paid off. A group of five officers came upon a cold campfire. They called for a bloodhound named Symbol and allowed the dog to smell clothing which had been taken from the suspect's Lopez Street house. The animal soon struck the trail and led the officers to the outlaws who were hiding on a silt island in the middle of an irrigation ditch about two miles south of Isleta. The criminals, under the officer's guns, offered no resistance. They were forced to wade in waist deep in icy cold water from the island to shore. The time was about 11:00 a.m., December 3, 1954. Officer Frank Sjolander's funeral had just concluded.

Once in custody, Isted admitted that he shot officers Sjolander and Casey. Spahr was known to have fired only one shot before his gun jammed. The weapon, containing seven live rounds, was found under his body. Isted fired eight times, emptying his gun. Officer Casey was hit five times and Sjolander was hit four times. Isted said he'd smoked marijuana before the shooting, and he was drunk, too. On April 11, 1955, Isted pleaded guilty to first degree murder and was promptly sentenced to life in prison. Lawrence Snow pleaded guilty to armed robbery and was sentenced to five to 15 years in prison.

A native of Texas, Frank Sjolander had been with the Albuquerque Police Department for about 13 months at the time of his death. He was survived by his wife, Helen, 28, one son, Guy, 10, and daughters Helen, 3, and Mary Agnes, 2. He was buried at Baytown, Texas.

Albuquerque *Journal*, December 2, 3 & 4, 1954; April 12, 1955
Albuquerque Police Department

CHARLES B. SMITH

Deputy Sheriff
Grant County, New Mexico

Joe Malloy returned to Silver City in late July, 1907, from Las Vegas where he participated in the territorial encampment of the New Mexico National Guard, Company D. On July 28 he began a drinking binge which continued most of the day on the 29th. Late in the day he purchased a bottle of whiskey and returned to the small house he shared with his mother and a man named Percy Thomas. Crazed with liquor, he found his revolver in a bureau drawer and announced that everybody in town had been "doing him dirt" and he was going to set matters right.

Malloy's mother and Thomas both attempted to dissuade him, but to no avail. Malloy took a shot at a lighted lamp, and missed. Then he stepped onto the front porch. A citizen by the name of J. E. Harwell had the bad luck to be passing by just then and Malloy shot him, inflicting a minor wound in the side. Malloy retreated back into the house as Harwell ran off in search of an officer. He soon found Grant County Deputy Sheriff Charles Smith.

Smith was unarmed at the time, but borrowed a pistol from another deputy before he went to Malloy's house. It was not of much use to him. When he stepped onto the front porch, Smith noted that the blinds were drawn and the door closed. He pushed the door open, and as he did so, Malloy opened fire, shooting rapidly and emptying the gun. One bullet struck Deputy Smith in the chest, severing the pulmonary artery; a second bullet hit the officer in the jaw. He died at the scene.

Malloy ran to an area near the courthouse where he held officers at bay for a short time with his empty pistol. He was soon disarmed and arrested. He claimed that he hadn't shot anyone, but a stranger who had fled over the hills had done the shooting. The coroner's jury, however, found Malloy was responsible for the killing. Available resources do not indicate what became of Malloy.

Charles Smith, 27, was described as a fearless and dutiful officer, quiet, sober and industrious. He had worked for the Victorio Land and Cattle Company before joining the sheriff's department. Unmarried, he was survived by two sisters and one brother, all residing in Texas.

"His death [was] much deplored and the citizens of Silver City [were] indignant over the killing as such occurrences [were] getting to be common in that section."

It was thought for a time that local citizens would take Malloy from the jail and exact vigilante justice, but extra officers prevented that happening.

Albuquerque *Journal*, July 31, 1907
Deming *Headlight*, August 1, 1907
Silver City *Independent*, July 30, 1907

DAVID SMITH

Patrolman
New Mexico State Police

Patrolman David Smith served as spotter for State Police Officer and pilot Lowell Howard as they conducted an airborne check for speeding motorists on U. S. Highway 550 just east of Farmington on August 6, 1984. The plane crashed killing both men. See page 143 for details.

David Smith, 29, was born in Colorado, but his family moved to New Mexico when he was one year old. He graduated from Aztec High School in 1975. He joined the State Police in 1978 and was stationed in Jal and Aztec. His wife, Jennifer and twin children, David Jr., and Sally, aged 7, survived him. Officer Smith's father, William E. Smith, Sr., served as chief of the Aztec Police Department. His brother, Thomas, served as an officer with the Farmington Police Department and another brother, William E. Smith, Jr., served as chief of the Aztec Fire Department. Officer David M. Smith was buried at the Aztec Cemetery.

Albuquerque *Journal*, August 7, 1984
Farmington *Daily Times*, August 6, 7, 8 & 10, 1984
The Roadrunner (New Mexico State Police Association, Vol. 3, No. 2, Summer, 1992)

DOMINIQUE J. SMITH

Deputy

Torrance County, New Mexico, Sheriff's Department

On the evening of January 19, 2009, Deputy Smith was a part of the investigation of a vehicle involved in transporting illegal narcotics. The vehicle was stopped near an entrance ramp along Interstate Highway 40 near the town of Moriarty, in Torrance County. As the inquiry continued, three law enforcement units were parked near the suspect vehicle, along with a flat-bed tow vehicle. All of them had emergency lights engaged. Deputy Smith stepped onto the roadway to take a picture of the vehicle in question. He was struck by a van operated by a Santa Rosa woman who failed to reduce her speed as she approached the scene. Deputy Smith died of his injuries. The driver of the car that hit the deputy was charged with failure to yield to an emergency vehicle.

Subsequent State Police investigation indicated that emergency vehicle flashing lights were visible for more than half a mile, as well as from the top of the eastbound ramp.

Deputy Smith, 32, was originally certified as a police officer in 2001 and had previously worked for the Estancia Police Department. He was survived by his wife, Heather, and two children.

Albuquerque *Journal*, January 20 & 21, 2009
New Mexico State Police Uniform Crash Report, January 20, 2009

RICHARD SMITH

Officer
Albuquerque, New Mexico, Police Department

At about 10:15 p.m. on Wednesday, August 18, 2005, Albuquerque Police Officers Richard Smith and Michael King were dispatched to an address on Gold Street SE to pick up a mental patient named John Hyde, 48. For complete details, see page 170.

A native of Albuquerque, Richard W. Smith joined the Albuquerque Police Department in 1980 and retired in 2000. He was rehired in 2004. He held a variety of assignments during his career and received a number of commendations. He made a perfect score in firearms proficiency in 1985. He was survived by his widow, Susan, and 13 year old daughter.

Police Chief Ray Schultz said, "Richard loved this job. Richard loved this community. He loved this department. He loved traffic enforcement and making the streets safer."

Albuquerque *Journal*, August 19 to 28; November 30, 2005; August 14 & 15, 2009
Albuquerque Police Department
Albuquerque *Tribune*, August 19 & 20, 2005
Santa Fe *New Mexican*, August 20, 2005

A. L. SMITHERS

Deputy Sheriff
Luna County, New Mexico

Deputy Smithers and Deputy Thomas H. Hall were killed during a gun battle with jail escapees on November 18, 1911, in the Black Mountains of Socorro County. For details see page 121.

RAMON ROBERT SOLIS

Patrolman
New Mexico State Police

Officers Ramon Robert Solis, Jennifer Schurman and Damon Talbot (see page 306) all completed the 64th State Police Recruit School in Santa Fe in December of 2000 and were assigned to the Roswell State Police District.

On Friday, October 19, 2001 all three were engaged in a training exercise on helicopter landing-zone safety. Upon completion of the training, the medical helicopter pilot, Shawn Kling, asked the officers if they would like to go for a ride. They agreed and the helicopter took off to the west of the Roswell State Police Office. It crashed within a few minutes. Officers Solis and Talbott were killed and Officer Schurman was seriously injured. Kling was also badly injured. The cause of the crash was not immediately determined. Both Schurman and Kling survived their injuries.

Officer Solis, 30, was born in Roswell and graduated from Goddard High School and the New Mexico Military Institute. He served in the U. S. Army from 1993 to 1996 and attained the rank of sergeant. His official biography described him as a "well-liked officer in the community and very motivated."

Both officers were buried with full law enforcement honors and both were interred in Roswell's South Park Cemetery. The Roswell State Police office was named in honor of the two officers.

Albuquerque *Journal*, October 20, 21, 22 & 24, 2001; February 5, 2002
Roswell *Daily Record*, October 24, 2001

WILLIAM THOMAS SPEIGHT

Patrolman
New Mexico State Police

When the State Police Department erected a 200-foot radio tower on Wolford Mountain near Cloudcroft, Officer Bill Speight assumed responsibility for maintaining it. Electric lines did not reach the top of the mountain and the Air Force had provided a generator which kept the beacon on top of the tower working. The officer could drive part of the way to the tower through Silver Spring Canyon but had to walk some distance to reach the generator.

Deep snow covered the ground when Officer Speight set out for the tower late Monday or early Tuesday, February 21 or 22, 1949. When he failed to return home as scheduled, a search was undertaken. Members of the search party included State Police Chief Hubert Beasley and Captain Al Hathaway, other State Police officers and Otero County Sheriff's Deputies. Officer Speight's body was found on the morning of Thursday, February 24. He was about a quarter mile from his car and it appeared that he'd sat down to rest and died. His car was stuck in the snow and he'd struggled to reach the place where he was found. A coroner's jury ruled that the officer died of a heart attack induced by exhaustion.

Bill Speight joined the State Police in 1937. He left the department and returned several times during his career, including a stint in the army during World War II when he served as a military policeman. In 1939, he engaged in a gunfight at an Alamogordo residence in which he was shot in the leg with a shotgun. He shot and killed his assailant. Doctors were unable to remove all of the bird shot from the wound and it caused him discomfort for the rest of his life. In 1947, as he assisted the Border Patrol in pursuing some illegal aliens aboard a freight train, his leg gave out and he fell off the top of a boxcar. He broke his neck and severely damaged his spine. He recovered from those injuries well enough to return to duty, but he suffered occasional blackouts. On one occasion, he blacked-out and drove his patrol car into a concrete embankment. State Police officers did not have sick or injury leave benefits at the time so Chief Beasley allowed Officer Speight to continue working for the department, but he would not issue him a car. Any work Speight did was done in his personal car.

In the course of his career, Officer Speight was awarded a Certificate of Distinguished Service for the shooting in 1939 and Certificate of Commendation for a cattle stealing case.

Bill Speight, 38, was born in Wellington, Texas. He moved to Las Vegas, New Mexico, in 1933. In his state police career he was stationed at Estancia, Alamogordo, Raton and Tucumcari. He was survived by his daughter, Billy Ann, 15. His wife, Annie, died of a heart attack in 1947. He was also survived by his parents, Mr. & Mrs. T. H. Speight of Clovis and a brother, Jack, of Albuquerque. Speight was buried at Alamogordo.

Albuquerque *Journal*, February 25, 1949
The Roadrunner (New Mexico State Police Association, Vol. 3, No. 2, Summer, 1992)

WILLIAM M. STEDMAN, JR.

Officer

Bloomfield, New Mexico, Police Department

Officer Stedman was killed on February 27, 1982, when his departmental vehicle was involved in an accident on State Road 44 about one mile north of Bloomfield. Officer Stedman had his emergency equipment activated at the time his vehicle was struck broadside by a dump truck. No citations were issued.

Officer Stedman, a native of North Carolina, was survived by his wife, Marie, and an 18 month old son, William Wayne. The Bloomfield Police Department established a trust fund for his wife and son. Officer Stedman was buried at Memory Gardens.

Farmington *Daily Times*, February 28, March 1 & 3, 1982

DWIGHT B. STEPHENS

Sheriff
Luna County, New Mexico

Things were astir in Deming on Sunday morning, February 20, 1916. Members of the New Mexico Cattle and Horse Growers Association were beginning to arrive for their annual convention and the Great Council of the Improved Order of Red Men would also meet in town during the following week. Dr. Fred Stephens and his wife were in town visiting his brother, Luna County Sheriff Dwight Stephens and his family.

Things were astir over at the Luna County jail, too.

One cell in the lock-up housed three prisoners: Jesse O. Starr and C. Schmidt, burglars who'd robbed the Palace Saloon, and W. F. Dashley a forger and embezzler. Jailer Emzie Tabor opened the cell door so Schmidt could empty the chamber pot. The burglar waited until Tabor turned his back to re-open the cell door then he grabbed the jailer and pinned his arms to his sides. Starr and Dashley helped out. They took Tabor's guns and keys and robbed him of his watch and five dollars in cash. The three outlaws were in control of the jail.

They locked Tabor in their former cell and unlocked all the other cells. Two prisoners elected to join the little gang in escaping: Francisco Acosta, accused of a murder at Spalding, New Mexico, and Joe Cranston, a vagrant. (The story goes that Cranston was reluctant to participate, but the others persuaded him to go along by promising that he could drive the getaway car.) They broke into the jail's armory and took rifles, handguns and a large supply of ammunition before they crossed the jail yard and broke into the office where there was a telephone.

Dashley called Del Snodgrass, owner of the Park Garage and Ford Dealership. He ordered that a car be brought around to the jail so that a sick prisoner could be taken to Faywood Hot Springs, northwest of Deming in Grant County. Dashley requested a full gas tank and extra tires. He also asked Snodgrass to bring change of a twenty-dollar bill so he could settle up for use of the car right away.

Busy getting ready to provide garage space and automotive services to arriving cattlemen and conventioneers, Snodgrass didn't suspect a thing. He arrived at the jail only to be confronted by five men pointing guns in his direction. He, too, was robbed and locked up with Emzie Tabor. The bandits cut the phone lines, threw the jailhouse keys into a gopher hole, and set off to the northeast, toward the town of Rincon, 50 miles away.

Tabor and Snodgrass set up a racket to attract attention to their plight, but no one could hear them. Half an hour passed. Then the wife of one of the prisoners who'd elected to remain in jail arrived for her weekly visit. She freed Tabor and Snodgrass who soon sounded the alarm.

Sheriff Dwight Stephens first assumed the outlaws would head for the Mexican border, thirty miles south. He alerted all crossing points by telephone. Then he set about assembling a posse. Witnesses reported seeing the Ford with five men heading northeast, and the six-man posse gave chase in their own machine (automobiles were called *machines* in 1916). The escapees had more than an hour head start, but it wasn't enough. The Deming *Headlight* for February 25, 1916, reported what happened next:

> ...[T]he posse took the trail, finally running on their quarry in a narrow cañon where they had stopped to eat lunch. Deputy sheriff[s] John T. Kelley and Wayne Estes, who had dropped off the car and had tried to outflank the outlaws, scrambled to the top of the hill overlooking the cañon where they were seated. At the same time Sheriff Stephens, Buck Sevier and [Deming town] Marshal Tabor came up the cañon, walking to within a few feet of the men before they saw them. Sevier immediately ordered them to throw up their hands, but the only reply was a fusillade of shots. Sheriff Stephens dropped at the first exchange of shots, dying instantly, and Sevier received a scalp wound that stunned him, and that came within an ace of taking off the side of his head. From the top of the bluff overlooking the cañon deputy sheriff Kelley, Marshal Tabor, Jack Arnold and Wayne Estes poured a hot fire into the outlaws, wounding Starr and killing Cranson. The other three men, Dashley, Schmidt and Acosta broke for the brush and made their escape.

What followed was a manhunt of gigantic proportions. Several carloads of men arrived from Deming along with a U. S. Army detachment under Lt. Clyde Earl Ely. Since the gunfight took place in Doña Ana County, Sheriff Felipe Lucero and his posse became very active in the search, too.

W. C. Simpson, a cattle inspector, and Fred Sherman, both of Deming, joined

Marshal Tabor in the search for Schmidt. They found him at 7:00 o'clock the following morning. He'd made it just sixteen miles, to the east and south of Rincon. He offered no resistance when they arrested him.

Three days later, late in the afternoon, Sheriff Lucero and Las Cruces city marshal Adolfo Sainz caught Acosta's trail on the Flat Lake Ranch, northeast of Rincon. They trailed the fugitive throughout the night, across the San Andres Mountains and into Otero County, a distance of 35 or 40 miles. At noon the following day they located Acosta on the J. B. Baird Ranch. Suffering from hunger and exhaustion, the killer submitted meekly to arrest. He joined Schmidt in the Doña Ana County jail.

Newspapers speculated that the fifth outlaw would be soon captured. One even speculated that W. F. Dashley would be back in jail within 48 hours. It wasn't to be.

W. C. Simpson succeeded Dwight Stephens as Luna County Sheriff. He and Doña Ana County Sheriff Lucero kept up the search for Dashley in the weeks and months that followed. At one point, Simpson traced Dashley to Venice, California, but police there failed to act in a timely way and the fugitive escaped. The same thing happened in San Francisco. On August 26, Dashley's luck ran out. Authorities in Reno, Nevada, arrested him and held him for Sheriffs Simpson and Lucero who happily escorted him back to New Mexico.

After Dashley's arrest and conviction, the *Deming Headlight* commented: "The perfect understanding which exists between the peace officers of Luna, Doña Ana and Grant counties is a powerful aid in the ferreting out of criminals who may be tempted to operate in the southwestern portion of the state, and is an assurance that there is no twilight zone in these parts where outlaws can operate with impunity and feel secure from capture."

In March, 1916, J. O. Starr, C. Schmidt and Francisco Acosta were tried for the murder of Sheriff Stephens. Starr admitted firing shots and seeing Stephens and Sevier fall. He claimed he fired in self-defense after the officers fired first. The jury didn't buy it. Starr was convicted and sentenced to hang. Schmidt was convicted of second degree murder and sentenced to life in prison. Acosta was acquitted of killing Stephens, but was immediately arrested by Luna County authorities for the killing at Spalding the year before. He was tried and sentenced to 20 years in prison on that charge.

Dashley, whose real name was A. B. Smith, generally considered the leader of the gang and the brains behind the escape was also convicted of murder in March, 1917 and sentenced to death. Documentation has not been found that shows that either Starr or Smith were executed for the murder of Sheriff Stephens.

A word is in order about Sheriff Dwight Stephens. A 43 year old native of Ohio, he'd lived in Deming for about 25 years at the time of his death. First appointed sheriff by Governor Miguel A. Otero in 1904, he served continuously, except for two years, until his death. Sheriff Stephens participated in a gunfight with jail escapees in November of 1911 in which his deputies Tom Hall (page 123) and A. L. Smithers (page 292) were killed.

Well liked and respected, the Albuquerque *Journal* reported that Stephens' funeral was the largest in Deming history, attended by the entire community.

Fred Fornoff, former captain of the New Mexico Mounted Police said this: "Sheriff Stephens was not a gunman in any sense to which odium might attach. The Luna County Sheriff was a fearless man and had a high sense of duty."

Dwight B. Stephens was survived by a wife and four children, aged three to 12 years. He was also survived by his parents who resided with his family in Deming.

Albuquerque *Morning Journal*, February 21, 22, 24, 25 & 26, 1916

Deming *Graphic*, March 16, 1904, February 25 & September 1, 1916

Deming *Headlight*, February 25, & September 8, 1916; March 9 & 23; April 6 & 13, 1917 Captain Jack Coussons, Luna County Sheriff's Department, correspondence, May 22, 1991

William Kuehl, Deming Police Department

RAYMOND SUTTON, SR.

Agent
Prohibition Bureau, U. S. Department Of The Treasury

The 18th Amendment—The Volstead Act—became the law of the land on January 18, 1920. It made the manufacture, transportation, and/or sale of alcoholic beverages illegal in the United States. To enforce the act, the Prohibition Bureau was created within the U. S. Department of the Treasury.

One of the first agents appointed in 1920 was rancher, banker, and former sheriff of Union County, New Mexico, Raymond Sutton, Sr., of Clayton. His territory covered the five northeastern New Mexico counties. He maintained his headquarters at his home, but often stayed overnight in towns across his assigned area. He was staying at the Seaberg Hotel in Ratón on August, 28, 1930. He expected to meet with Trinidad, Colorado, Police Officer Oscar Vanderberg that evening. The two of them planned to work in the Ratón Pass area in search of rumrunners.

But on that Thursday afternoon, Agent Sutton drove south out of Raton, toward Cimarron. At a point about seven miles from Dawson, he pulled off the road and parked. Colfax County Undersheriff Boots Fletcher saw him parked there, waved, and drove on. Fletcher was among the last people to see Agent Sutton alive. A week later, the district director of the Prohibition Bureau in Albuquerque, Charles Stearns, became concerned about the agent. His last report had been filed on August 27, and Sutton had uncharacteristically failed to appear for a district court hearing in Clayton. Stearns contacted Colfax County Sheriff Al Davis.

Sheriff Davis discovered that all of Sutton's belongings remained unpacked in his hotel room and some reports upon which the agent had been working seemed to be undisturbed. The sheriff called Mrs. Sutton in Clayton and asked if she knew her husband's whereabouts. She had not heard from him in several days.

By Friday, September 5, Stearns, Davis and Sheriff A. W. Turner of Union County headed up a party of about a 100 men and a search in the mountains around Raton began. The Colorado National Guard sent an airplane to help out and a posse of horsemen joined in. Other law enforcement agencies also participated: Mora County Sheriff's Department, the sheriff from Trinidad, Colorado and federal agents from across the Rocky Mountain States. Several groups offered rewards which totaled more than $500. By September 18, when no trace of Agent Sutton, or his car, had been found, the search was all but called off.

But the case took on a new dimension on September 19 when a subject by the name of James Caldwell was arrested. He'd cashed Sutton's last paycheck some four days after the agent disappeared. Caldwell used Sutton's Masonic membership card as identification. Specifically, Caldwell was charged with passing a false check and forgery.

On October 18, 1930, a cowboy named Rafael Zamora found Agent Sutton's car in a deep arroyo some 18 miles southwest of Raton. Lodged between two piñon trees and covered with brush, the Pontiac was so well concealed that drivers of cars on the Taos-Raton highway passing by only ten yards away could not see it. Search parties had also covered the area without seeing it. Fingerprint experts went over the car with care, but rain had done much to wash away usable prints. The ominous thing about the car was the discovery of blood in the back seat. Investigators surmised that Agent Sutton had been killed outside the car, and then the vehicle used to haul his body away. Searchers hoped the body would be found near the car. It was not.

A federal grand jury indicted James Perry Caldwell in December, 1930, and he was tried at Pueblo, Colorado, in January, 1931. The witness who originally saw him cash Sutton's check suddenly could not identify Caldwell as the culprit. The passing a false check charge was dismissed. The trial continued on forgery charges. Expert witnesses testified that the signature on the check was not Ray Sutton's; that Sutton's name had been forged by Caldwell. Even so, the jury took about 20 hours to acquit Caldwell.

Agent Sutton had been very active in enforcing the Volstead Act; in raiding stills and disrupting liquor traffic. Speculation at the time was that one of the major bootleggers in the area was responsible for Sutton's death, and James Perry Caldwell was involved in it. There were countless theories concerning where the body had been disposed of but none were ever proven because the body was never found. There was little doubt, however, among those familiar with the case, that Ray Sutton was murdered, and most likely on the afternoon of August 28, 1930. No one else was ever prosecuted in the case.

The 18th amendment was repealed on December 5, 1933.

Ray Sutton was born in Woodward County, Oklahoma in 1873. In 1910 he was appointed the first sheriff of Ellis County, Oklahoma, and two years later elected to the position and reelected in 1914. He moved to New Mexico after leaving office in Oklahoma and in 1916 he was elected sheriff of Union County. He was reelected in 1918. He joined the Prohibition Bureau after leaving office. His wife, Margaret, a son, Ray Jr., and a daughter, Nello, survived him. He was preceded in death by a daughter, Hazel, who died at 14 in 1919.

Albuquerque *Journal*, December 23, 1930; January 17, 1934

Mrs. N. H. Click, Compiler, Mrs. Charles E. Leierer, Editor, "Tragedies in Our County," *Us*

Nesters in the Land of Enchantment, (First person accounts of early life in northeastern New Mexico, copyright 1980, Cora Glenn Click.)

Chuck Hornung, "The Mystery Death of Federal Prohibition Officer Ray Sutton," National Association & Center for Outlaw and Lawman History, University of Wyoming, Laramie, April-June, 1991

Mike Pappas, "Officer Vanishes in Prohibition Drama," Raton *Range*, January 31, February 8 & February 14, 1989

WALTER GRANGE TABER

Patrolman
New Mexico State Police

Patrolman Walter Taber, 40, was stationed in Grants but he'd been at State Police headquarters in Santa Fe for training in September 1937. On Wednesday, September 22, he started for home. Only a few blocks from headquarters, at the inter-section of Cerrillos and Indian School Roads, a car pulled out in front of his motorcycle. The collision was unavoidable. Officer Taber suffered a broken hip, lacerations and contusions on the face and head. He was taken to St. Vincent's Hospital where he died a week later on September 29.

Walter Taber joined the State Police in June 1935. A member of the second State Police training school,* he was the first State Police officer killed in the line of duty. He was survived by his wife, Evelyn, and a daughter, Elizabeth.

* The first State Police training school ran from April to May, 1935. It pro-duced eight officers.

Albuquerque *Journal*, September 23 & 30, 1937
The Roadrunner (New Mexico State Police Association, Vol. 3, No. 2, Summer 1992)

DAMON KYLE TALBOTT

Patrolman
New Mexico State Police

Officers Damon Talbot, Jennifer Schurman and Ramon Robert Solis (see page 294) all completed the 64th State Police Recruit School in Santa Fe in December of 2000 and were assigned to the Roswell State Police District.

On Friday, October 19, 2001 all three were engaged in a training exercise on helicopter landing-zone safety. Upon completion of the training, the medical helicopter pilot, Shawn Kling, asked the officers if they would like to go for a ride. They agreed and the helicopter took off to the west of the Roswell State Police Office. It crashed within a few minutes. Officers Talbott and Solis and were killed and Officer Schurman was seriously injured. Kling was also badly injured. The cause of the crash was not immediately determined. Both Schurman and Kling survived their injuries.

Officer Talbott was born in Trinidad, Colorado, but graduated from Roswell High School. He was described as an "honest and trustworthy citizen." He was the youngest State Police officer ever killed in the line of duty.

Both officers were buried with full law enforcement honors and both were interred in Roswell's South Park Cemetery. The Roswell State Police office was named in honor of officers Talbott and Solis.

Albuquerque *Journal*, October 20, 21, 22 & 24, 2001; February 5, 2002
Roswell *Daily Record*, October 24, 2001

ANDREW "ANDY" FRANCIS TINGWALL
Sergeant/Pilot
New Mexico State Police

In the late afternoon of June 9, 2009, a University of New Mexico graduate student named Megumi Yamamoto, 26, dialed 911. She reported that she was stranded in the mountains above Santa Fe. The weather was deteriorating, and she was not equipped to spend the night where she was. After some missteps which involved incorrect routing of her request for help, the decision was finally made to use the State Police helicopter. Sergeant Andy Tingwall, 37, piloted the aircraft accompanied by Officer Wesley Cox, 29, who served as spotter.

As he flew toward the Sangre de Cristo Mountains, Sgt. Tingwall saw an opening in the clouds and landed near Spirit Lake (called *La Laguna del Espíritu Santo*, or The Lake of the Holy Spirit, by early Hispanic settlers). Ms. Yamamoto told the State Police dispatcher (who was coincidentally Sgt. Tingwall's wife, Leighann) by phone that she didn't think she could walk to the helicopter. Sgt. Tingwall was able to find her and carry her to the aircraft on his back. The time was just before 10:00 p.m.

The weather worsened with increased wind velocity, blowing snow and sleet and clouds moved in rapidly. While Sgt. Tingwall could see the lights of Santa Fe when he landed, that was not possible as he attempted to lift off. He was completely socked-in when the rear rotor apparently struck a tree and the helicopter crashed at above 12,000 feet on the mountainside and tumbled several hundred feet down into a ravine. Ms. Yamanoto and Sgt. Tingwall were thrown out while Officer Cox remained strapped in his seat.

Officer Cox stayed with the wreckage throughout the night, and discovered that Ms. Yamamoto was dead. Shortly after the crash, he was able to make voice contact with Tingwall further up on the mountain, but that ceased by morning. After sunrise, Cox determined that he would make his way down the mountain, in spite of a crushed leg and a severe back injury. He was suffering from hypothermia when he reached rescuers. He reported that he believed that Sgt. Tingwall was dead, too. Because of the weather and the terrain, rescue parties were not able to recover the bodies until the morning of June 11. Officer Cox survived his injuries.

Andy Tingwall was born in New York but raised in Big Sky, Montana. He graduated from the New Mexico Military Institute at Roswell in the early 1990s and served with the U. S. Marine Corps before he joined the New Mexico State Police in 1995. In his 14 years of service he served as public information officer, tactical team member, and training officer in State Police Recruit School. He was named State Police officer of the year for 2008 after the rescue of a man he pulled out a flooded Albuquerque arroyo. The New Mexico Sheriffs' and Police Association also named him officer of the year for 2009.

Albuquerque *Journal*, June 11, 12, 13, 15, 16, 19, 20, 2009
Barry Massey, Associated Press, June 11, 2009
Santa Fe *New Mexican*, June 15, 2009

WILLIAM EDWARD TIPTON

Deputy Sheriff
Roosevelt County, New Mexico

Will Tipton was a blacksmith by trade, but he was serving as constable in Portales when Roosevelt County Sheriff Joseph Lang appointed him deputy sheriff for the community of Texico.* On April 25, 1907, while going about his duties, Tipton encountered Portales town marshal Byron Parrish drinking whiskey in the White House Saloon in Texico. There was bad blood between the two men. Tipton, in his official capacity, ordered Parrish to surrender his gun to the bartender, in accordance with a town ordinance. Tipton was within his legal right to make this demand since a marshal from another town had no special right to go about Texico packing a gun. As a matter of courtesy, however, lawmen rarely disarmed one another.

Parrish, described as a dangerous and fearless man, took his gun from its holster and moved as if to hand it over to the bartender, but instead he hit Tipton alongside the head with the barrel. The blow staggered the deputy, a powerful man, but he didn't go down and he managed to knock the gun from Parish's hand before the two men grabbed each other and wrestled "breast to breast." Parrish managed to reach around Tipton and take the deputy's pistol from his hip pocket where he habitually carried it. Parrish brought the gun up and shot Tipton in the head, killing him instantly.

Parrish was tried for shooting Tipton, and acquitted.

Deputy Will Tipton was survived by a wife and six children.

* In 1907, Texico was in Roosevelt County. Curry County was not carved out of Quay and Roosevelt counties until 1909.

Clovis *News Journal*, February 20, 1981
Larry Ball, *Desert Lawmen, The High Sheriffs of New Mexico and Arizona,1846-1912*, University of New Mexico Press
James D. Hamlin, *The Flamboyant Judge, A Biography as Told to J. Evetts Halley and Wm. Curry Holden*, Palo Duro Press
Gilbert Holguin, Marshal, Texico, New Mexico, conversation, October 4, 1995

ESTHER TODECHEENE

Patrolman
Navajo Tribal Division Of Public Safety

Navajo Tribal Police Officer Esther Todecheene, 24, died on June 8, 1998 when the departmental vehicle she was driving rolled over several times, ejecting her. She was responding to a call for assistance from another officer at the time of the accident.

Officer Todecheene, a New Mexico certified peace officer, had been with the Navajo Division of Public Safety for less than one year when she was killed. Her parents, two brothers and three sisters survived her.

New Mexico Law Enforcement Academy records
Officer Down Memorial Page

SHERMAN LEE TOLER JR.

Patrolman
New Mexico State Police

On the morning of March 5, 1986, Captain Bill Butts, commander of the Tucumcari State Police District, commended Patrolman Sherman Toler for the young officer's efforts in interdicting drug traffic along Interstate Highway 40 in Eastern New Mexico. In 1985 alone, the young officer recovered more than 726 pounds of marijuana, more than six pounds of cocaine, and four ounces of PCP. The drugs had a combined street value of more than $1.3 million. Toler made more than $37,000 in cash seizures and was responsible for the confiscation of 10 vehicles valued at more than $46,000. He made 20 narcotics arrests in 1985.

On that same March morning, a convicted narcotics dealer and thug named Cloyd Norman Hall, Jr., 35, and a female companion, were driving from his residence in San Bernardino, California, to St. Louis, Missouri. Hall was first stopped by police in Arizona and cited for a traffic violation. He was stopped again at a New Mexico State Police license and registration roadblock near Grants. Because his car, a black Cadillac, sat low in the back, an officer asked for, and received, permission to search the trunk. Nothing was found. Hall and his companion were allowed to go after about 10 minutes. Just before 6:00 p.m. on Wednesday, March 5, Officer Sherman Toler stopped the 1974 Cadillac for the third time, about 11 miles west of Tucumcari. He'd clocked it on radar at 60 miles per hour in a 55 zone.

Officer Toler issued Hall a warning citation and asked if he could look in the trunk. Hall agreed and walked to the rear of the car with the officer and stood beside him as the luggage compartment was opened. No one but Hall knows exactly what happened then, but a struggle between the two men took place, and both ended up wrestling on the ground. Hall managed to take Toler's gun and stand. At a range of about five feet, Hall emptied the .357 caliber magnum revolver into Toler's body. The killer was careful to shoot the officer in places where his bullet proof vest would offer no protection. Still, the officer was able to raise himself. That's when Hall beat him severely about the head with the gun before he jumped into the Cadillac and fled the scene.

Several passing motorists, including a truck driver, observed the incident and noted the description of Hall's Cadillac. At 6:06 p.m., an off-duty Santa Rosa policeman, Marty Pacheco arrived on the scene. Several motorists had already stopped and some were trying to administer resuscitation measures. Pacheco used Toler's police radio to request assistance and he broadcast the description of the car. Quay County Sheriff Joel Garnett, en route to the scene of the shooting, spotted the black Cadillac parked at the Stuckey's Restaurant about two miles west of Tucumcari. He arrested Hall and his female companion without incident. Hall had given Toler's empty gun to a waitress saying there'd been an *accident*.

Sherman Toler was pronounced dead on arrival at Trigg Memorial Hospital in Tucumcari later that evening. Officers found Judy Marie Toler at a Tucumcari church where she and the Toler children waited in vain for Sherman to join them for Wednesday evening services.

Cloyd Norman Hall had a criminal record going back 18 years to St. Louis where he was arrested for possession of stolen property at age 17. He served time in California prisons for drug violations and assault on police officers. In the latter case, Hall and another man disarmed two San Bernardino officers and threatened to "off the pigs." One of the officers managed to pull his backup gun and shoot and wound Hall. Hall was also a suspect in the killing of a 17 year old cocaine dealer the year before he killed Toler. Hall had been freed from a California prison about three years before he killed the New Mexico officer.

On a change of venue, Hall was tried at Fort Sumner later in 1986. Defense attorneys convinced the jury that deliberation and premeditation were lacking in Hall's actions, and the jury convicted him of second degree murder instead of first degree murder as asked for by the prosecution. Hall was sentenced to 17 years in prison.

One attorney was quoted as saying that just because he (Hall) killed a police officer didn't mean he should spend the rest of his life in jail. Hall became eligible for parole in late 1994 after serving eight and one half years, and according to New Mexico's good-time law, he could not be denied freedom. Hall told the Parole Board that he felt as though *he* was the victim in this case, not Officer Toler.

On December 27, 1995, after serving one year of parole at the Central New Mexico Correctional Facility at Los Lunas—he had applied to do his parole in both California and Missouri and neither would have him—Cloyd Norman Hall Jr. was released from custody, a free man. He served less than 10 years for the murder of Officer Sherman Toler.

A native of Albuquerque, Sherman Toler Jr. 27, graduated from Valley High School in 1976 and joined the State Police in 1979. He was stationed at Moriarty,

Elida and Portales before being assigned to Tucumcari. Officer Toler was survived by his wife, Judy Marie, twin sons, David Scott and Daniel Vernon, 3, a daughter, Tabatha Marie, 2, and his parents, Mr. & Mrs. Sherman Toler, Sr. of Tijeras. He was buried at Moriarty.

Albuquerque *Journal*, March 6, 7, 8 1986; May 5, June 12, 1994; December 27 & 28, 1995

Albuquerque *Tribune*, December 12, 1994

The Roadrunner (New Mexico State Police Association, Vol. 3, No. 2, Summer, 1992).

Tom Romero, Commander, Alcohol & Gaming Enforcement Section, New Mexico Department of Public Safety (Romero was a Tucumcari Police Officer at the time of Officer Toler's murder.)

USA Today, March 7, 1986

ANTONIO LINO VALDEZ

Deputy Sheriff/Jailer
San Miguel County, New Mexico

Antonio Lino Valdez served San Miguel County Sheriff Desiderio Romero as deputy and jailer* at West Las Vegas, New Mexico. On the afternoon of April 2, 1880, two men came to the jail door and asked to visit prisoner J. J. Webb who was being held for the murder of Michael Keleher, a freighter and rancher from Dakota Territory. Valdez recognized the men as Dave Rudabaugh, a former part-time policeman from East Las Vegas, and John "Little Allen" Llewellyn, a local house painter. Both had been to the jail to visit Webb previously. Valdez admitted them and followed them to Webb's cell.

Once at the cell door, Llewellyn pulled his gun and ordered Valdez to surrender the keys to the cell. Valdez refused and Llewellyn and/or Rudabuagh shot the jailer and removed the keys from his body. One of the outlaws tossed the keys to Webb and bade him free himself and they fled to a waiting hack. Webb declined and remained in his cell. Antonio Lino Valdez, carried into the jail's kitchen, died there of a bullet wound to the chest.

Two successive posses pursued the killers, and both were unsuccessful. One version of the story goes that after Rudabaugh and Llewellyn evaded the posses, they continued south, toward Fort Sumner. Llewellyn ailed from consumption and rheumatism and suffered considerably from many hours on horseback. He begged Rudabaugh to shoot him and put him out of his misery. Rudabaugh obliged and buried Little Allen along the trail. Whether the story is true or not has always been in question. What is known for sure is that Little Allen was never seen again.

Rudabaugh next showed up riding with William H. Bonney (Billy the Kid). On December 24, 1880, at Stinking Springs (east of Fort Sumner), Rudabaugh, Bonney, and two other outlaws—Tom Pickett and Billy Wilson—were captured by a posse led by Deputy U. S. Marshal and Lincoln County Sheriff-elect Pat Garrett. The prisoners were taken to Las Vegas where they could board a train for points south. West Las Vegas citizens, along with Sheriff Romero, tried to take Rudabaugh into custody so that he could be tried for the murder of Jailer Valdez. Garrett, functioning as deputy U. S. Marshal, prevailed and took Rudabaugh on to Santa Fe to face federal charges of mail theft.

In March of 1881, after Rudabaugh was sentenced to life in prison on the federal charges, he was returned to Las Vegas to face territorial trial for the murder of Antonio Lino Valdez. He was promptly found guilty and sentenced to hang. On December 3, 1881, Rudabaugh, along with J. J. Webb and five others escaped from the San Miguel County jail. He was never recaptured. A report reached New Mexico in February, 1886, that Rudabaugh, while drunk in a Parral, Chihuahua, *cantina*, and after being caught cheating at cards, shot and killed two men. In retaliation, local citizens attacked the outlaw, killed him, cut off his head and paraded it through the town's streets on the end of a long pike.

History records nothing of Antonio Lino Valdez's personal life.

* Some sources indicate that Valdez served as San Miguel County jailer; others that he was a deputy sheriff. It is possible, of course, that he served in both capacities.

Larry D. Ball, *Desert Lawmen, The High Sheriffs of New Mexico and Arizona, 1846-1912*, University of New Mexico Press

Howard Bryan, *Wildest of The Wild West, True Tales of A Frontier Town on the Santa Fe Trail* Clear Light Publishers

Leon C. Metz, *Pat Garrett, The Story of a Western Lawman*, University of Oklahoma Press

Jay Robert Nash, *Encyclopedia of Western Lawmen & Outlaws*, De Capo Press

Bill O'Neal, *Encyclopedia of Western Gunfighters*, University of Oklahoma Press

Dan L. Thrapp, *Encyclopedia of Frontier Biography*, University of Nebraska Press

FRANK X. VIGIL

Chief Deputy Sheriff
Valencia County, New Mexico

At about a quarter before two on the morning of May 23, 1898, armed men boarded the engine of a passenger and express train at Belen, New Mexico. They forced the engineer to move the train on down the line about two miles where they separated the express car from the other cars. They blew a hole in the safe and stole the contents. The railroad at the time placed the loss at $500;* an Albuquerque newspaper reported it at about $3500; later historians say $20,000 to $50,000 was taken. The thieves rode off to the west.

A few hours later, Valencia County deputies Frank Vigil and Dan Bustamente set off from Belen in pursuit of the robbers. Socorro County Sheriff Holm Bursum and deputy U. S. Marshal Cipriano Baca set out from Socorro on the same mission but their horses gave out and they turned back to get fresh mounts and more men. Vigil and Bustamente made camp for the night and rode into the Alamo Navajo community early on the morning of May 25. They were joined by a group of Navajo men, only two of whom were armed. The Indians told the deputies where the outlaws were hiding nearby and they set out immediately.

The posse arrived at the outlaw camp on Alamosa Creek at about 6:00 a.m. Some of the Navajos were able to get in close enough to lead off the bandits' horses before Vigil, Bustamente and two Navajos surrounded the camp. At a range of more than 100 yards, Deputy Vigil called out to the men to surrender and the outlaws seemed to comply, standing with their arms at their sides, their rifles leaning against a tree about ten feet away. The officers approached. At a range of about 35 yards, the outlaws suddenly grabbed their rifles, ducked behind some cottonwood trees and opened fire. Frank Vigil and Dan Bustamente were scarcely able to return fire before they fell, mortally wounded. One of the bandits was hit in the neck and as his partner tended to his wound, one of the Navajo possemen, Vicente Guerro, opened fire, wounding the outlaw in the hip and shoulder. The bandit fired at the Navajo with his rifle and Guerro fell dead with a bullet in the head.

The other possemen retreated south to Magdalena where they put out the first word of the battle. They later returned and recovered the bodies of the fallen officers which they took to the mining village of Santa Rita (called Riley when it became a ghost town in the early 1930s), east of Alamo on the Río Salado. Vigil and Bustamente were buried there, although Vigil's remains were later removed to Belen.

Valencia County Sheriff Jesus Sanchez lauded the bravery of his men in their effort to arrest the bandits, but he pointed out that they put themselves in considerable jeopardy by not having armed themselves with rifles. All four possemen were armed with only revolvers and their handguns were no match for the "improved" Winchester rifles the outlaws used in the gunfight.

The gang of train robbers was made up of William E. "Bronco Bill" Walters, Daniel "Red" Pipkin and William "Kid" Johnson,** all of whom had long criminal records. Walters in particular, considered one of the worst New Mexico outlaws, had been ordered to "quit the territory" in 1897. He obviously didn't stay away for long. The outlaws were believed to have buried most of the loot from the Belen train robbery—keeping a few thousand dollars for immediate needs—before they limped away from Alamosa Creek. They made it to Datil, New Mexico, where they stole horses and rode on west to a hideout in eastern Arizona near the small town of Geronimo, northwest of Safford on the Gila River. They lived there openly and spent money freely and after they shot up a Fourth of July dance, their presence in Geronimo came to the attention of Wells Fargo detectives George Scarborough (see page 271) and Jeff Milton.

By July 29, 1898, Scarborough, Milton and two other men reached a horse camp on the Black River twenty-five miles south of Fort Apache. They spent the night there and the next morning, Walters, Pipkin and Johnson rode into the camp. Walters sensed that something was wrong, wheeled his horse and started to ride out, firing shots at Scarborough as he went. The Wells Fargo agents opened fire and Walters, hit twice, fell from his horse. Pipkin and Johnson took cover and made a fight of it but Johnson was soon hit and mortally wounded and Pipkin, his horse killed, fled into the brush on foot and made good his escape.

Walters survived his wounds, was arrested and returned to New Mexico. In November 1899, he pled guilty to one count of second degree murder and received a life sentence in the Territorial Penitentiary. He was thirty years old when he began his sentence. In spite of the fact that Walters escaped from the Santa Fe prison in 1911—he was captured three days later—Governor Washington E. Lindsey pardoned him and set him free on April 17, 1917. Walters, using the name W. C. "Bill" Brown although everyone knew who he really was, died in 1921 on a ranch where he worked near Hachita, New Mexico after he fell off a windmill and broke his neck. He'd never been able to find the loot he buried near Alamosa Creek in 1898.

Red Pipkin was captured in March, 1899 near Moab, Utah and returned to

Arizona. He served time in Yuma Prison until 1907. In the 1920s, Pipkin became a McKinley County, New Mexico, deputy under Sheriff Bob Roberts. He committed suicide by shooting himself in 1938 rather than await death from cancer.

Frank X. Vigil of Belen was survived by his wife. They had no children of their own but they had adopted an Indian girl from the Albuquerque Indian School. Deputy Vigil was described as "...one of the bravest officers in New Mexico."

Dan Bustamente, about 50 years old and a blacksmith by trade, resided in the village of Los Chavez between Belen and Los Lunas. He was survived by a wife and two children.

History records nothing of personal nature about posseman Vicente Guerro.

* The railroads usually reported $250 to $500 taken in any robbery, no matter the actual amount. This was intended to show that train robbery was *not* a profitable business.

** This William "Kid" Johnson should not be confused with John "Kid" Johnson who participated in the killings of Albuquerque Marshal Bob McGuire and Deputy Marshal E. D. Henry in November, 1886. John "Kid" Johnson is known to have lived well into the 1920s.

Albuquerque *Morning Democrat*, May 25, 27 & 28, 1898

Larry D. Ball, *Desert Lawmen, The High Sheriffs of New Mexico and Arizona, 1846-1912* University of New Mexico Press

Howard Bryan, *Robbers, Rogues and Ruffians, True Tales of the Wild West*, Clear Light Publishers

Dan L.Thrapp, *Encyclopedia of Frontier Biography*, University of Nebraska Press

JAMES MONROE VIGIL

Lieutenant
Alamogordo, New Mexico, Department of Public Safety

Patrolling along U. S. Route 54 near the Alamogordo city limit on Wednesday, August 29, 1973, Lt. Jim Vigil stopped a light colored car bearing Kansas license plates for a routine traffic check. The car's driver, Alfredo Salinas, opened fire as Lt. Vigil approached on foot and two bullets from a .22 caliber pistol hit the officer. Lt. Vigil drew and fired three times and one of his bullets hit the assailant in the chest. Salinas, though wounded, got out of his car, removed the officer's pistol and shot him two more times with his own gun. A passing motorist found the officer lying alongside the road and called for help. Jim Vigil was pronounced dead at 1:30 p.m. at Gerald Champion Memorial Hospital of bullet wounds to the chest and head.

An illegal alien from Mexico, Salinas, 27, had been living in Wichita, Kansas. On Monday, August 27, after a domestic dispute, he shot and severely wounded his 16 year old wife, Connie, and fled toward Old Mexico believing he'd killed her. He apparently thought Officer Vigil stopped him because of the Kansas shooting.

Two hours after the shooting of Lt. Vigil, Alamogordo Mayor Eddie Olson—who participated in the search for the killer—and Officer Bill Woltz found Salinas in his car, parked along the road, dead. He'd suffered two bullet wounds: the one in his chest was believed to have been delivered by the officer before he fell; the second wound, to his head, was caused by Lt. Vigil's gun, probably self-inflicted. Officers found Lt. Vigil's gun in Salinas' car.

Jim Vigil, 29, was a six and one half year veteran of the Alamogordo DPS. His wife, Brenda, and two children, a girl aged seven and a boy aged three, survived him.

Alamogordo DPS Director Rex Carroll said: "[Vigil] was a very dedicated officer; very easy going and quiet. He was a man who enjoyed his work."

Alamogordo Department of Public Safety
Albuquerque *Journal*, August 30 & 31, 1973
Las Cruces *Sun News*, August 30, 1973
Officer Bill Woltz, conversation, March 8, 1996

CARL EMANUEL VOCALE

Deputy Sheriff
Doña Ana County, New Mexico

Deputy Vocale reported for duty at 10:00 p.m. on Saturday, July 15, 1989. He was first dispatched to assist other officers at a loud party which seemed to be getting out of control. While he was there, he received his second call of the shift, to assist another unit on a burglary call. The main route away from the party was clogged with traffic so the deputy took an alternate route along the side of a pecan orchard and then across a railroad track at a point marked only by an unlighted warning sign. He probably never saw the locomotive before it struck the right side of his patrol car, just behind the wheel well. Deputy Vocale died at the scene.

Carl Vocale, 44, was born at Deming and graduated from Deming High School in 1963. In July, 1979, he joined the Luna County Sheriff's Department. He was the department's chief investigator from 1983 to 1987. He joined the Doña Ana County Sheriff's Department in January of 1989. He was active in the Fraternal Order of Police, Law Enforcement Rodeo Association and the New Mexico Mounted Patrol.

He was survived by his wife, Kathy, and three children: Dave, 22, Richard, 21, and Sharon 16.

Captain Jim Clay of the Luna County Sheriff's Department quoted Carl Vocale as often saying, "I was a human being a long time before I became a cop." Sergeant Edward Lerma of the Doña Ana County Sheriff's Department said, "A good human being and a good cop he was!"

Albuquerque *Journal,* July 19, 1989
Las Cruces *Sun News,* July 18, 1989
State Police Reports, July 16, 1989
Edward Lerma, Sergeant, "Why Now? The Life/Death of Deputy Carl Emanuel Vocale," *Employee Newsletter,* Doña Ana County Sheriff's Department, August, 1989, Vol. 3
Cooney Sarracino, Doña Ana County Sheriff, correspondence, October 24, 1989
Dave Vocale (son), correspondence, May 28, June 29 & July 9, 1990

CHARLES WALKER

City Marshal
San Marcial, New Mexico

Accounts of the demise of Marshal Walker differ somewhat in the two news-papers which reported the affair. An item which appeared in the Dallas (Texas) *Weekly Herald* under the dateline, San Marcial, N. M., June 24 (1881), reported thus:

> Charles Walker, city marshal [*sic*], was shot and killed last night by Paddy Ryan, who but recently escaped from jail at El Paso Del Norte, Mexico, where he was confined for shooting a Mex-ican. Ryan was beating his wife and Walker went into the house to stop him. After remonstrating with Ryan he turned to leave, when Ryan drew his pistol and emptied it into Walker's back. Five shots lodged in a space that could be covered by a man's hand. Ryan then ran for the mountains pursued by a number of men, but owing to the darkness he succeeded in making his escape.

New Mexico's Rio Grande *Republican* for June 25, 1881, offered its version of the affray.

> Ryan who was under the influence of liquor and mad about something went into the dining room where his family were [*sic*] seated at dinner, and finding one of his children crying he brutally knocked it out of the chair. His wife interfered to protect the child when Ryan drew his pistol and struck her a cruel blow on the head, felling her to the floor. The screams of the woman and child brought Walker to the scene, whereupon Ryan ordered him to leave the room saying "this is a family affair and you have no business here," or words to that effect. Walker answered that it was his business as an officer to keep the peace. At this, Ryan commenced firing at Walker, shooting five bullets into different parts of his body. Walker died from the effects of his wounds a few hours afterwards. Ryan fled after the shooting and several of the citizens fired at him as he ran, but the bullets all flew wide of the mark and he escaped out of

town unhurt. Both the murdered man and the murderer were regarded as hard characters. Walker was an overbearing pistol slinger and Ryan was a brute when drunk. The killing is considered wholly unjustifiable, and if Ryan is caught he will probably fare badly.

Efforts to learn what became of Paddy Ryan have been unsuccessful. It is noteworthy that in July 1881, the month following this shooting, a fire nearly destroyed the entire town of San Marcial. The murder of Marshal Walker may have simply been lost in the shuffle.

In addition to the two sources noted above, a thin volume called *Outlaws of New Mexico*, complied by Peter Hertzog and published by Sunstone Press in 1884, notes only that "[P. Ryan] killed Charles Walker at San Marcial. June 23, 1881."

CHARLES E. WASMER

Patrolman
Bosque Farms, New Mexico, Police Department

August 18, 1977, early evening. Officer Charles Wasmer and citizen patrol officer Rick Switzer were driving on Loop Road in Bosque Farms when a car came around a curve and nearly hit their police vehicle. The officers had no more than stopped the car when another driver approached and complained that the same car had sideswiped her pickup and fled the scene. The officers, in talking to the driver of the errant vehicle, learned that she was Ruth Manus, 51, who lived only about 150 yards from where they stopped her. She had obviously been drinking.

At about 9:00 p.m., as the officers continued their investigation of the accident and Mrs. Manus' driving habits, William Manus, 58, her husband, approached the group and opened fire with a double barrel 12 gauge shotgun. He hit Officer Wasmer with both barrels, once in the chest and once in the face. The officer managed to shoot Manus and get to his police car and call for help before he died. Officer Switzer also shot Manus. Manus, however, survived his wounds and was charged with first degree murder, attempted murder and aggravated assault. Ruth Manus was charged with driving while intoxicated, reckless driving and leaving the scene of an accident.

District Attorney Tom Esquibel said at the time that he thought Manus had a grudge against Wasmer because he, Manus, had been cited for driving while intoxicated in the recent past. Manus, a retired air traffic controller, was convicted of first degree murder and sentenced to life in prison by District Court Judge George Perez in February 1978. He was also sentenced to 10 to 50 years for the attempted murder of Officer Switzer, the sentences to be served consecutively. Manus appealed the verdict but the New Mexico Supreme Court upheld it in May of 1979.

Officer Wasmer, 36, was survived by his wife, Carrie, a Valencia County Sheriff's dispatcher, and two sons by a previous marriage. He had been with the Bosque Farms Police Department for about two years at the time of his death. He was described as a good officer, one who would have "gone down fighting."

Albuquerque *Journal*, August 19 & 21, 1977
Hastings Hutchins, Chief, Bosque Farms Police Dept., Jan. 25, 1996
Santa Fe *New Mexican*, January 26 & February 23, 1978; May 10, 1979

WILLIAM F. WHITE

Inspector
New Mexico Alcohol Beverage Control Department

State Liquor Inspectors Chris Ortiz, Sonny Carter and Bill White met for breakfast at the Portales Inn on Sunday morning, December 8, 1985. The three agents planned to catch a Clovis bootlegger who was believed to regularly sell alcoholic beverages on Sunday. Bill White paid for breakfast. The three drove to Clovis in Sonny Carter's car.

Carter made the first effort to illegally purchase booze at 324 Second Street in Clovis but the suspect wouldn't sell to him. Ortiz tried next with the same result. Bill White was unsuccessful, too, and he returned to the car which was parked at the corner of Grand and Conley. He commented that he'd try again, another time, after he'd let his beard grow for a few days.

Suddenly, without warning, White was stricken with a massive heart attack which immediately rendered him unconscious. Inspectors Ortiz and Carter managed to get him out of the car and onto the ground and they administered CPR until fire and rescue personnel arrived on the scene. Bill White was transported to the hospital, but he died before regaining consciousness.

Inspector White was normally stationed in Hobbs where his wife, Francis, served as chief dispatcher for the Hobbs Police Department. He was also survived by 11 children and stepchildren: Carla, Laura, Anita, Beckey, Barbara, Sharon, Tracy, Ronnie, Max, Damon and Lonnie.

Agent Chris Ortiz, Alcohol & Gaming Enforcement Section, New Mexico Department
     of Public Safety, conversation, March 21, 1996
Sheriff Bill Lane, Lea County, conversation, March, 1996

JAY "JERRY" ELMO WIGNALL

Sergeant

Tucumcari, New Mexico, Police Department

Bobby Gene Garcia, 20, began his crime spree about 6:00 p.m. on November 9, 1966. He first went to the home of his mother-in-law, Annie Apalacio, in a rage. He shot and killed his sister-in-law, Josie Baker, and left, dragging his wife along with him. Walking, he started for the city hall about five blocks away but left his wife behind in an alley. Garcia met two former schoolmates, Steve Grau and Ralph Murray, near a stairway in city hall leading up to the police department and jail on the second floor. He forced them, at gunpoint, to accompany him up the stairs. Once in the police office, Garcia demanded that either Mary Simpson, the dispatcher, or Jerry Wignall, the desk sergeant, give him the key to the jail. Garcia wanted to free his brother, Albert, who had been jailed the day before for assault with a deadly weapon and disorderly conduct. Neither Simpson nor Wignall moved fast enough to suit Bobby Garcia so he blasted a hole in the wall with his 12 gauge automatic shotgun.

Sergeant Wignall took Garcia seriously then, and removed the jail key from his desk drawer. Garcia thought Wignall had pulled a gun and he shot the officer in the lower right back. Then he forced the others into the hall and opened the jail door. He discovered that brother Albert was not in the Tucumcari jail. He'd been transferred to the county jail earlier in the day. Garcia grabbed Mrs. Simpson and forced her to accompany him as he fled down the back stairs. He met police officer Max Crespin along the way and promptly shot him in the leg. Grau and Murray broadcast a call for help. Wignall, at that point, remained conscious.

State Police officer Jack Kelly arrived on the scene in time to see Garcia heading down the street with his hostage. Kelly followed along, shouting at Garcia to put his gun down, to let Mrs. Simpson go. Garcia ignored the officer. He reached the Sands Dorsey Drug Store with his hostage still in tow, and ran inside, pushing patrons aside. Quay County Sheriff Claude Moncus arrived and he and Officer Kelly followed Garcia inside. Other officers arrived. Garcia threatened to kill the officers if they didn't stay back. Finally, in the face of guns pointed at him, Garcia agreed to surrender to Moncus and he gave the sheriff his gun. Mrs. Simpson was not injured.

Efforts to arraign Bobby Garcia on Thursday, the 10th, were not successful. It took five officers to drag him from jail to court and once there he refused to cooperate. When Judge J. V. Gallegos suggested that Garcia take a drink of water and calm himself, the killer became violent. "It's poison," he screamed. "You're trying to kill me!" Garcia was returned to jail to await arraignment at a later time.

Sgt. Jerry Wignall died of his wound on Friday, November 11 at 5:45 a.m.

Tried and convicted of first degree murder, Bobby Gene Garcia was sentenced to life in prison. He escaped twice and after being recaptured the last time, he was confined to the federal prison at Terre Haute, Indiana. Garcia committed suicide there by hanging himself on December 13, 1980.

Jerry Wignall, 57, was survived by his wife, Anna Belle, one son, two step-children and his mother, Lenore Wignall of Oxnard, California.

Albuquerque *Journal*, November 10 & 11, 1966
Tucumcari *Daily News*, November 10 & 11, 1966
Marilyn Parker, The Quay County *Sun*, correspondence, November 21, 1989

BENNIE DELL WILLIAMS

Patrolman
New Mexico State Police

Officer Ben Williams was south bound on U. S. Route 70 at about 4:00 p.m. on July 9, 1963. The road was wet from a summer rain. At a point about nine miles south of Portales, he lost control of his 1962 Dodge police car and skidded sideways across the roadway before the vehicle rolled over, twice, coming to rest on its top. The officer was out of the car, and staggering, when a passing motorist stopped to assist. Williams collapsed and the woman went for help. About seven miles north she found police officers Bill Eddleman and Fred White investigating another accident. They called for an ambulance and returned to the scene of the accident. Officer Williams was alive when they got to him, but he died in the ambulance en route to the hospital.

A native of Washington State, Patrolman Williams moved to Lordsburg at a young age and graduated from high school there in 1956. He joined the State Police in 1960. His wife, Rita, one daughter, Tamara, 5, and two sons, James Craig, 3, and Bennie Eric 2, survived the officer. He was buried at Lordsburg.

Albuquerque *Journal*, July 10, 1963
The Roadrunner (New Mexico State Police Association, Vol. 3, No. 2, Summer, 1992)

HORST H. "WOODY" WOODS

Officer
U.S. Veterans Administration Police Department

Woody Woods served as a police officer at the Veterans Administration Hospital in Albuquerque. He worked the graveyard shift in the early morning hours of January 10, 1996. A hospital patient stepped outside one of the buildings to smoke a cigarette at about 1:45 a.m. and noticed a suspicious man in the parking lot. He told Woods about it and the officer approached an elderly man crouched down beside a Veterans Administration police car. As the officer spoke, the man shot him in the head with a .380 caliber semi-automatic pistol.

The Kirtland Air Force Base Police arrived minutes later. The suspect, William L. Smith, 76, of Farmington, New Mexico, was still at the scene and a standoff quickly developed. For about 20 minutes Smith would not let anyone close to the wounded man. Officers finally convinced Smith to surrender his weapons—which included two guns and a machete—and medical personnel attended to Officer Woods. He was declared dead almost immediately. It was determined that his wound was so severe that he could not have been saved even without the delay.

Four hours after the shooting, medical technicians drew blood from the suspect and found his blood-alcohol level at nearly .19, more than twice the legal limit for intoxication in New Mexico. Smith, an outpatient at the VA hospital, often visited the facility because of heart and kidney problems. He would drive from Farmington in a recreational vehicle early in the morning so he could park near the door. A search of Smith's vehicle conducted after his arrest produced a rifle, three pistols, ammunition, and a supply of liquor. A federal grand jury, on February 9, 1996, indicted Smith on charges of first degree murder and using a firearm during a crime of violence.

Smith had a prior record of aberrant behavior. In June of 1995, a Farmington police officer was injured slightly when he responded to a complaint that Smith was threatening to shoot cars speeding on the street in his upper middle class neighborhood. Smith struck the officer with his cane and was charged with misdemeanor battery. Reports described Smith as intoxicated at the time. In September, 1995, officials had to disarm Smith when he showed up at the VA hospital emergency room carrying two handguns and a Bowie knife.

Woody Woods, 46, had resided in Los Lunas for about a year and a half at the time of his death. He retired from the U. S. Navy after 25 years of service in 1993 with the rank of master chief petty officer, the highest enlisted rank. Woods was a veteran of five tours of duty in Viet Nam and the Persian Gulf War. He attended the Veterans Administration Law Enforcement Academy in Little Rock, Arkansas and had only returned to the job two weeks before the shooting that took his life. VA police officers are not permitted to carry firearms but they have full arrest powers within their jurisdiction.

In May, 1997, a park at the Veterans Affairs hospital, named Woody's Woods, was dedicated to officer Woods.

Officer Horst Woods was survived by his wife Linda; a son Matthew of Virginia Beach, VA; a daughter, Summer, of Los Lunas; and parents, Leo and Hildegard Woods of Albuquerque.

All who knew Woody described him as a friendly and outgoing man. His father said this: "[Woody was] a loving person who would probably do anything for anyone—even the bastard that shot him."

Albuquerque *Journal*, January 11, 12, 13 & 17; February 10; April 19, 1996, and May 10, 1997

H. Douglas Beldon, Chief Division Counsel & Supervisory Special Agent, Federal Bureau of Investigation, Albuquerque, New Mexico; correspondence, February 1, 1996

ROY WOOFTER

Marshal
Roswell, New Mexico

The city of Roswell in southeastern New Mexico enacted a prohibition ordinance in 1910 that made illegal the sale of beer and liquor within the community. While the law was supported by a sizable segment of citizens, especially the churches, it was strongly opposed by others, and several bootleggers continued to sell booze.

City Marshal Roy Woofter was earnest in enforcing the law. His investigation led him to suspect that Jim Lynch was selling beer from his boarding house at the corner of First Street and Richardson Avenue. Lynch apparently knew that Marshal Woofter was aware of his illegal activities. One mid-week evening in late May, 1911, Lynch was heard to say, "I'll shoot that star full of holes if I catch him peeping around my house."

Upon a complaint made by Marshal Woofter, a warrant was issued for a search of Lynch's house. On May 26, 1911, around 5:00 in the afternoon, Marshal Woofter along with Roswell city policemen—and brothers—Ed and Henry Carmichael arrived to execute the search. They found Lynch in an alley behind the Smoke House, near his residence, with two other men, Fred Higgins and Red Preston. Lynch objected to the search at a time when his wife was out of town. Woofter assured him that the search *would* be conducted. Lynch, along with Higgins and Preston accompanied the officers to the Lynch house. Lynch told the officers they had nothing to fear from him and he opened his coat to show them he was not armed.

The group of six entered by the front door. They found nothing in the first room they entered and before Woofter could enter the second room, Lynch went through the door, slammed it in the marshal's face and locked it. Woofter knocked on the door and kicked it several times but Lynch would not open up or respond. One of the Carmichael brothers went out the front door and around the house toward the back door while Woofter went around the house, along the porch, in the opposite direction. Witnesses said the marshal's hands were at his sides and he had not drawn his gun.

As he passed a window, a voice called out: "Keep off my back porch!" A shot fired from inside hit the marshal in the stomach.

Woofter clutched his stomach and faltered but did not fall. He managed to stagger to where Henry Carmichael stood. "Lynch has shot me. Save me. Let Lynch go."

The Carmichael brothers along with Higgins and Preston managed to get the marshal to the house next door. They summoned an ambulance and Woofter was taken to St. Mary's Hospital where he was attended by four surgeons. The .45 caliber rifle bullet, a U. S. A. ball weighing 405 grains, had done great damage. One doctor reported that the exit wound was large enough that three fingers could be inserted into it. In spite of the doctors' best efforts, the officer died the next morning about 5:00 o'clock. Before he died, however, he made a long and specific statement in which he identified the voice of the man who shot him as belonging to Jim Lynch.

Chaves County sheriff's deputies Jim Johnson and Clarence Young arrived at the scene to find Lynch in his house, behind a locked door, holding the Winchester rifle in his hands. They ordered Lynch out of the house, and he told them to come in. Deputies responded that the door was locked. Lynch told them use a knife to unhook the screen door. They declined. At last, Lynch opened the door and handed one of the deputies his rifle. He was arrested and taken to jail.

After Lynch was removed from the scene, the Carmichael brothers and a fireman completed the search of the house. They found a barrel of beer and an ice box containing a large amount of bottled of beer.

On a change of venue, Lynch was tried at Carlsbad in mid October, 1911. The defendant's family engaged the services of high-priced Texas legal talent to make the case that Lynch acted only in defense of his home. He claimed that he believed the officers had no right to be there. Lynch also claimed that he fired only when Woofter reached for his gun. The jury didn't believe any of it and took only one hour to convict Lynch of murder in the first degree.

Roy Woofter had resided in Roswell for about five years at the time of his death. A native of West Virginia, he'd previously served as a peace officer at Albia in southeastern Iowa. He'd moved to Roswell for his health and joined the Police Department in July, 1909, and became city marshal in October of the same year. He married Margaret Forsyth three years before his death. They had no children. His remains were returned to Iowa for burial.

A Roswell newspaper reported that Reverend P. T. Ramsey said of Marshal Woofter that he "submerged every private interest, the comforts of home and his own personal safety to act against the criminal element. Fearless in his duty he had gone forth and because of that duty he now lay cold in death."

Sgt. John Halvorson, Roswell Police Department, "Woofter only Roswell lawman killed in performance of duty," Roswell *Daily Record*, September 24, 1995
Roswell *Daily Record*, May 27, 29, 30, 31; June 19 & 26; October, 13, 14, 16 & 19, 1911

NEW MEXICO PEACE OFFICERS
KILLED IN THE LINE OF DUTY
BY DEPARTMENT

Alamogordo Dept. of Public Safety
Bruce A. Richard (1984)
James Monroe Vigil (1973)

Albuquerque Police Dept.
Richard Armijo (1958)
John Arthur Carrillo (1987)
Philip H. Chacon (1980)
Gerald Eugene Cline (1983)
E. D. Henry (1886)
Michael R. King (2005)
Lewis Alexander Knapp (1912)
Michael R. McGuire (1886)
Kenneth Shawn McWethy (1986)
Max Ray Oldham (1959)
Donald W. Redfern (1951)
Jeffrey C. Russell (2002)
Frank A. Sjolander (1954)
Richard Smith (2005)

**Atchison, Topeka & Santa Fe Railroad
  Police**
Louis McCamant (1924)
J. A. McClure (1911)
Lewis H. Mickey (1925)

Bernalillo Town Marshal's Office
Clemente Salazar (1950)

Bernalillo County Sheriff's Dept.
Emilio Candelaria (1930)
Ray Davis (1968)
Angelic S. Garcia (2001)
James McGrane Jr. (2006)
Julian Narvaez (1969)
William Sibrava (1994)

Bloomfield Police Dept.
William M. Stedman, Jr. (1982)

Bosque Farms Police Dept.
Charles E. Wasmer (1977)

Carlsbad Police Dept.
Melvin Lee Hodges (1962)

Chaves County Sheriff's Dept.
Rufus J. Dunnahoo (1931)
Barney F. Leonard (1933)
William Rainbolt (1901)

Clayton Police Dept.
Emilio Mestas (1973)

Clovis Police Dept.
Rodolfo Ledezma (1995)

Colfax County Sheriff's Dept.
William A. Burgen (1882)
Henry M. Love (1899)

Deming Police Dept.
Royce Bennett (1979)

District Attorneys/Prosecutors
Victor C. Breen (1971)
Albert J. Fountain (1896)
David A. Lane (1986)
E. C. Serna (1977)

Doña Ana County Sheriff's Dept.
Ruben Carbajal (1990)
Patrick F. Garrett (1908)
Ralph R. Higginbotham (1952)
W. L. Jerrell (1884)
Kent Kearney (1896)
Robert P. Larson (1982)
Tranquilino Compos Lopez (1911)
Robert A. Olinger (1881)
Carl Emanuel Vocale (1989)

Eddy County Sheriff's Dept.
George Washington Batton (1922)
James Leslie Dow (1897)
Bud Johnson (1898)

Eunice Police Dept.
Leonard E. Daniel (1953)

Farmington Police Dept.
Victoria Chavez (1992)
Ben Herrera (1962)
Owen Landdeck (1979)

Gallup Police Department
John B. Arvizo (1965)
Ronald T. Baca (1986)
Larry Bryan Mitchell (2001)
Barney D. Montoya (1977)
Louis Silva (1930)

Grant County Sheriff'S Dept.
Ventura Bencoma (1921)
Benjamin L. Green (1981)
Thomas Hall (1886)
William D. Johnson (1900)
George A. Scarborough (1900)
Charles B. Smith (1907)

Hobbs Police Dept.
Robert B. Butler (1951)

Huerfano County, Colorado, Sheriff's Dept.
Edward J. Farr (1899)

Isleta Pueblo
Luis Abeyta (1921)

Jal Police Dept.
Luis Castillo (2001)

Jicarilla Apache Police Dept.
Ishkoten Koteen (1961)

Lamb County, Texas, Sheriff's Dept.
Harvey Samuel Bolin (1932)

Las Vegas Marshal's Office
Joe Carson (1880)

Lea County Sheriff's Dept.
J. M. Clifton (1932)

Lincoln County Constable's Office
Juan Martinez (1873)

Lincoln County Sheriff's Dept.
Thomas C. Bedford, Jr. (1979)
James W. Bell (1881)
William Brady (1878)
James Carlyle (1880)
Jasper Corn (1884)
Patrick F. Garrett (1908)
George Hindman (1878)
John Hurley (1885)
Tom Jones (1933)
Lyon Phillipowsky (1874)

Loma Parda Marshal's Office
Edward Seaman (1872)

Lordsburg Constable
C. B. Schutz (1893)

Luna County Sheriff's Dept.
Thomas H. Hall (1911
A. L. Smithers (1911)
Dwight B. Stephens (1916)

McKinley County Sheriff's Dept.
Mack R. Carmichael (1935)

Mesilla Marshal's Office
Philip Olivas (1992)
Thomas A. Richmond (1988)

Moriarty Police Dept.
Gilbert Montoya (1967)

Mountainair Police Dept.
Stephen Sandlin (1988)

Navajo Dept. of Law Enforcement
Winsonfred A. Filfred (1999)
Hoskie Gene (1996)
Samuel Redhouse (1997)
Esther Todecheene (1998)

New Mexico Alcohol Beverage Control Dept.
Edward L. Moreno (1970)
William F. White (1985)

New Mexico Corrections Officers
Ralph Garcia (1999)
Louis Franklin Jewett, Jr. (1981)
Gerald Peter Magee (1981)
Filimon J. Ortiz (1952)
Joseph Ralph Silva (1987)

New Mexico Game & Fish Dept.
O. C. Gray (1960)
Austin A. Roberts (1960)

New Mexico Livestock Board
James B. Jones (1981)

New Mexico Mounted Police
J. B. Rusk (1912)

New Mexico Transportation Dept.
Gregory A. Geoffrion (1997)
Daniel C. Rivera, Jr. (1989)

New Mexico State Police
Wayne G. Allison (1988)
Lloyd Rafael Aragon (2001)
James Archuleta (2006)
Joe Aven, Jr. (1953)
Michael C. Avilucea (2008)
Leslie Delbert Bugg (1946)
Mackie C de Baca (1944)
James E. Clark (1960)
David Coker (1979)
Nash Phillip Garcia (1952)
Richard Gomez (1980)
Lowell D. Howard (1984)
Glen Huber (1991)
Antonio Jaramillo (1965)
Robert Earle Lee (1960)
Christopher Mirabal (2007)
Manuel Olivas (1985)
José Francisco Quintana (1944)
John T. Ramsey (1953)
Robert Seth Romero (1967)
Robert Rosenbloom (1971)

Peter Ross (2005)
David Smith (1984)
Ramon Robert Solis (2001)
William T. Speight (1949)
Walter Grange Taber (1937)
Damon Kyle Talbott (2001)
Andrew F. Tingwall (2009)
Sherman L. Toler, Jr. (1986)
Bennie Dell Williams (1963)

Otero County Sheriff's Dept.
James F. Haynes (1934)
Robert Hedman (2004)
William L. Rutherford (1923)

Pojoaque Police Dept.
John "Kevin" Schultz (2002)

Quay County Sheriff's Dept.
Travis Haynes (1972)

Questa Police Dept.
Ronald E. Shores (1977)

Los Ranchos de Albuquerque Constable
Manuel Garcia y Griego (1868)

Raton Police Dept.
Oscar Davis (1923)

Rio Arriba County Sheriff's Dept.
Jerry Martinez (1991)

Rio Rancho Police Dept.
Germaine Casey (2007)

Roosevelt County Sheriff's Dept.
William E. Tipton (1907)

Roswell Marshal's Office
Roy Woofter (1911)

Sandoval County Sheriff's Dept.
Joseph A. Harris (2009)

San Ildefonso Police Dept.
Issac Benjamin Martinez (1994)

San Marcial Marshal's Office
Charles Walker (1881)

San Miguel County Sheriff's Dept.
Juan Leo Ortiz (1978)
Antonio Lino Valdez (1880)

Santa Fe County Sheriff's Dept.
Ike Alarid (1932)
Leopoldo C. Gurule (1980)

Santa Rosa Marshal's Office
José María Gonzales (1949)

Sierra County ShEriff's Dept.
Kelly Fay Clark (1999)
Warren Ruiz (1942)

Silver City Constable
Perfecto Rodriguez (1904)

Silver City Marshal's Office
William Harvey Kilburn (1904)

Taos Marshal's Office
Lee Vicente Peña (1944)

Taos County Sheriff's Dept.
Stephen Louis Lee (1847)
Elfego Martínez (1882)

Torrence County Sheriff's Dept.
James M. Chase (1905)
William Meador (1933)
Dominique J. Smith (2009)

Tucimcari Police Dept.
Jay "Jerry" E. Wignall (1966)

Union County Sheriff's Dept.
J. V. Cogdill (1937)
Luciano B. Gallegos (1897)
James I. Kent (1909)

U. S. Atomic Energy Commission
Warren Gray Fleshman (1950)
Robert F. Purcell (1950)

U. S. Bureau Narcotics & Dangerous Drugs
Andrew P. Sanderson (1944)

U. S. Customs Service
J. H. Heard (1932)

U. S. Federal Bureau of Investigation
Truett Eugene Rowe (1937)

U. S. Prohibition Bureau, Dept. of Treasury
Raymond Sutton, Sr. (1930)

U. S. Veterans Administration Police Dept.
Horst H. Woods (1996)

Valencia County Sheriff's Dept.
Dan Bustamente (1898)
Andres Chavez (1934)
Leo Chavez (1986)
Charles Cunningham (1930)
Vicente Guerro (1898)
Frank X. Vigil (1898)

NEW MEXICO PEACE OFFICERS
KILLED IN THE LINE OF DUTY
BY YEAR OF OCCURANCE

1847
Stephen Louis Lee

1868
Manuel Garcia y Griego

1872
Edward Seaman

1873
Juan Martinez

1874
Lyon Phillipowsky

1878
William Brady
George Hindman

1880
James Carlyle
Joe Carson
Antonio Lino Valdez

1881
James W. Bell
Robert A. Olinger
Charles Walker

1882
William A. Burgen
Elfego Martinez

1884
W. L. Jerrell
Jasper Corn

1885
John Hurley

1886
E. D. Henry
Michael R. McGuire
Thomas Hall

1893
C. B. Schutz

1896
Albert J. Fountain
Kent Kearney

1896
James Leslie Dow

1897
Luciano B. Gallegos

1898
Dan Bustamente
Vicente Guerro
Bud Johnson
Frank X. Vigil

1899
Henry M. Love
Edward J. Farr

1900
William D. Johnson
George Scarborough

1901
William Rainbolt

1904
William H. Kilburn
Perfecto Rodriguez

1905
James M. Case
1907
Charles B. Smith
William E. Tipton

1908
Patrick F. Garrett

1909
James I. Kent

1911
Thomas H. Hall
Tranquilino Lopez
J. A. McClure
A. L. Smithers
Roy Woofter

1912
Lewis A. Knapp
J. B. Rusk

1916
Dwight B. Stephens

1921
Ventura Bencoma
Luis Abeyta

1922
George W. Batton

1923
Oscar Davis
William L. Rutherford

1924
Louis McCamant

1925
Lewis H. Mickey

1930
Emilio Candelaria
Charles Cunningham
Louis Silva
Raymond Sutton, Sr.

1931
Rufus J. Dunnahoo

1932
Ike Alarid
Harvey S. Bolin
J. M. Clifton
J. H. Heard

1933
Tom Jones
Barney Leonard
William Meador

1934
James F. Haynes
Andres Chavez

1935
Mack R. Carmichael

1937
J. V. Cogdill
Truett E. Rowe
Walter G. Taber

1942
Warren Ruiz

1944
Mackie C de Baca
Lee Vicente Peña
José Francisco Quintana
Andrew P. Sanderson

1946
Leslie Delbert Bugg

1949
José María Gonzales
William T. Speight

1950
Warren G. Fleshman
Robert Purcell
Clemente Salazar

1951
Donald W. Redfern
Robert B. Butler

1952
Nash P. Garcia
Ralph R. Higginbotham
Filimon J. Ortiz

1953
Joe Aven, Jr.
Leonard E. Daniel
John T. Ramsey

1954
Frank Sjolander

1958
Richard Armijo

1959
Max Ray Oldham

1960
James E. Clark
O. C. Gray
Robert E. Lee
Austin A. Roberts

1961
Ishkoten Koteen

1962
Ben Herrera
Melvin Lee Hodges

1963
Bennie Dell Williams

1965
John B. Arvizo
Antonio Jaramillo

1966
Jay "Jerry" Wignall

1967
Gilbert Montoya
Robert S. Romero

1968
Ray Davis

1969
Julian Narvaez

1970
Edward Moreno

1971
Victor C. Breen
Robert Rosenbloom

1972
Travis Haynes

1973
James Monroe Vigil
Emilio Mestas

1977
Barney D. Montoya
E. C. Serna
Ronald E. Shores
Charles E. Wasmer

1978
Juan Leo Ortiz

1979
Thomas C. Bedford
Royce Bennett
David Coker
Owen Landdeck

1980
Philip H. Chacon
Richard Gomez
Leopoldo C. Gurule

1981
Benjamin L. Green
Louis F. Jewett Jr.
Gerald P. Magee
James B. Jones

1982
William M. Stedman Jr.
Robert P. Larson

1983
Gerald E. Cline

1984
Lowell D. Howard
Bruce A. Richard
David Smith

1985
Manuel Olivas
William F. White

1986
Ronald T. Baca
Leo Chavez
David A. Lane
Kenneth S. McWethy
Sherman L. Toler

1987
John Arthur Carrillo
Joseph Ralph Silva

1988
Wayne G. Allison
Thomas A. Richmond
Stephen Sandlin

1989
Daniel C. Rivera Jr.
Carl E. Vocale

1990
Ruben Carbajal

1991
Glen Huber
Jerry Martinez

1992
Victoria Chavez
Philip Olivas

1994
Issac B. Martinez

1995
Rodolfo Ledezma

1996
Hoskie Gene
Horst H. Woods

1997
Gregory A. Geoffrion
Samuel Redhouse

1998
Esther Todecheene

1999
Kelly Fay Clark
Winsonfred A. Filfred
Ralph Garcia

2001
Lloyd R. Aragon
Luis Castillo
Angelic S. Garcia
Larry B. Mitchell
Ramon R. Solis
Damon K. Talbott

2002
Jeffrey C. Russell
John "Kevin" Schultz

2004
Robert Hedman

2005
Michael R. King
Peter Ross
Richard Smith

2006
James Archuleta
James McGrane

2007
Christopher Mirabal
Germaine Casey

2008
Michael C. Avilucea

2009
Joseph Harris
Dominique J. Smith
Andrew F. Tingwall

SELECTED BIBLIOGRAPHY

Alexander, Bob. *Dangerous Dan Tucker: New Mexico's Deadly Lawman*, High-Lonesome Books, 2001.

_____. *Desert Desperadoes: The Banditti of Southwestern New Mexico*, Gila Books, 2006.

_____. *Lawmen, Outlaws, and S. O. Bs.: Gunfighters of the Old Southwest*, (Two Volumes) High-Lonesome Books, 2007.

_____. *Sheriff Harvey Whitehill: Silver City Stalwart*, High-Lonesome Books, 2005.

Ball, Larry D. *Desert Lawmen, The High Sheriffs of New Mexico and Arizona, 1846-1912*, University of New Mexico Press, 1992.

_____. *The United States Marshals of New Mexico & Arizona Territories 1846-1912*, University of New Mexico Press, 1978.

Bryan, Howard. *Robbers, Rogues and Ruffians, True Tales of the Wild West*, Clear Light Publishers, 1991.

_____. *Wildest of the Wild West, True Tales Of A Frontier Town On The Santa Fe Trail*, Clear Light Publishers, 1988.

_____. *Incredible Elfego Baca, Good Man, Bad Man of the Old West*, Clear Light Publishers, 1993.

Bullis, Don. *Duels, "Gunfights & Shoot-outs*, Rio Grande Books, 2010.

_____. *New Mexico & Politicians of the Past*, Rio Grande Press, 2009.

Cline, Donald. *Alias Billy the Kid, The Man Behind The Legend*, Sunstone Press, 1986.

Crutchfield, James A. *Tragedy at Taos, The Revolt of 1847*, Republic of Texas Press, 1995.

Curry, George. *1861-1947, An Autobiography*, University of New Mexico Press, 1958.

DeArment, Robert K. *George Scarborough: The Life and Death of a Lawman on the Closing Frontier*, University of Oklahoma Press, 1992.

DeMattos, Jack. *Mysterious Gunfighter, The Story of Dave Mather*, The Early West, 1992.

Fergusson, Erna. *Murder & Mystery in New Mexico*, Lightning Tree Press, 1948.

Gamber, Glenn, & Clark, Connie. *To Serve And Protect*, D. C., National Law Enforcement Memorial Fund, 1995.

Garst, Shannon. *William Bent and His Adobe Empire*, Julian Messner, Inc., 1957.

Gibson, A. M. *The Life and Death of Colonel Albert Jennings Fountain*, University of Oklahoma Press, 1965.

Gillett, James B. *Six Years with the Texas Rangers, 1875 to 1881*, University of Nebraska Press, 1921.

Harkey, Dee. *Mean as Hell*, Ancient City Press, 1989.

Harrison, Fred. *Hell Holes and Hangings*, Clarendon Press, 1968.

Hornung, Chuck. *Fullerton's Rangers: A History of the New Mexico Territorial Mounted Police*, McFarland & Company, Publishers, 2005.

_____. *The Thin Gray Line—The New Mexico Mounted Police*, Western Heritage Press, 1971.

Jenkins, Myra Ellen, Albert H. Schroeder. *A Brief History of New Mexico*, University of New Mexico Press, 1974.

Julyan, Robert. *The Place Names of New Mexico*, University of New Mexico Press, 1996.

Keleher, William A. *The Fabulous Frontier, Twelve New Mexico Items*, University of New Mexico Press, 1962.

_____. *Turmoil in New Mexico, 1846-1868*, University of New Mexico Press, 1952.

_____. *Violence in Lincoln County, 1869-1881*, University of New Mexico Press, 1957.

Kelly, Charles. *The Outlaw Trail, A History of Butch Cassidy and His Wild Bunch*, Bonanza Books, 1959.

Klasner, Lily. *My Girlhood Among Outlaws*, University of Arizona Press, 1972.

Lacy, Ann and Anne Valley-Fox, Eds. *Outlaws & Desperados*, A New Mexico Federal Writers Project Book, Sunstone Press, 2008.

Larson, Carole. *Forgotten Frontier, The Story of Southeastern New Mexico*, University of New Mexico Press, 1993.

Lavish, Donald R. *William Brady, Tragic Hero of The Lincoln County War*, Sunstone Press, 1986.

McLoughlin, Denis. *Wild and Woolly, An Encyclopedia of the Old West*, Barnes & Noble, 1975.

Meketa, Jacqueline. *From Martyrs to Murderers, The Old Southwest's Saints, Sinners & Scalawags*, Yucca Tree Press, 1993.

Metz, Leon Claire. *Encyclopedia of Lawmen, Outlaws, and Gunfighters*, Checkmark Books, 2003.

_____. *John Selman, Gunfighter*, University of Oklahoma Press, 1976.

_____. *Pat Garrett, The Story of a Western Lawman*, University of Oklahoma Press, 1973.

_____. *The Shooters*, Mangan Books, 1976.

Mullin, Robert N. *A Chronology of The Lincoln County War*, The Press of the Territorian, 1966.

Nash, Jay Robert. *Encyclopedia of Western Lawmen & Outlaws*, Da Capo Press, 1994.

New Mexico State Police 60th Anniversary Yearbook, 1995.

O'Neal, Bill. *Encyclopedia of Western Gunfighters*. Norman & London, University of Oklahoma Press, 1979.

Otero, Miguel Antonio. *My Nine Years As Governor of the Territory of New Mexico, 1897-1906*, University of New Mexico Press, 1904.

Pearce, T. M. (ed). *New Mexico Place Names, A Geographical Dictionary*, University of New Mexico Press, 1965.

Prassel, Frank Richard. *The Western Peace Officer, A Legacy of Law and Order*, University of Oklahoma Press, 1972.

Rickards, Colin. *Sheriff Pat Garrett's Last Days*, Sunstone Press, 1986.

Scanland, John Milton. *Life of Pat F. Garrett and the Taming of the Border Outlaw*, Carleton F. Hodge, 1971.

Simmons, Marc. *Albuquerque, A Narrative History*, University of New Mexico Press, 1982.

_____. (ed). *On The Santa Fe Trail*, University Press of Kansas, 1986.

_____. *New Mexico, An Interpretive History*, University of New Mexico Press, 1977.

_____. *Ranchers, Ramblers and Renegades, True Tales of Territorial New Mexico*, Ancient City Press, 1984.

_____. *When Six-Guns Ruled, Outlaw Tales of the Southwest*, Ancient City Press, 1990.

Sonnichsen, C. L. *I'll Die Before I'll Run, The Story of the Great Feuds of Texas*, University of Nebraska Press, 1951.

_____ & Morrison, William V., *Alias Billy the Kid*, University of New Mexico Press, 1955.

Thrapp, Dan L. *Encyclopedia of Frontier Biography*, Three Volumes, University of Nebraska Press, 1988.

Utley, Robert M. *High Noon in Lincoln, Violence of the Western Frontier*, University of New Mexico Press, 1987.

Webb, Walter Prescott Webb. *The Texas Rangers, A Century of Frontier Defense*, University of Texas Press, 1935.

Wilson, John P. *Merchants, Guns & Money, The Story of Lincoln County and Its Wars*, Museum of New Mexico Press, 1987.

Index

R

Rainbolt, Will 239
Ramczyk, Daniel 171
Ramires, David 274
Ramsey, John "Jake" 11, 241
Randall, William "Big" 49
Raney, Ray 222
Redfern, Donald W. 242
Redhouse, Samuel 243
Redman, James 42
Reed, George 116
Reed, Ivan 37
Register, Lamar 224
Reidy, Robert W. 225
Reinhart, Lambert 187
Rendon, Cheryl 145
Rendon, Nikki 145
Reno, W. H. 90
Reynolds, Hubert 159, 160
Rhoudes, Deborah 134
Rice, Frank 212
Richard, Bruce 244
Richmond, Tom 245
Rider, Allan 280
Rivera, Danny 247
Rivera, Ray 224
Roach, Joe 100
Roberts, Austin 115, 248
Roberts, Dee 44
Robinson, Van Bering 55
Rocha, Jesus 21
Rodriguez, Perfecto 167, 249
Rogers, Waldo H. 174
Romero, Ablencio 39
Romero, Albert 279
Romero, Desiderio 314
Romero, Hilario 76
Romero, Robert Seth 250
Rosenblatt, Paul 109
Rosenbloom, Bob 252
Ross, Charlie 205
Ross, Gary 59
Ross, Pete 254
Rowe, Truett E. 256
Roybal, Carol 119
Roybal, Joe 119
Roybal, Silviano 260
Rudabaugh, Dave 42, 314
Ruiz, Warren 259
Runnels, Mike 64
Runyan, Dave 155
Runyan, Norman 129
Rusk, Jerry 260
Russell, Jeff 262

Rutherford, Bill 263
Ryan, Paddy 321

S

Sadecki, John R. 230
Sainz, Adolfo 300
Saiz, Pilar 122
Salandre, Louie 17
Salas, Benito 23
Salazar, Clemente 268
Salinas, Alfredo 319
Salopek, Billy 245
Sanchez, Abel 113
Sanchez, Abelicio 57
Sanchez, Daniel 78
Sanchez, Jesus 317
Sanchez, Lalo 223
Sanderson, Andrew P. 269
Sandlin, Stephen 270
Sandoval, Eloy 145
Sandoval, Ignacita 145, 195
Sandoval, Maryellen 145
Scarborough, Ed 156
Scarborough, George 271, 317
Schmidt, C. 298
Schultz, Kevin 273
Schurman, Jennifer 294, 306
Schutz, C. B. 274
Scroggin, Robert 128
Scroggins, John 27
Seaman, Edward 276
Segotta, Faron 216
Seligman, Arthur 265
Selman, John 271
Serna, Dave 278
Sherman, Fred 299
Shores, Ron 279
Sibrava, Bill 280
Sierra, U. 274
Silva, Louis 284
Silva, Manuel 284
Silva, Ralph 282
Simms, John 45
Simpson, Mary 325
Simpson, W. C. 123, 299
Sjolander, Frank 286
Smelcer, Charles Hollis 263
Smith, Bill 85
Smith, Charles 288
Smith, David 143, 290
Smith, Dominique J. 291
Smithers, A. L. 123, 293
Smith, F. H. 90
Smith, Gary 146, 195

Smith, O. M. 264
Smith, Richard 170, 292
Smith, Richard Roy 243
Smith, William L. 328
Snodgrass, Del 298
Snow, Lawrence Jay 286
Snyder, D. W. 163
Solis, Ramon Robert 294, 306
Sour, Abe 39
Spahr, James Leroy 286
Speight, Bill 295
Speight, William 101
Spencer, Charles 209
Stanton, Ed "Pearchmouth" 159, 185
Starr, Jesse O. 298
Starr, Leslie 215
Stearns, Charles 302
Steck, Joe 42
Stedman, William M. 297
Stephens, Dwight 124, 298
Stephens, Dwight B. 123
Sterns, Charles 39
Stevenson, George 271
Stewart, Cicero 91
Stewart, Miles Cicero 124, 155
Stiles, William 271
Stout, Donald 190
Stover, Bob 55
Sullivan, Jack 25
Sutherland, Norma 244
Sutton, Raymond 302
Switzer, Rick 323

T

Taber, Walter 101, 305
Tabor, Emzie 298
Tackett, Paul 267
Talbot, Damon 294, 306
Tapia, Tom 193
Taylor, Joe 154
Thomas, Percy 288
Thomas, Rufus 91
Tijerina, Reyes López 111, 250
Tingley, Clyde 26, 45
Tingwall, Andy 143, 307
Tipton, Will 309
Todecheene, Esther 310
Toler, Sherman Lee 311
Torres, Bonifacio 78
Trujillo, Diego 57
Trujillo, Frank 232
Trujillo, Jesse 152
Trujillo, Michael 5

Tunstall, John Henry 27
Turnbo, L. S. 150
Turner, A. W. 302

U

Udall, Tom 270
Ulibarri, Harold 119

V

Valdez, Antonio Lino 314
Valdez, C. y Sanchez y 61
Valerio, Harold 158
Vanderberg, Oscar 302
Vaughn, J. F. 198
Velarde, Ignacio 44
Velarde, Leandro 46
Verner, Phil 37
Viarrial, Gerald James 193
Viarrial, Jacob 193
Vigil, Cornelio 183
Vigil, Donaciano 184
Vigil, Frank 316
Vigil, Jim 319
Vigil, Lawrence Eugene "Larry" 213
Vocale, Carl 320

W

Waite, Fred 27
Walker, Charles 321, 322
Wallace, Allen C. 33
Wallace, Frank 185
Walters, William E. "Bronco Bill" 317
Warner, Dave 197
Wasmer, Charles 323
Watson, Fred J. 172
Weaver, Red 91
Webb, J. J. 314
Welch, Gilford 87
White, Bill 324
White, Dennis 109
White, Fred 327
Widenmann, Robert 27
Wignall, Jerry 325
Wilburn, C. 155
Wilburn, Stone 15
Williams, Al 9
Williams, Ben 95, 161, 201, 327
Williams, Charles 167
Williams, H. M. 163
Williams, Hugh 237

Williams, James 1
Williams, Thomas 197
Willis, Greg 176
Wilson, Billy 42, 314
Wilson, Jim 83
Wilson, Lawrence E. "Bobcat" 44, 257
Winans, Harvey 190
Wolfinger, Louis 264
Woltz, Bill 319
Woodruff, K. S. 62
Woods, James B. 121
Woods, Woody 328
Woodward, Hugh 45
Woofter, Roy 188, 330

Y

Yamamoto, Megumi 307
Young, Clarence 331
Young, Frank 185
Yrait, Graciano 263

Z

Zamora, Felipe 209
Zamora, Rafael 303

Don Bullis retired from the Special Investigations Division, Intelligence Section, New Mexico Department of Public Safety, in 2002. He had previously served as a Sandoval County, New Mexico, deputy sheriff and Village of San Ysidro, New Mexico, town marshal. He served as commissioner on the New Mexico Governor's Organized Crime Prevention Commission from 1987 to 1989. A graduate of Eastern New Mexico University, Bullis is the author of the award-winning series, *New Mexico: A Biographical Dictionary* (Vol. I & II), *Duels, Gunfights & Shoot-Outs, New Mexico and the Politicians of the Past*, and the novels *Bloodville* and *Bull's Eye*. His historical items appear in *New Mexico Stockman* and *Tradición Revista* magazines and his interviews of important New Mexicans have appeared in *New Mexico Magazine*. He serves as Second Vice President of the Historical Society of New Mexico and Sheriff (President) of the Central New Mexico Corral of Westerners International. He resides and writes in Rio Rancho where he lives with his wife, Gloria, an award-winning photographer.